KU-591-630

To Laugh or To Weep

A Biography of

Conor Cruise O'Brien

Anthony J Jordan

BLACKWATER PRESS

Acknowledgements

I want to thank the following for assistance in the course of writing this book.

Mary Kelligher and Gerard Whelan of the Royal Dublin Society Library; Maire Kennedy of Dublin Corporation Gilbert Library; Bernie Costello, Margaret McHugh and Chris White of Claremorris Public Library; the staffs of the ILAC, Pembroke and Ringsend Public Libraries: also Walter Brooks, Alan Fletcher, Eamon O' Murchu, Jeremy Addis, Teresa MacManus, Micheal O Dubhshlainte, Pat O'Keeffe, Sean Haran, Patrick Cruise O'Brien, Christine Hetherington, Conor Cruise O'Brien.

Editor
Hilda O'Sullivan

Design & Layout
Edward Callan

ISBN
0 86121 443 9

© – Anthony J Jordan 1994

Produced in Ireland by
Blackwater Press
c/o Folens Publishers
8 Broomhill Business Park,
Tallaght, Dublin 24.

All rights reserved. No part of this publication may be reproduced, stored in a retrieval system, or transmitted in any form or by any means, electronic, mechanical, photocopying, recording, or otherwise, without the prior written permission of the publisher.
This book is sold subject to the conditions that it shall not, by way of trade or otherwise, be lent, re-sold, hired out or otherwise circulated with the Publishers' prior consent in any form of binding or cover other than that in which it is published and without a similar condition including this condition being imposed on the subsequent purchaser.

While considerable effort has been made to locate all holders of copyright material used in this text, we have failed to contact some of these. Should they wish to contact Blackwater Press, we will be glad to come to some arrangement.

Contents

Foreword

Howth,
Dublin.
January 11, 1993

Dear Mr. Jordan,

     Thank you for your letter and manuscript. I think you have approached what you rightly called my "varied career" in a spirit of fair inquiry and given a good account of it. I wouldn't of course agree with everything you say, but then it wouldn't be healthy ever for a biographer and his subject to be in entire agreement about everything. In this case by quoting relevant statements of mine at length you give your reader an opportunity to decide between us. I know only too well that many will complain that your approach is too indulgent...

     Yours sincerely,

     Conor Cruise O'Brien

Subsequent to recieving the above letter and taking into account the implied advice about quoting Dr. O'Brien's speeches in full, I have revised the text, with some additional material and some omissions. I have, however, included all of the commentary and elucidation of the text which Dr. O'Brien was so kind to give me. This runs to about four thousand words and is incorporated at the relevant points in my text.

     Tony Jordan

Dedication

In memory of
the late lamented
Cardinal Tomas O'Fiaich
who remembered my song.

Introduction

CONOR CRUISE O'BRIEN

During the academic year of 1962-63, a student at St. Patrick's College, Maynooth, circulated an autograph album among his fellow clerical students. We were invited to sign our names and enter an appropriate comment. I had recently finished reading *To Katanga and Back* by Conor Cruise O'Brien. I selected a passage from that book for my entry to the album. It read, 'I have long thought it one of my country's misfortunes, that so much that is best in the Irish Church departs for the mission field, while among those who remain at home, there will always be some whose favourite music is the anthem, Ecce Sacerdos Magnus'[1]. At that time, little did I know that Dr O'Brien would become one of the most virulent critics of the Irish Catholic Church over the succeeding thirty years. When I related this story to Dr O'Brien in 1992, he laughed heartily.

Conor Cruise O'Brien has had a multi-faceted career as a scholar, diplomat, UN Representative, Educationalist, Politician, Government Minister, Journalist and Critic. Throughout his life, he has been true to his chosen heritage, that of liberal agnostic, Home Ruler and rationalist. He inherited his father's confrontational-like manner, totally confident in his ability to out talk and put down any opponent, with style. Though rejecting much of this mother's heritage, he retained the Sheehy sense of pride and position. As a diplomat, he served four Ministers at External Affairs, de Valera, Liam Cosgrave, Sean MacBride and Frank Aiken. He played a role in the Anti-Partition campaign of the late forties. It was with Ireland's accession to United Nations membership and the creation of a UN desk at External Affairs, that O'Brien's star began to shine. Out of this came his controversial tenure as UN Representative in Katanga in 1961. A subsequent career change took him to Kwame Nkrumah's Ghana, ravaged by corruption. Later he lectured in the USA, then embroiled in the Vietnam War. Ireland celebrated the fiftieth anniversary of the 1916 Easter Rising in a triumphal fashion. *The Irish Times* published a special supplement to mark the occasion. Cruise O'Brien contributed a devastatingly bitter account of the country as it might appear to Patrick Pearse and James Connolly. Two years later, he returned to Ireland and rejoined the Labour Party, intent on playing his part in changing the face of Irish society. His successful entry into politics coincided with the advent of the Civil Rights Movement in Northern Ireland and the subsequent troubles there. This became his almost personal crusade, as he worked to prevent Ireland becoming embroiled in a civil war. He devoted himself to demythologising Irish History, though his over-zealousness may have been counterproductive. He made bitter enemies as his attacks on the IRA, and on Irish Nationalism itself, became more pronounced. He came to Government at a critical time on the security front as kidnappings and assassinations occurred. Then, suddenly, he was thrown out of public office. He left politics to become a brilliant journalist with Irish and British newspapers. When his *bête noire*, Charles J Haughey, became Taoiseach, in 1981, O'Brien conducted a relentless campaign, warning against the dangerous tendencies of the man. He recalled that Edmund Burke, who pursued Warren Hastings over ten years, referred to Hastings as 'the Captain General of iniquity'. O'Brien implied that this term 'sets off rather nicely'[2] his own feelings about Mr Haughey.

Dr O'Brien has described his life in Ireland as 'trying to see, can you, in fact, get on in Ireland without either the Catholic Church or the Fenians. I have found I can get along pretty well. I love the Enlightenment ideas of tolerance, mutual forbearance, responsibility and freedom of expression'[3]. This statement puts into focus what is the main theme of Dr O'Brien's life, as portrayed in this text, that of rejection. In his youth, by rejecting the Catholic faith he was reared in, he was unconsciously rejecting his own mother. His continuing outspoken anti-Catholicism forced many of the Irish people to reject him. He rejected the Sheehy family record of betrayal of Parnell, admitting to me that as a youth, this record weighed heavily on his mind[4]. After a brief flirtation with de Valera and Fianna Fail, he rejected that party with a life-long vehemence. At a most critical period of his life, Dr O'Brien found himself rejected publicly by the United Nations and by his own Government. At this time, too, he endured the personal rejection of his first wife. He subsequently rejected a man who had supported him throughout the Congo debacle, and given him a prestigious appointment, Kwame Nkrumah. Later came his public rejection of Irish Nationalism and his apparent espousal of Unionism. Most recently he has rejected a long-time association with the Irish Anti-Apartheid Association, resigning from that group in 1992. He has also rejected the Labour Party, resigning from that body at the time of the New Irish Forum in 1983. He opposed that party's present Coalition Government with Fianna Fail, saying, 'I opposed it from the beginning. I predicted it and saw it as a disaster coming'[5].

One of the great and sustaining characteristics of Dr O'Brien is his sense of humour, his sense of fun, even mischievousness. This is not always readily apparent, being usually understated, as with many intellectuals, but it is never far from the surface. When it is obvious, particularly in a self deprecatory way, as in his descriptions of himself being assaulted by the police in New York in 1967, and at an Apprentice Boys gathering in Derry in 1971, it is hilarious. But it is never far from the surface and to his great joy, it is shared by his present wife, the poet, Maire Mhac an tSaoi. It is a sign of Dr O'Brien's maturity and that of Irish society, that amidst all these rejections, he has remained domiciled in Ireland. Today, were it not for his continuing provocative disposition, he would have attained the stature of admired elder statesman. Instead, he is rightly regarded as one who is still capable of further rejections. In this, I feel sure, he is exceedingly content.

Chapter One

FAMILY BACKGROUND

CHILDHOOD

EDUCATION

FIRST MARRIAGE

Donal Conor David Dermot Donat Francis Cruise O'Brien was born on 3 November 1917. He was the only child of Francis Cruise O'Brien and Kathleen Sheehy. His father came from Ennistymon in Clare where the family lived in a large house which is now the Falls Hotel. Francis came to Dublin to attend the Royal University of Ireland, a Catholic institution founded by Cardinal Cullen and Cardinal Newman. Among his contemporaries were James Joyce, Tom Kettle and Francis Skeffington. O'Brien became auditor of the University Literary and Historical Society. He joined the Irish Party and was described as 'one of the most obnoxious of the new intellectuals in the Irish party organisation, poor, but with the power to say wounding things in a memorable manner'[1]. After completing university he became a journalist.

Kathleen Sheehy was the youngest child of David and Bessie Sheehy. David had been a Member of Parliament for the Irish Party since 1885. His wife was a very formidable matriarch, who had great expectations for each of her two sons and four daughters. James Joyce and his brother Stanislaus were regular guests at the Sheehy home. James had a secret passion for one of the daughters, Mary, but he never acted on it[2]. Mrs Sheehy herself features in Joyce's *Ulysses*, when Fr Conmee, a Jesuit, meets her. Joyce's eye for detail gives us a vivid picture of the good woman.

1

[Father Conmee, SJ] walked up the avenue of sunnywinking leaves and towards him came the wife of David Sheehy MP.

– Very well, indeed, father. And you, father?

Father Conmee was wonderfully well indeed. He would go to Buxton probably for the waters. And her boys, were they getting on well at Belvedere? Was that so? Father Conmee was very glad indeed to hear that. And Mr Sheehy himself. Still in London. The house was still sitting, to be sure it was. Beautiful weather it was, delightful indeed. Yes, it was very probable that Father Bernard Vaughan would come again to preach. O, yes: a very great success. A wonderful man really.

Father Conmee was very glad to see the wife of Mr David Sheehy MP looking so well and he begged to be remembered to Mr David Sheehy, MP. Yes, he would certainly call.

– Good afternoon, Mrs Sheehy.

Father Conmee doffed his silk hat, as he took leave, at the jet beads of her mantilla glistening in the sun[3].

The Sheehy children did not disappoint Mrs Sheehy. The male children were of course able to choose worthy partners for themselves. The two older girls made very suitable matches. Mary married Tom Kettle, who was then an MP with the Irish Party and later a professor of Economics at University College Dublin. Hanna married Francis Skeffington in 1903. He was Registrar at the same university and a noted writer. He adopted his wife's name, becoming Francis Sheehy-Skeffington. But a controversy arose in the Sheehy family when the youngest daughter, Kathleen, accepted the proposal of Francis Cruise O'Brien. Mrs Sheehy had disapproved strongly of this suitor and had done her best to thwart the courtship. She disliked O'Brien intensely, as did her daughter

Mary. The attitude of the family to the proposal is summed up in the biography of Tom Kettle thus:

> Mary and Dick sided with their parents against the marriage. Margaret and Eugene's objections were less inflexible. Tom Kettle's heart went out to Kathleen and Cruise, but his head forbade him to disagree openly with Mary. Hanna and Frank Sheehy-Skeffington, vehement partisans, supported the lovers against parental interference[4].

The Sheehy-Skeffingtons were both agnostics, like O'Brien. But it was not the difference of religion which was Mrs Sheehy's main objection to O'Brien. It was more a matter of social snobbery. O'Brien was an unknown countryman with little prospects. His provocative predisposition did not endear him to those conservative people, who took their position in society so seriously. This familial opposition left Cruise O'Brien angry and unforgiving[5]. Neither did it prevent the marriage, which was noted by James Joyce in a letter to Stanislaus[6]. In James Joyces's *The Dead* the character of Miss Ivors is based on Kathleen Sheehy, who became committed to the Irish language after a visit to Inishmaan in the Aran Islands. Kathleen's parents found that that visit had made her more independent-minded than she had previously been. Cruise O'Brien had been working as the editor of the *Wexford People*, but then became a leader writer for the *Freeman's Journal*, the organ of the Irish Party in Dublin.

Two major tragedies, which were to have a major impact on the still unborn Conor Cruise O'Brien, befell the extended Sheehy family during 1916. During the Easter Rising, Francis Sheehy-Skeffington, a noted pacifist, was murdered in appalling circumstances by a British Army officer, Captain Bowen-Colthurst. An offer of compensation by the British government was refused by his widow, Hanna. Tom Kettle had felt the Rising was a betrayal of all those who had worked so assiduously for Home Rule. He had earlier joined the Dublin Fusiliers, as a sign of good faith to the British authorities, then engaged in the major war on the continent. As a result of the Easter Rising, he volunteered for active service. He was killed in action in September 1916 at Givenchy in the Battle of the Somme. Two years later in 1918, Sinn Fein, the inheritors of the Easter Rising, swept to power in the general election, almost wiping out totally the old Irish Party. David Sheehy, who had held his parliamentary seat for thirty-three years, was among the losers. The old order, which the Sheehy family had thrived on, was gone.

Francis Cruise O'Brien accepted the Anglo-Irish Treaty. His old paper had its premises burned down. He transferred to the *Irish Independent* where he generally supported the new government. The main aspect of the new State which displeased him most was the clericalism, which became all pervasive. He began to confine his social life to his membership of the United Arts Club where he would usually meet only those of a liberal outlook. Many Protestants were members and spoke of their fears in the new State. Lady Gregory and Lennox Robinson once composed a letter of protest about government treatment of prisoners on hunger strike in Mountjoy Jail. They showed it to Cruise O'Brien at the Arts Club, who made a few alterations and said that he felt his paper would publish it[7]. Conor Cruise O'Brien has made reference to his father's poking gentle fun at WB Yeats' fascism, at the Arts Club[8]. Hanna Sheehy-Skeffington opposed the treaty, while her brother, David, accepted it and became a Circuit Court Judge.

Conor Cruise O'Brien has described his childhood thus:

> I was an only child and I think probably spoiled; certainly my mother and my father were very fond of me. Two members of our extended family were very

4

important to my upbringing, Hanna Sheehy-Skeffington and Mary Kettle, my mother's eldest sisters. Both had been widowed in the same year... Those bereavements had a great bearing on my life and cast a kind of shadow through these powerful widows. They were very strong personalities, much more so than my mother, who was rather quiet and retiring. She was a Catholic and Aunt Mary was a Catholic too. My father was an agnostic and so was Aunt Hanna. She and my father tended to be allies. Mary was definitely not an ally for my father. They were rarely in the same room if they could avoid it. Their main difference was one of temperament[9].

Kathleen Cruise O' Brien, despite some early misgivings, was a devout Catholic, in the family tradition. Her husband's agnosticism was a continuing cause of grief to her. He agreed to his son's baptism, First Holy Communion (at the Dominican Convent Muckross Park) and Confirmation (St. Mary's Church Haddington Road). But at her husband's wish she agreed to send her son to 'a non sectarian school of Protestant ethos, Sandford Park'[10]. Conor Cruise relates that his father thought that his secondary education should not be in a Catholic establishment, because there they would try to close his mind. His father wanted his mind to stay open. Sandford Park School was set up in 1922 by a Mr Le Pen, who with finance from interested parents bought a house in Ranelagh. The house was set in over eight acres and had a relaxed family atmosphere where most boys blossomed. It provided a privileged education with a true sense of equality and tolerance. It was a very pro-British school, where poppies were worn on Armistice Day and the British National Anthem played. Conor's first cousin, Owen Sheehy-Skeffington, whom Conor admired greatly, had attended the same school nine years earlier and been Head Boy. Neither attended the religion classes. The total number of boys attending the school was about one hundred.

Conor has said of it:

Sandford Park School was bursting with agnostics, agnostic Catholics, agnostic Protestants and agnostic Jews: about one third of each. But we all felt we were marginal to the society out there, where there were millions of Catholics. We felt collectively lonely but not individually so[11].

Apart from his own father, the O'Brien family seem to have contributed little to the make up of the young boy. Conor has said that his father:

> ... used to talk to him a bit about his background. All the O'Briens of my time consisted of my father and his sister who was married to the novelist, Emar O'Duffy. They lived in London, with only occasional contact.[12]

The Sheehy family were the prepondering influence on the boy, or certainly tried to be. Conor Cruise recalled that:

> ... family gatherings were overpoweringly Sheehy. I remember one Christmas, 1926 indeed, the Sheehy family assembled, praised themselves; they were distinguished people and rightly proud of themselves. I'm not knocking them. Then they started singing 'For We Are Jolly Good Fellows'. This was for the assembled Sheehys. This was a bit too much Sheehy for me and I went across the room and took my father's hand. He was very pleased. But what astounded me was that the Sheehys were pleased, because this showed that I had character and could go against public opinion. I was a good Sheehy, which was not the point I intended to make[13].

Francis Cruise O'Brien had been chronically ill with tuberculosis for some years, but his son remembers him as being great fun and usually in high spirits. On Christmas Day 1927, Francis was trying to bend a bow he had cut as a present for Conor, when he got a seizure and died before his son's eyes. This death, at the age of forty-two years, took a great deal out of the joy of the boy's youth.

Francis Cruise O'Brien's friends organised that Conor's school fees would be paid, so that he could continue on at Sandford Park[14]. But Conor's mother came under renewed pressure to move the boy to a Catholic school. He recalled that one mother of a boy at Sandford had been told that her dead husband was still in Purgatory because she left her Catholic boy at the school. Conor had reason to believe that the same was said to his mother. He knew of first hand experience that his mother had to negotiate his Confirmation with the Parish Priest of Rathmines, while standing outside the door of the presbytery[15]. Despite her own strong religious feelings and the pressure exerted from her family and the clergy, Kathleen Cruise O'Brien continued to honour her husband's wish. In later life her son was exceedingly grateful for her strength of character on this point. But he realised too that his mother did suffer visibly and was depressed in her bereavement and trials. He has expressed his deep personal regret over his own attitude to his grieving mother, saying:

> I have remorse as I look back on that, because I never properly appreciated her position during her life. I saw her as being pushed around by her stronger minded sisters and as what they were pushing her around about was how I ought to be brought up, I resented this and I was not as nice to my mother as I ought to have been[16].

The attitude of the Catholic clergy to his mother led to a strong distaste in her son for the Irish Catholic Church. This built up into a deep cold resentment, which has only tempered very slightly with time.

Conor's family home was on Leinster Road in Rathmines, where his mother taught Irish in the nearby School of Commerce. The three widowed sisters gathered regularly at Kathleen's house for long Sunday dinners and teas, where there was always a warm welcome for family and friends. The long mahogany table could accommodate twelve quite easily and although dinner was, as a rule, confined to members of the family, the Sunday table often had its full complement of guests for tea – plain bread and butter and home-made scones and big cupfuls of strong tea. Conversation never lagged. Opinions differed widely on politics but were united on the feminist front. The young people, Conor, Owen, Betty Kettle and their friends, were often not able to get a word in edgeways, but they took their revenge in parlour games and charades. Owen was like an older understanding brother to Conor, particularly after the death of Conor's father.

As Conor was to assert many times, the year 1932 was a watershed one for politics in the young State, when the electorate made a decisive shift of allegiance and gave Eamon de Valera power. Among the people who rejoiced at this victory was the fifteen year old Conor, since it was nice, 'to be even remotely on the side of someone who was winning[17].

His mother had voted for de Valera because he was a gentleman and a good Catholic, though like herself, with sometimes strained relations with the clergy. Conor was fed up with the history of defeat within the family and wanted to be on the side of a winner who had brought legitimacy to the State for many erstwhile dissidents. He wrote:

> In my own family, for example, while criticism of Mr de Valera continued lively, the State itself was no longer treated dismissivly or derisively. It was now a State it would be proper to serve, as our family had believed it would be proper to serve a Home Rule State[18].

The boy even decided that he wanted to pursue a career in the Irish Foreign Service, when he graduated from university. The entire family thought this a laudable amibition. Even his unrepentant republican aunt, Hanna, who had broken with de Valera in 1926 when he led Fianna Fail into the Dail, was temporarily caught up in the euphoria of the defeat of the hated Cosgrave government and the release of republican prisoners by de Valera.

After Sandford Park, Conor entered Trinity College Dublin. This was a Protestant establishment not usually frequented by Catholics. Again he was following in the path of Owen Sheehy-Skeffington who had gone there on scholarship in 1927, and was appointed lecturer in French there in 1933. It is worth looking some years ahead at Owen Sheehy-Skeffington, since he was such a definite role model for Conor, particularly in his earlier years. Owen was a complex man, a staunch republican, who chose to go to Trinity because he would be able to continue playing cricket. He was quite a sportsman. He also swam, boxed, played rugby and became a member of the hurling club at Trinity. He was an ardent feminist, a skilled debater and a writer of note. In 1934 he joined the Irish Labour Party as a committed socialist. He married in a registry office in 1935. He opposed the Spanish Civil War and had contacts with the Republican Congress. He opposed the 1937 Constitution on feminist grounds and because of an absence of unity proposals. That same year he contracted tuberculosis and went to a Swiss clinic to convalesce.

The young Conor was never wealthy. As a student he only got by on an allowance from a relative. At Trinity he won a scholarship, which helped greatly. He became a resident of the college during his second year. It was at this time his mother died after a brief illness. His residency eased the difficulty of bereavement. To earn some money, he became the Trinity correspondent for *The Irish Times*, reporting on various aspects of College life. He later became Editor of the College magazine *TCD*. He was a frequent debater at College societies, being a rather boisterous student, intent on making all aware of his presence.

While at Trinity, Conor joined the Labour Party. This gave him another forum at which to display himself and his radical ideas before the student body. But he also got the opportunity to speak before a national audience in 1938, when he attended the

Annual Party Conference in Galway as a delegate from the College Branch. A burning topic of the day was the rise of Fascism in Europe and the Spanish Civil war which led so many young Irishmen to Spain, to fight on either side of that terrible war. The fact that the Fascist side was also seen as the Catholic side, made it a delicate matter in Ireland. The Labour Party had planned to avoid any debate on the Spanish War at its conference. Instead, it allowed a motion through, which congratulated the Labour Party in the Dail on their resistance to the recognition by Ireland of Italy's conquest of Abyssinia. The role of proposing the motion was that of the young Trinity delegate. He was not going to allow the Party hierarchy to stifle his greatest opportunity to achieve wide recognition for his intellectual and public speaking attributes. He had reached the national stage and he intended that the occasion would be remembered. This he succeeded in doing to a degree which caused a major furore at Conference, sorely embarrassed the Party, and captured newspapers headlines for himself. His 1938 performance foreshadowed accurately so many future interventions which caused so many people so much angst. The *Irish Weekly Independent*, which carried a large report under banner headlines said:

> References to the Spanish War by a Trinity College delegate at the conference on Wednesday led to a heated interlude, in which a prominent Labour deputy figured...

> Mr DC Cruise O'Brien, proposing the resolution, referred to the Spanish War and Mr McGowan TD, after some exchanges had taken place, stated that he felt it his duty as a citizen and a Catholic to protest against the remarks of the proposer. Moving the resolution, Mr DC Cruise O'Brien observed that all the progressive movements in Ireland for the past one hundred and fifty years came from Trinity College, and this observation was received with laughter by some delegates. Mr

O'Brien, continuing, pointed out that Wolfe Tone, Davis and other national leaders came from Trinity and the Citizen Army had its birth in rooms there (applause).

Having referred to recent events in Italy and Austria, Mr O'Brien went on to say that in the more controversial country of Spain, Fascism was militant. A civil war had been let loose wantonly by a clique of generals for their own ends and financed by a millionaire who made his money out of smuggling and the white slave traffic.

The revolution against a democratically elected government was being supported by Nazis and Italian troops. He was not there to defend Red atrocities, he was merely saying that these atrocities were all let loose by this small clique of Fascist generals. If one agreed with the judgement of votes rather than force of ballots against bullets, it was his duty to hold out against Fascism in all its forms, even in Spain.

The speaker resumed his seat amidst applause. Mr Frank Robbins, ITGWU, seconded the motion. Mr GL McGowan TD jumped to his feet and speaking with heat and vehemence opposed the speaker from Trinity College. He objected to the extraneous matter brought forward by the proposer and he would not accept it.

The Chairman said that there was no reference to Spain in the motion and could not be referred to by other speakers. Amid interruptions and jeers, Mr Norton appealed to Mr McGowan to remember the Press are present and he ought not say anything calculated to damage the Party outside.

Mr McGowan said that 'a motion proposed in such a

manner as has been done here today is going to do more to damage the Labour movement than anything I can say. I feel it my duty as a citizen and a Catholic to protect against the remarks of the Trinity college delegate. While we respect everybody's religious beliefs, we are Catholics first and politicians afterwards'[19].

The newspaper headlines came as a shock to most of Conor's family. His Aunt Mary, who since the death of his mother, felt she was responsible for his well-being, was not at all pleased. She interviewed the young man and told him what she thought of his speech. But within the family he also found support, particularly from Owen Sheehy-Skeffington, who was still recuperating in a Swiss clinic[20].

It was at Trinity that O'Brien first came into contact with many Protestants from Northern Ireland. These had a tradition of coming south for their university education. One very special Northern Protestant student, for Conor, was named Christine Foster. Her father, Alex, was the Principal of the Belfast Royal Academy, a rather well-known secondary school. She and Conor began to go out together. Christine's family, on both sides, but particularly on her mother's side, had as rich a history as that of Conor's relations. There were also interconnections between the families. Christine Foster, now in her seventies, and still an extremely attractive woman, described her family background and her first meeting with Conor thus:

> My father's family were from Derry. His father was Registrar of Births, Deaths, Marriages in Derry. They were rather narrow Presbyterians. My father was very much a scholarship boy. They were poor enough. He got a scholarship to Foyle College and then to Queens University. He was capped seventeen times for Ireland between 1910 and 1921, and played twice for the Lions

12

in South Africa. He was really very much a self-made man. He met my mother in Queens University. She was the daughter of Dr Lynd, who was an Honorary Moderator of the General Assembly of the Presbyterian Church. His family of seven, all very gifted and liberal people, included the well-known Robert Lynd. They all had similar views to Robert. They were in no way narrow Protestant Unionist, very far from it. They were very much in the Gaelic League, friends of Roger Casement, that sort of ambience.

Christine's father was born in Derry, where his first teaching post was in Foyle College. He later taught in Glasgow and then became Principal of Belfast Royal Academy. Christine came to Trinity College Dublin in 1936 to read Modern Languages, French and German. She knew Dublin well, saying, 'Two aunts and one uncle, all Lynds, lived in Dublin. One in the Civil Service, one teaching in Celbridge'. Her uncle was a Principal Officer in the Department of Finance. Her aunts had a flat in Ely Place. Christine herself stayed in Trinity Hall, which was the women's student residence on the outskirts of Dublin. It only entertained male guests for dinner. Her aunts and uncle provided a second home for Christine, there never being much of a generation gap in the Lynd family. They were all very friendly. Christine recalls her first sighting of Conor and their developing relationship towards marriage:

I remember seeing Conor when we were doing our entrance examinations. I think we were in College about two years before we became friendly at all. We moved in other kinds of circles. He always stood out because he was always first in whatever he was doing. He was also very much of a personality. He was not a person to be passed over in a crowd... We were not going out much more than a year and a half before we were married in 1939. It was unusual at the time for students to marry. It was probably a *cause celebre*. A curious thing was that Conor's uncle, Tom Kettle, was a very close friend of my uncle, Robert Lynd. In fact Kettle spent his last night in London, before he went to the War front to be killed, in Robert Lynd's house.

To begin with Conor was an extremely interesting kind of individual, intellectually very stimulating. I met his aunt, his father's sister, who worked in the Embassy in London and her son. They both had pretty acid tongues, which I think is characteristic of the O'Briens. [21]

The marriage of Christine and Conor was, like that of Owen Sheehy-Skeffington, a civil ceremony only. This relationship brought Conor into very close contact with the Protestant ethos of the North. In Belfast he became acclimatised to the comfortable life of middle class Protestants, as he wrote in his 1972 book, *States of Ireland*. That book states:

> The Northern Ireland that I came to know through Christine's relatives was that of the Protestant middle class, mainly in Belfast. Many of them were people of liberal views: nobody spoke unkindly of Papists; everyone was kind, or at worst polite to me personally. But somehow there were no Catholics around.[22]

This particular description and allied passages are hotly disputed by Christine, who is also annoyed that her mother's attitude to Britain during the war is not accurately portrayed in the same book. Of the quoted passage, Christine says,

> That is not so. We had plenty of Catholic friends in Belfast, unlike what Conor wrote in *States of Ireland*. He also very much misrepresents my mother in that book. My

mother was very much in favour of the Allied cause as we all were. But she was by no means the rabid pro-British person she is portrayed in that book. I had a terrible row with Conor over that book. I jolly well nearly...[23]

Conor had expected to enter the Diplomatic Service after graduating from Trinity. He did exceptionally well in his degree examinations, but he failed to pass the subsequent entrance test for the Civil Service. He decided to remain on at Trinity and take another degree in History and Politics. During this period, to keep himself and his wife, he did various part-time jobs, including teaching in his father-in-law's school in Belfast. His intention was to resit the civil service examination at a later stage.

Conor's doctoral thesis was on Charles Stewart Parnell. This afforded him the opportunity to study his own family history, on the Sheehy side particularly. His work on the period brought him to admire Parnell for his parliamentary leadership of the Irish party at Westminster. He saw how Parnell, though Protestant, led the Irish people and beat the British at their own parliamentary game of politics. He saw how his maternal grandfather's brother, Fr Eugene Sheehy, played a major part as a priest of the Land League, and pursued a role independent of the Vatican. But the black side of Conor's adulation of Parnell, was the fact that his maternal grandfather, David Sheehy MP had voted against Parnell, when he was being hounded by both Gladstone and the Catholic Church. He could not understand how this could have occurred. This weighed heavily on the young man, as he so clearly felt that Parnell had been betrayed by a motley set of cliques at the moment when he was about to achieve ultimate victory. Conor believed that Parnell had to win out or die [24]. His defeat led to the undermining of the Irish Party and the democratic process itself. Constitutional politicians sacrificed the greatest of Irish leaders at the bidding of Gladstone and earned contempt in their own country. Revolutionary politics got a huge fillip out of the debacle. Conor believed that if the Home Rule policy had been allowed to mature, unhindered by the 1916 Rising and Sinn Fein, a similar though less painful result would have emerged in a new State. He believed that both Home Rule and Sinn Fein were grounded in the soil of Catholic Ireland. He has written:

> I believe that the political independence of a twenty-six county state — which is what we have – could and would have been obtained peacefully on the basis of the Home Rule proposals reluctantly accepted by the Irish Party in 1914. The subsequent armed struggle was waged not to bring our present twenty-six county state into being, but to avert substantially that outcome, adumbrated in the proposals of 1914. This recourse to violence was a failure. It ended in the acceptance by a majority in the Dail and of the people, of a settlement based in substance though not in form, on Lloyd George's Parliament of Southern Ireland, which in turn was essentially what was offered to Redmond in 1914. Subsequent improvement on the Treaty settlement was won by negotiation and could, obviously, have been won in the same way on the basis of the 1914 Home Rule proposals [25].

Chapter Two

---◆---

---◆---

When Eamon de Valera became Taoiseach in 1932, he also took on the portfolio of the Minister of External Affairs. This enabled him to present himself as the embodiment of the nation, defending its interests against the usurping Saxon and also guarding against being outflanked by any zealot[1]. De Valera also embarked on establishing his 'External Association' with the British, though still being linked with the Commonwealth. He played an active role at the League of Nations, arguing that it could become a form of world government. But these fine sentiments were not followed up by the Department of External Affairs. Sean Lester, who was a long-time Irish Representative at the League in Geneva was 'persistently critical of the lack of interest of Irish policy-makers in the broader aspects of the League of Nations'[2]. Though de Valera became President of the League in 1938, he had lost confidence in it by 18 June 1936 when he spoke in Dail Eireann[3]. He maintained a neutral non-intervention policy amid various crises, most especially World War Two, which brought severe international criticism on him. Because of Partition, Ireland was the only Dominion to remain neutral, marking her out as quite different among the other Commonwealth countries.

17

In 1942, at the age of twenty-four, Conor again applied to join the Civil Service. This time he was successful and entered the Department of Finance. Much later he was to recall this period in a reflection on the 1970 Arms Crisis. He wrote: 'I served as a Junior Administrative Officer in Finance. J J McGelliot was Secretary in those days and Arthur D Codling an Assistant Secretary. They were two gentlemen of awesome probity and they impressed on me that there was scarcely anything worse a public servant could do than to apply money to a purpose other than that for which the Dail had voted it. If any such enormity occurred under that austere dispensation, a footnote in the Appropriations Account would read: The officer responsible has since left the Service[4]. Conor did not wish to remain in Finance. He again applied to join the Department of External Affairs. The basic qualification for application was a good honours university degree, with an upper age limit of thirty. An open competitive examination was followed by an oral Irish test. This led to the post of Third Secretary, which was the bottom rung of a career topped by that of ambassador. The entry process was very competitive, though given the few people attending university and emerging with a first or second class honours degree, it made the staff of the Department of External Affairs into a very esoteric and privileged group. On this second occasion Conor was a successful candidate. The extra few years may have matured him and the episode of his controversial speech in Galway in 1938, if it counted against him at all, was long since past. Once selected for the position, there was no training for new staff, apart from training on the job. They were placed in various sections within the Department for six month periods and expected to learn that way. There was a probation period of two years, though it was almost unheard of for a Third Secretary to be let go. As long as staff attended to their duties and behaved in an unobtrusive and diplomatic fashion, not engaging in any public controversy, they were assured of gainful employment. Thus, Conor Cruise O'Brien settled down to the relative anonymity of life as a privileged civil servant. He was ambitious to prove himself and gain

18

promotion, but that only came slowly within such a conservative body, where length of service was the main criterion for success.

Christine recalls the early days of their married life:

We were very happy early on. We had lots of friends in common. Although the War was on, it was a bad time to get a job, unless you went over and joined the War effort, which neither of us wished to do. It was difficult financially but my family helped a great deal. As soon as Conor joined the Civil Service, things were more or less comfortable. Donal was born in 1942, two years after we were married. I taught for some time after we were married. We had a flat in Fitzwilliam Square and later on Pembroke Road. Conor was always writing. He was a somewhat distant father in the rearing of the children. Young children, I think, bored him. He got on very well in the Diplomatic Service. We both had many friends there. He was unconventional from the point of view of that service. I don't know how much that weighed with his superiors. He was never a careful man[5].

They had two more children within a short space of time, both girls, Fedelma and Kate.

By 1948 de Valera had been Minister for External Affairs for sixteen years. The political problems there had almost exclusively been concerned with the government of the United Kingdom. The Coalition Government which ousted Fianna Fail that year gave the Ministry of External Affairs to Sean MacBride, the leader of Clann na Poblachta, and bitter opponent of de Valera. MacBride's four years at Iveagh House brought about a major expansion of the role and influence of the Department affecting the lives of all the staff there enormously. The major concerns of External Affairs still remained relations with the UK. But, in the post World War era MacBride played a major role in the OEEC (Organisation for European Economic Cooperation) recovery programme filtering Marshal Aid from the USA to a war-torn continent.

He also participated in the new Council of Europe, being President of the Council of Foreign Ministers in 1950. He was party to several fundamental European conventions signed during those years. He was instrumental in the Declaration of the Republic in 1949 and the crucial decision to remain outside NATO. All of this activity had to be serviced by an expanded department. The total expenditure for the department doubled. New forms of diplomatic activity developed especially on the information, publicity and cultural sides. MacBride spoke at length in the Dail and generally won support for its new role in the wider world.

In July 1949 MacBride announced that he was setting up two new sections within the Department, the Political Division and the Information Division. Conor was given charge of the latter. MacBride said that Ireland suffered from a wall of silence and indeed misrepresentation concerning Partition. He said that when he took over the Department it had no press attachés or information officers or a member of the diplomatic staff specially trained to deal with the Press and public relations. MacBride well realised that information was vital to the formation of public opinion which influenced public policy.[6]

Among the initiatives Conor was involved in at the Department, was the formation of an Irish News Agency and an anti-partition campaign. MacBride persuaded the Government that Ireland's case on partition and other matters was being presented to the wider world through British news agencies. He argued that Ireland needed to challenge this position. The Dail passed an 'Irish News Agency Act 1949'. Conor got the job of supervising the new agency, which had a short and chequered life. Brian Inglis was asked to work for the agency by Conor. He covered the first full meeting of the Council of Europe in 1950 where the honour of chairing the session fell to MacBride. Inglis writes of MacBride's address:

> ...irritating the English delegates who thought he

was being pretentious or offensive and puzzling the French, who found his treatment of their language stilted. And in a carelessly supercilious phrase MacBride allowed himself to give the impression that the Ministers regarded themselves as wise parents controlling the childish whims of their unruly children – the Assembly delegates[7].

Inglis goes on to say that when the defence debate took place several of the Irish delegates spoke, including Eamon de Valera, William Norton and Sean MacEntee, deploring the fact that Ireland was unable to participate in European defence while it was partitioned and part of it occupied by another member state of the Council of Europe. According to Inglis these contributions were received very badly by the assembled delegates but the Irish felt obliged to use the occasion to make their point. The report of proceedings issued by the Irish News Agency and carried on its front page by *The Irish Times*, made it clear that the Irish delegates had been met with hostility. This led to the Agency itself being treated in a hostile fashion by the Irish delegates. Inglis writes that MacBride had already been disillusioned by the Agency's failure to meet the Irish delegation on its arrival in Strasbourg[8].

The Anti-Partition Campaign was more overtly party political in nature. De Valera, still smarting from defeat at the polls, feared that MacBride would steal Fianna Fail clothes on anti-partition. De Valera began an international tour of India, Australia, New Zealand and the USA arguing the anti-partition case. MacBride had to pursue the matter publicly as well, airing the issue at various international fora. Conor had a domestic role in the campaign. He began to liaise with Northern Ireland politicians for his Minister travelling extensively throughout the north. Eddie McAteer, who had been returned unopposed to Stormont as MP for Mid-Derry, and Senator JG Lennon, were among the people Conor saw regularly. These visits were quite an education for him as it was his first major exposure to nationalists in the north. The

Unionists he had long since known. The difference between the two groups was most pronounced, the Unionists being by far the best well off, with all the connotations that implied for social and cultural intercourse. Conor also had the task of taking visitors to Ireland northwards, to see at first hand the injustices perpetrated by partition. He later wrote that he blushes to recall the amount of his professional time that was devoted between 1947 and 1951 to 'anti-partition'[9]. The only positive result of this activity, so far as he was concerned, was that it led him to discover the cavernous inanities of anti-partition and of government propaganda generally. Writing in 1972 he said that in 1951 he realised propaganda about 'Ireland's right to Unity was futile'.[10] Writing of MacBride in 1972 he described him as 'an attractive and dashing figure'[11].

Many years later in 1961, de Valera recalled to Conor a huge All-Party meeting on Partition in Dublin's Mansion House, in 1949. He told Conor that he had watched him enter the Hall with his Minister, MacBride. But, de Valera noted that all during MacBride's speech, Conor never took his eyes off himself, de Valera. De Valera said that he then remarked to himself, that that young man will definitely become a politician.[12]

Though being in full time employment, Conor was also writing seriously, like several others within the Department. In 1952 he had a book, called *Maria Cross*, published under the pseudonym of Donat O'Donnell. It was dedicated to Christine, his wife. It was an elaborate literary exercise devoted to criticism of the work of eight writers who were Catholics. These were François Mauriac, Georges Bernanos, Graham Greene, Sean O'Faolain, Evelyn Waugh, Charles Peguy, Paul Claudel and Leon Bloy. Conor considered whether the imaginative work of these Catholic writers is affected by their religion. He concluded by writing:

> The power of conviction which the best in these writers has over the others, who are not conscious of sharing either their religious outlook or their pattern of feeling, comes, I think, from this intuitive harmony of mystery

and suffering, the reverbation, even at the oblique touch of a fingernail, of the great Catholic bell. However much we may disclaim the tie, we are all related, like Raymond and his father – through Maria Cross[13].

Promotion within the Department was usually slow. An official's career up to the post of counsellor, which still entailed being directly supervised whether at home or abroad, generally took about twelve years. After that an official assumed direct personal responsibility either as head of a branch at Iveagh House, or as a *chargé d'affaires* or ambassador in charge of an overseas posting. Conor was Counsellor in Charge of Information at the Department and later in 1955 at the Paris embassy.

When I spoke to Christine about the wonderful time she must have had living in Paris, she said,

We were together in Paris for the year 1955-56. It wasn't enjoyable because by that time I was sure that the marriage was at an end. It was a difficult and unhappy time. Paris was dreadful. It was then I decided that something had to be done. It became increasingly difficult over a number of years. I took the initiative. The feeling of relief that I had was just as if some huge weight had been taken off... I did my very very best to accommodate..., but you find it a shade difficult to live... with God.[14]

Conor was very upset by this turn of events and was most hurt by the rejection involved. For one who was so brilliant and successful, it was a personal rebuff of the greatest proportions. The couple gradually came to a mutual agreement to end the marriage over a period of a few years, as we shall see later.

Conor and the family returned from Paris to Dublin, where he became Head of the United Nations Section at the Department. He also became a member of succeeding delegations to the General Assembly in New York. In 1960 he became Assistant Secretary with responsibility for Northern Ireland.

Chapter Three

The debate on UN membership for Ireland began in Dail Eireann on 24 July 1946. The Taoiseach Eamon de Valera, after the failure of the League of Nations to secure peace, was not very hopeful about the new body. He said 'In our circumstances, although it is impossible to be enthusiastic, I think we have a duty as a member of the world community to do our share'[1]. Ireland's application to become a member of the UN was vetoed by the USSR because there were no diplomatic relations between the two countries. Despite Ireland's active role under MacBride's ministry, or maybe because of it, since Ireland was so clearly with the Western democracies, the USSR continued to cast its veto over Ireland's subsequent applications. It was not until December 1955, when a deal was done at the UN allowing a corresponding number of countries from each side of the Iron Curtain to join, that Ireland was finally successful. In 1956 Ireland attended its first UN session. Much of the preparatory groundwork had been done by Conor Cruise O'Brien as Head of the UN section of the ministry in Dublin. The Irish delegation was led by Liam Cosgrave, the current Minister. It was guided by three principles: first, a scrupulous fidelity to the obligations of the UN Charter; second, Ireland should try to maintain an independent stance, with the intention of avoiding becoming associated with particular blocks or groups so far as possible; thirdly, Ireland was to do what she could to preserve Christian civilisation and to support wherever she could those powers primarily charged with the defence of the free world against communism. As Liam Cosgrave had said in the Dail, 'we belong to the great community of states made up of the USA, Canada and Western Europe'.[2]

Conor believed that in the early days the UN had to fit in with whatever the American view of a situation was. In 1950 the USA got the UN to support it in the Korean War, risking a confrontation with China. But in 1956 the USA refused to get involved in Hungary and risk a war with the USSR. The influx of Afro/Asian members ended the power of the USA to be the sole determinant of General Assembly decisions. Then the USA had to, as Conor saw it, at least manipulate sections of the new members against each other, in order to get its own way[3]. This situation also led to the Secretary General's Office belief, that it could play a more dynamic role between the power blocks. Liam Cosgrave condemned the Anglo-French invasion of Suez and the Russian invasion of Hungary in 1956.

The second Coalition Government fell in 1957 and the new Minister at External Affairs was Frank Aiken. (He was also Minister from 1951-1954). Mr Aiken was to retain this post continually until 1969. Aiken had been a close associate of de Valera's since the Civil War. He was well aware of how de Valera sought to pursue an independent policy at the old League of Nations. Aiken resolved to do the same at the UN and came to take an independent position on many issues much to the consternation of some Western nations. Conor regarded Aiken as a natural neutralist who required little, if any, advice from his juniors and subordinates.[4] Professor Joseph Lee has written of this period: 'Conor Cruise O'Brien provided Aiken with cerebral support. O'Brien, in particular, sought to model Ireland's international role on that of Sweden.' Lee also writes: 'Not even his most severe critics could accuse him (Conor) of unremitting self-effacement'[5]. Professor TD Williams writes: 'It was a period also when the Irish delegation influenced by Conor Cruise O'Brien, did a magnificent job of public relations'.[6]

Conor attended every UN General Assembly from 1956 to 1961. Those were exciting years for the diplomats at External Affairs. Ireland began to undertake an independent foreign policy, speaking out fearlessly on the major issues facing the world. Though Mr Aiken spoke the words and agreed with them, it was commonly believed that the detailed composition, the nuances, the points to emphasise belonged to the senior officials who sat behind him as he spoke. Dr O'Brien has given me the following comment on the previous paragraph:

I think the form of words used here in the passage beginning 'Though Mr Aiken spoke the words', present Aiken's role as more passive than it actually was. The way it worked was this: Aiken was responsible for the basic policy decision, that of pursuing an independent line, a position which was strongly opposed by two of the senior officials: FH Boland, Permanent Representative of Ireland at the UN and Eamonn Kennedy, Counsellor at the Permanent Mission. In relation to every question on the agenda of the General Assembly or any of its seven plenary Committees meeting simultaneously, Aiken would hold regular delegation meetings to consider Ireland's policy on the matter in question. He would hear reports from the Irish representative on the Committee in question and would invite the views of the other members of the delegation. When he had listened to the argument and put questions to the participants he would give a decision on the general line to be taken. If the matter was of sufficient importance for the Irish delegate to speak, instead of casting a silent vote, he would ask someone, usually the Irish delegate on the relevant Committee, to prepare a draft speech and show it to him. I used to draft his own speeches, after hearing from him an indication of his general thinking. He would go over the draft with me line by line, often suggesting changes, never insisting on these until he had heard my objection to the changes. He was an excellent Head of Delegation – firm without being overbearing, and considerate without being weak.

For Conor these were very fulfilling years as he reached an international audience with his own ideas. Ireland was in a unique position to speak and be listened to. It was clearly part of the western world but yet was only a new member. It had a very recent colonial past, when by force of arms, it had expelled one of the permanent members of the Security Council from part of its territory. Yet it was now on excellent terms with that same power. It was a model for so many countries which were in the process of untying colonial chains. It clearly had a foot in both blocks at the UN. As Mr Aiken put it at the UN:

> We know what imperialism is and what resistance to it involves. We do not hear with indifference, the voices of those spokesmen of African and Asian countries who passionately champion the right to independence of millions who are still, unfortunately under foreign rule... More than eighty years ago the then leader of the Irish nation Charles Stewart Parnell, proclaimed the principle that 'the cause of nationality is sacred, in Asia and Africa as in Ireland'. That is still a basic principle of our political thinking in Ireland today, as it was with those of my generation who felt impelled to assert in arms the right of our country to independence.[7]

One topic Aiken referred to every year, was that of the danger to the whole world of the spread of nuclear weapons. His policy was that of non-profilertion of them. In this he shared the view of all small and exposed nations. He also spoke on disengagement by colonial powers from their overseas colonies and earned mild disapproval from the United Kingdom delegation.[8]

But it was on the question of admission of the People's Republic of China (Red China) to the UN that really highlighted Ireland's independent role and brought the wrath of other Western nations upon it. The Chinese seat on the Security Council and in the General Assembly, was held by Chiang Kai Shek's ousted regime, which was based on the island of Formosa off the

Chinese mainland. This was very firmly American policy. Each year the matter of whether there should be a debate on the matter was voted upon at the UN and each year it was heavily defeated. In 1957 Ireland informed the USA that it proposed to vote in favour of a discussion on the matter and intended to vote accordingly. The USA was very displeased and tried to get the Irish to change. Cardinal Spellman of New York brought American displeasure into the public domain, when he spoke about the possible boycott of Aer Lingus and Bord Failte by Americans. This did frighten some people in Ireland who were directly concerned. But it did not affect Aiken's position. A motion of 'Disapproval of the Government Foreign Policy' was taken in the Dail, in government time on 28 November 1957, where Mr Aiken explained in detail what his policy was. Cardinal Spellman contacted the Irish Consul-General in New York on the matter.[9] A Monsignor from the Cardinal's diocese phoned Maire MacEntee, whose uncle was a Cardinal, and whose father was a minister in the Irish government. Maire MacEntee was a member of the Irish UN delegation and a formidable person in her own right. The Monsignor explained that the Cardinal could hardly attend the reception for the Irish delegation, if Ireland was to vote for Red China. Ireland voted as intended but as usual the matter was defeated. There was plenty of criticism from Ireland as well as from America. Many people chose to ignore the fact that all Ireland was voting for, was that a discussion should take place on the matter. When Liam Cosgrave spoke at the UN in December 1955 he adverted to the strange situation where the government of one quarter of the people of the world, the Chinese, was absent. When de Valera spoke at the League of Nations in 1934, he advocated the entry of the USSR to that body. On the particular vote Professor TD Williams writes: 'It was often loosely and exaggeratedly thought that Conor Cruise O'Brien had played the decisive part in influencing the Minister on this point ... the truth is that the Minister himself was in theory and in fact responsible'. [10]

Dr O'Brien has given me this comment on the China vote:

I happen to be the only surviving primary source for the origins of what became rather grandly known as 'Ireland's China Policy' for it originated in a conversation between me, as the then head of the newly created UN Desk at Iveagh House, and Frank Aiken as incoming Minister for External Affairs, in 1957. Aiken called me into his office on the first day, I believe, of his new term to discuss the agenda for the coming General Assembly. He began by telling me that he proposed to take a somewhat different line from his predecessor, Liam Cosgrave. Cosgrave had spoken and voted as part of 'the West'; he proposed to take a more independent line. I told him that in that case the most important item on the whole agenda, by far, was 'the question of the representation of China'. The vote was always taken on the question of 'whether to discuss the representation of China' – a formula designed to save Britain from the embarrassment of choosing between voting for the seating of Peking and displeasing America, and voting against the seating of Peking and possibly losing Hong Kong. This vote was always taken as the acid test of the independence of a delegation. Hardly any delegates thought it sensible to exclude Peking and seat Taiwan as a Permanent Member of the Security Council. Those who voted did so because they were afraid to displease the United States. This annual vote was one of the few in the General Assembly on which the White House kept a watchful eye because it was rightly regarded as an index on the international influence of the United States. Any change in Ireland's position would be strongly resented by the United States. On the other hand if we voted against discussion we would not be taken seriously over our claim to independence. After listening to me carefully and after having put a few questions, Aiken told

29

me he would vote for a discussion on the question of Chinese representation. We both fastened our seat belts.

It was clear that the major powers regarded their 'spheres of influence' as sacrosanct in the Cold War. The rights and wrongs of an issue were not necessarily important. The current national interest of a major power took precedence over the morality of any single issue anywhere. When Mr Aiken criticised the Chinese for aggression against Tibet, the USSR accused him of being a lackey of the USA. He retorted that peace in the world is indivisible saying:

> If the Assembly demonstrates that it is prepared to condemn wholesale violations of human rights, wherever they are perpetrated, it will be maintaining intact that invisible but effective barrier against further acts of aggression, which is constituted by a vigilant world public opinion. If, on the other hand, it chooses to ignore a flagrant denial of human rights to an entire people, then it weakens that barrier and must render further violations of human rights a little easier and a little more likely. [11]

The Chinese-Formosa situation was very volatile as in August 1958 the Communists launched air, sea and artillery attacks against another island held by its opponents, Quemoy, killing over two hundred people in one day.

The Irish role at the UN may have counted for very little, in fact, on any international level. It was the major powers which dominated. But for Ireland itself, and for many individual Irish people, it counted for a lot. For the Irish people it was heartening to see that, like at the Council of Europe, it could at least make its presence felt at the UN. It became a help to national morale to look outwards and not always be totally concerned by local problems. One point which requires explanation is why Ireland did not raise the problem of Partition at the UN where it would have received widespread sympathy. A conscious decision was taken that the internationalisation of this matter was not the way forward. Conor had reached that conclusion several years earlier and was able to convince his Minister on the correctness of the strategy. There were very obvious practical reasons for this as the Taoiseach, Sean Lemass, explained to Patrick Hillery TD, when he asked: 'Why don't you go the UN over the North?' Lemass replied that Ireland should do that 'only if you're ready to accept the decision for all time'. He explained that the British would win any vote in the security council where they have a veto. Ireland would lose on the matter and it would be copper-fastened for all time in the UN. [12]

In 1960 FH Boland became the President of the General Assembly and in 1962 Ireland served on the Security Council. In 1960 too, the UN became embroiled in a peace-keeping exercise in the newly independent Congo. General Sean McKeown served as a Commander-in-Chief of the multi-national UN forces. Ireland itself was happy to contribute troops to that UN force. The *Irish Press* editorialised thus in September 1960:

> Ireland's stature within the United Nations has been growing steadily. We can be proud that in tackling the Congo crisis the Secretary-General has again requested the contribution of Irish troops. That request arises out of the special position we have established for ourselves within the international community. We have, as the Taoiseach said last week, tried to deal with world problems and issues on their merits and arrive at fair and impartial conclusion.
>
> The UN request also reflects our special position as one of the few white peoples with no imperialist background. Our own history has taught us to reject the shoddy evasions of colonialism and our men go to the Congo with no illusions about the kind of breakdown that has taken place there and no secret ambitions to remain.

This sympathy and understanding for the aspirations of Afro-Asia is our troops greatest asset in helping to ease the birth-pangs of the new Congo. The Irish force to the Congo can be proud to follow the lead given by the Irish contingent to the Lebanon. Their job will be difficult, beset with hardship and unpleasant conditions. They go, secure in the knowledge that the nation appreciates their efforts and salutes their cause.[13]

Within a short space of time Conor himself would be singled out by the UN as it looked for specific people to serve it in the troubled Congo.

Chapter Four

BELGIAN CONGO IN CRISIS
IRISH TROOPS MASSACRED

❖

The Congo (known as Zaire since 1971) is a vast country in central Africa just edging far enough westwards to have a coastline on the Atlantic. It is rich in minerals particularly copper. It attracted many colonists especially from Belgium. It was called the Belgian Congo from 1908 when Belgium annexed it to its overseas territory. The winds of change for independence for African countries blew strongly at the start of the 1960s. In the Belgian Congo a mission educated trade unionist named Patrice Lumumba was very active in agitating for independence. In this he was supported by the ruler of newly independent Ghana, Mr Nkrumah. But it was as late as March 1960 before Lumumba was allowed to address a public meeting in the Congo. Riots followed and the Belgian authorities, highly nervous, declared martial law. Lumumba's party got control of large areas of the country very quickly as Belgian rule collapsed. The Belgians made a snap decision to grant the country independence and prepared to leave expeditiously. A teacher named Joseph Kasavubu was chosen as President with Lumumba as Prime Minister. Belgium handed over power that same year in June. King Baudouin attended the ceremony where, to the consternation of most, Lumumba criticised the departing colonial power in vicious terms. Within days the Congolese national army had mutinied against the government. European settlers feared for their lives and property. To try to quell the mutiny, all the white army officers were sacked. This succeeded in stopping the mutiny but did nothing to ease the fears of the Europeans, many of whom fled to the capital Leopoldville.

The richest and most advanced of the provinces of the Congo was Katanga in the South East. The valuable copper mines were there. The local political leader was Moise Tshombe, the son of a wealthy businessman. He suffered no inferiority complex with Europeans, treating them as equals. His most powerful ally was Godefroid Munongo, the grandson of the Paramount Chief of the Bayeke people. The most powerful economic unit in the entire country was the Union Miniere (mining company) in Katanga. The aim of this company, in the new situation, was to continue to prosper for its mostly foreign investors. It was prepared to take independent action to see that this would happen. It imported two hundred foreign mercenaries in June to protect its interests. It influenced Tshombe and Munongo to declare Katangan independence and to invite back the departed Belgian troops to safeguard the people against the mutinous Congolese national army. Tshombe had earlier refused to attend the Leopoldville independence ceremony. He claimed that the central government was plotting with his political enemies within Katanga and had already plundered Katanganese funds[1]. Kasavubu and Lumumba flew to Elizabethville, the capital of Katanga, but Munongo refused to allow their aircraft to land. Then the Vice Prime Minister asked for US troops to restore order. The US was reluctant to get involved, where it might come into conflict with a NATO partner, Belgium. But at the same time the US feared that the Russians would get involved. Something had to be done. The US then agreed that there was a role for the UN in a peace-keeping role. At this time Mr Nkrumah was warning against US involvement. He informed the Secretary General Dag Hammarskjold that only African troops should be sent in. Belgian troops arrived at Leopoldville airport uninvited. Lumumba declared martial law and threatened to ask Mr Khrushchev to send help. On 14 July the Security Council asked Belgian troops to withdraw and said the UN would send in military help. Less than two weeks later a UN force of over eight thousand European and African soldiers took up positions in the Congo, apart from Katanga. Russian supplies arrived for the Congolese army which invaded South Kasai, which had also declared its independence. Many people were killed especially Balubas. Katanganese gendarmerie, led by Belgian officers, repulsed a national army attack on Katanga. Hammarskjold visited Elizabethville in August to talk to Tshombe. There was pressure on UN troops to go in to Katanga. Hammarskjold announced that the UN would send an advance party to Elizabethville under Ralph Bunche. Tshombe declared Katanga an independent, sovereign and constitutional state.

In November of that year the whole Irish nation was horror stricken when it was announced that a group of Irish soldiers serving with the UN in the Congo had been ambushed at Niemba by Baluba warriors. Many of them were killed and some remained missing for a time. Their deaths shocked the country and their state funeral to Glasnevin cemetery was one of the biggest ever seen in Dublin. Paradoxically their deaths seemed to stiffen the resolve of the country to remain totally committed to service with the UN, as a new battalion was preparing to leave early in the new year.

In the Congo political events were reaching farcical proportions. President Kasavubu decided to sack Lumumba, who refused to accept the dismissal. Each came to be protected from the other by UN forces. Political stalemate ensued for some months as the various factions and their international backers jockeyed for power. In Ireland the time had come for the new Irish battalion to travel to the Congo. The *Irish Independent* editorialised on the situation:

> Tomorrow the troops of the thirty-fourth battalion will begin leaving for the Congo. They will join the UN forces just as General Sean McKeown is settling in to his new post as Commander-in-Chief... Mr Kasavubu has called a round-table conference of the opposing political leaders, to begin on 25 January. Merely to place the Army Commander, Colonel Mobutu, across the table to Mr Lumumba and the Premiers of Kasai and Katanga is not

35

to guarantee agreement...   The eight African and
Asian states that met in Casablanca at the week-end
declared violently and unhelpfully for Mr Lumumba.
Last month, eleven African States, all former French
colonies, declared for President Kasavubu. Their
decision was welcomed by the Western Bloc, while the
Soviet Bloc clearly favoured the Casablanca states. It is
time for the Congolese to grow tired of being the pawns
of world and African political chess... No news could be
more welcome to those Congolese lacking food and
medicine or to the UN contingent, now undergoing
major changes of personnel, or to the men of the thirty-
fourth battalion.[2]

The farce and tragedy continued in the Congo. The Congolese
army captured Lumumba. He later escaped to Stanleyville only to
be recaptured and returned to Leopoldville. Almost all the
Congolese factions wanted rid of him. They were afraid of his
personal power. The central government wanted Tshombe to take
custody of him, but Tshombe refused. Later Kasavubu and
Mobutu had Lumumba flown to Katanga anyway. Whether
Tshombe had agreed to this is unknown. But Lumumba did not
survive for very long after he disembarked at Elizabethville. His
body was never produced[3]. His death was announced in February
1961.

    The UN were studying the situation in Katanga very carefully.
On 21 February the Security Council passed a vital resolution
urging 'measures for the immediate withdrawal and evacuation
from the Congo of all Belgian and other foreign military and para-
military personnel and political advisers not under the UN
command, and mercenaries'. It 'urged that the UN take
immediately all appropriate measures to prevent the occurence of
civil war in the Congo, including arrangements for ceasefires, the
halting of all military operations, the prevention of clashes, and
the use of force, if necessary in the last resort'. It also noted with
deep regret the killing of Patrice Lumumba.

In March Hammarskjold asked the Irish Government to release Conor Cruise O'Brien to serve as the UN Representative in Katanga. He was agreeable to the proposal but the Government refused the request. It felt that Ireland was heavily enough involved already in the Congo. In May the UN Secretariat renewed its request for O'Brien. This time it asked for him to be allowed join the UN staff, making no mention of the Congo. The Irish Government agreed to second him for a two year period. O'Brien flew to New York that same month. There he was briefed on the Congo situation. The UN was insistent that it would come well out of its operation there. It agreed with the American view that the secession of Katanga must be ended so that Communism would not get a foothold in Africa.

O'Brien has speculated that the choice of UN Representative in Katanga lay between himself and another Irish diplomat, Mr Eamonn Kennedy. He surmised that though the latter knew more about the African situation than he, and would have been the 'safer' man, he, O'Brien, was chosen because he was regarded as the 'radical' member of the Irish delegation given to be open about being anti-colonial. He surmises that if Mr Kennedy was unable to implement the UN resolutions peacefully, he would accept the *status quo* in Katanga, but that he, O'Brien, would act if necessary, at grave risk to that (Katangan) law and order. O'Brien believed these were among the reasons why he was the chosen one by Hammarskjold. O'Brien has also written that Hammarskjold had also liked his earlier book *Maria Cross*. It was also felt that an Irishman was an obvious choice for the post.[4]

O'Brien was in fact replacing a Mr Dayal of India who had been the UN representative in the Congo. He had run into criticism from Western countries, particularly during the stand-off between Kasavubu and Lumumba, when he refused to execute a warrant to have Lumumba arrested, but sought instead to have all Congolese leaders talk together. Conor found Dayal, despite his recent ordeal, extremely impressive. He did not appear to have let his removal upset or embitter him. Dayal told Conor that the West had supported Kasavubu against Lumumba. He emphasised to Conor that 'the essential thing is to safeguard the office of the Secretary-General'[5]. Ian Colvin, who was in Katanga for the duration and wrote a biography of Tshombe, believed that warning to have meant that Hammarskjold was going to countenance secret military operations in Katanga[6]. O'Brien read the warning as meaning that the Office of the Secretary-General must be preserved as an independent focus of supranational loyalty[7]. Whether Conor knew that he was about to enter a very dangerous minefield, on which there might be casualties, is not absolutely clear, but he was ready for action.

Dr O'Brien informs me that he regards my earlier description of Mr Tshombe as 'not reliable'. He writes:

> This is how the people who controlled Tshombe liked to present him. And the people who controlled him were undoubtedly the European financial interests in Katanga, primarily the Union Miniere... Tshombe was essentially a servant of the powers that were, in whatever place he was. In Leopoldville he said what the UN wanted him to say. In Elizabethville he said what the Union Miniere wanted him to say and in Rhodesia, later, he said whatever the British wanted him to say.

Dr O'Brien also writes that Mr Dayal:

> ...had been Special Representative in the entire Congo in Leopoldville. Hammarskjold did not want to replace him in that office for fear of giving offense to the Indian government whose support was most important to him. He downgraded the Leopoldville post to an officer in charge and appointed me as his personal representative in Katanga.

Dr O'Brien also adds that he knew alright that he was about to enter a very dangerous minefield.

SUDAN

CENTRAL
AFRICAN
REPUBLIC

PEOPLE'S REP.
OF THE CONGO

River Congo

REP. OF THE CONGO

UGANDA

•Stanleyville   Lake Victoria

Equator

RWANDA

Goma ●

BURUNDI

Kindu ●

Niemba ●

TANZANIA

Lake Tanganika

KASAI

■LEOPOLDVILLE

Kananga ●

Albertrville

Kamina ●

KATANGA   Lake Mweru

Jadotville●

Elizabethville

●Ndola

ANGOLA

SOUTH ATLANTIC OCEAN

NORTHERN RHODESIA
(ZAMBIA)

Tropic of Capricorn

Approximate scale: 35 mm : 800 km

Chapter Five

---◆---

---◆---

Conor Cruise O'Brien first arrived in Elizabethville on 14 June 1961 as special representative of the UN. He was welcomed on arrival by a guard of honour from the Irish UN contingent. He took up residence at the Villa des Roches, an expansive single storey building which included a swimming pool. Up to seven or eight UN personnel also lived at the house. Elizabethville was a mining town founded in 1910. It had a cathedral and a university. It was a pleasant place to live, situated about four thousand feet above sea level. The shops were well stocked with consumer goods; there was an excellent golf course. There was a large expatriate European population enjoying a high standard of living. Up to thirty-two thousand Europeans lived in the province of Katanga.

The man O'Brien most wanted to meet on his arrival was absent from Elizabethville just then. Moise Tshombe was in jail in Leopoldville. In the previous April, Tshombe had left Katanga to meet central government leaders in Coquillatville, capital of Equateur Province. After disagreement at the talks, Tshombe walked out only to be arrested and taken to Leopoldville. In May he was charged with rebellion, repression and use of illegal currency. But on 22 June in the presence of new Prime Minister Ileo and General Mobutu, he was set free. Then he said, 'Katanga is ready to end its secession, the armed forces of Katanga will be put under the command of General Mobutu. I will return to Katanga to give effect to these decisions and then visit Leopoldville and work for Congo unity'.

41

For O'Brien waiting in Elizabethville, this was very good news indeed. The UN mission was to assist and encourage precisely this to happen. Four days later Tshombe met O'Brien in Elizabethville for an exchange of views. But now that he was back safely in Katanga, Tshombe saw the situation rather differently. He felt that Katanga would remain independent. In early July the Katangan National Assembly repudiated the agreement Tshombe had made with the central government. It also refused to send any representatives to the central parliament in Leopoldville.

O'Brien continued to negotiate with Tshombe on his immediate mission, to get rid of the foreigners assisting the Katangan forces. There were reckoned to be about five hundred of them left, mostly Belgians. Protracted negotiations went on with little positive outcome. O'Brien also continued to advise Tshombe to go to Leopoldville and accept the authority of the central government.

Mahmoud Khiary, a Tunisian UN diplomat, came to Elizabethville to consult O'Brien who told him that the Katangans felt that the UN was merely playing games. He felt that it had to be demonstrated to them that this was not so[1]. Khiary was acting head of UN Civil Operations in the Congo. He had come as a special delegate of the Secretary-General, Hammarskjold, to invite Tshombe to attend a summit meeting in Leopoldville. O'Brien later passed on this invitation. O'Brien felt that Tshombe was a virtual prisoner of the Europeans in Elizabethville and of Munongo, his colleague. O'Brien offered Tshombe a safe UN passage but felt there was little hope of progress.[2] To make matters worse, Radio Katanga reported O'Brien's exhortations as orders to Tshombe. Tshombe did offer to meet the central government leaders outside the country or in Katanga but not in Leopoldville. But O'Brien told him this would be unacceptable to central government.

O'Brien's son, Donal, a university student at Cambridge, was staying at Villa des Roches with his father during his summer holidays. Together they toured much of Northern Katanga to see conditions on the ground. The following month, August, O'Brien took a few weeks home leave. He was content to bide his time for a while. The London *Times* in an editorial (31 July) said: 'Unfortunately, the creaking civil administration of the UN in Katanga, overstaffed and with too high a proportion of mediocrities engaged in a Parkinsonian paper-chase, does not inspire much confidence'.

In late August O'Brien announced the arrival of a battalion of Indian troops from North Katanga to Elizabethville. Mahmoud Khiary gave authority for a UN operation to apprehend all foreign officers. O'Brien proposed extra action so as to lessen the risk of bloodshed. He got authorisation from Khiary to detain Munongo temporarily and to take control of the Radio Station and Post Office. On the morning of 28 August, Indian and Swedish UN troops attained all objectives. O'Brien received a telegram of congratulations from Hammarskjold on an exceedingly sensitive operation carried through with skill and courage. Two hundred and seventy-three foreigners were apprehended. Seventy others had sought sanctuary in the Belgian consulate. Then the Belgian Consul, backed by other Western Consuls, appealed to the UN to allow the Belgian mercenaries to leave the country voluntarily and avoid the indignity of arrest. This was agreed over O'Brien's head. Belgium later repudiated this agreement to have them leave voluntarily[3].

The Western Consuls proceeded to put pressure on O'Brien concerning the safety of their citizens in the new situation. There were also about four thousand Balubas living in a UN protected camp who were afraid of Katangan forces. This placed the UN in the position of being regarded as the enemies of the Katangan forces.

Tshombe offered to announce his agreement to the departure of Belgian officers, if the UN returned the Post Office and the Radio Station. He announced over the air:

> My dear compatriots, I wish to explain the situation in view of the false reports circulating... the United Nations is at present engaged in withdrawing military personnel of foreign nationality serving in the Katangan gendarmerie. The Government bows to the decision of the UN. It wishes to thank the officers, non-commissioned officers and men of foreign nationality for the services that they have rendered to Katanga, and to pay tribute to their ability and devotion. They can rest assured that the Government will not forget them. The Government appeals to the population to maintain calm. Katanganese will henceforth be in command of the armed forces of Katanga at all ranks. These forces will continue to maintain order and protect lives and property[4].

In his commentary on my text, Dr O'Brien says the UN initiative was not lost as the Belgian officers were in fact expelled.

O'Brien tried to get Tshombe to sack Munongo as Minister of the Interior on the grounds of plotting against the UN and because of atrocities committed against the Balubas. As O'Brien wrote: 'The thing to do with Munongo was not to investigate his impartiality... but to get him behind bars ... I was now seeking authority through Leopoldville, from New York, to arrest Munongo'[5]. On 9 September, Tshombe told Ian Colvin of the *Daily Telegraph* that he had learned of a plot by the central government in concert with the UN to invade Katanga and that he had confronted O'Brien with it. Two days later Khiary arrived at Elizabethville with authorisation for further military action if Tshombe continued to prove intransigent. Main installations were to be taken and most government ministers, except Tshombe, were to be arrested. Khiary said Hammarskjold had given authority for these operations. But since the Secretary-General was due in Leopoldville in two days time, the action should precede his arrival or occur after his departure[6]. The next day O'Brien again met Tshombe and invited him to go to Leopoldville. Ian Colvin, who also met Tshombe that day, later met O'Brien also. Colvin reports O'Brien as saying to him: 'I merely told Tshombe, if you refuse this proposal, I will take your refusal as definite and final'[7]. Khiary and O'Brien together, met Tshombe where Khiary invited Tshombe to come to Leopoldville to meet Hammarskjold.

The next morning, Irish, Indian and Swedish UN troops took over targeted buildings. Much shooting and killing occurred. At 4am Tshombe phoned O'Brien to find out what was happening. O'Brien told him of the UN objectives. He asked Tshombe to agree to issue an unconditional ceasefire and end the secession. Tshombe agreed to do so on the radio. O'Brien then sent for Tshombe. Unfortunately Tshombe could not be located nor did it appear that UN soldiers were in the vicinity of his palace. O'Brien later went with an escort to Tshombe's house but no contact was made. The only government minister the UN had managed to arrest was Kibwe, the Minister for Finance. Later that morning O'Brien gave a press conference. He said that the first shots that morning were fired from the Belgian Consulate by unknown Europeans. He said the action had been taken on a request from the central government which was sending a Commissioner to Elizabethville. He added that the secession of Katanga was ended. He also appeared to think that all military operations were also finished[8].

That evening the Katangan UN reported to the UN at Leopoldville on the mornings action. The report read:

1920 from HQ Katanga Command Eville to ONUC Leopoldville.

Info: HQ Sector A Aville, HQ Sector B Eville, HQ Sector C Kamina.

Sitrep from 121600 Z to 131600 Z

45

FIRSTLY for OP. Morthor plan as follows. Alpha. 1 Dogra Bn Gp with under cmd one coy 3/1 AR. task. seize. one. EVILLE post office and Radio installation in vicinity. two. Radio Katanga studio. three. Take in UN custody minister of info SAMALENGHE. four. secure air field² five custody of arrested personnel. BRAVO. 35 Irish battalion Gp. task. seize. one. Radio transmitter at college St Francois. two. take into UN custody Minister of Finance KIBWE three seize and est rd bloc railway tunnel. four secure refugee camp at factory and own line. charlie 12 SWED battalion Gp with one coy of 3/1 AR task to seize. one. radio transmitter en route de Kilobelobe. two take into UN custody Minister interior MUNONGO. officers of sûreté white personnel working and African chiefs. three secure refugee camp. SECONDLY first shot was fired from Belgian Consulate³ building near post office at 130400 B at DOGRAS. THIRDLY radio Katanga studio and post office captured by DOGRA by 130500 b after heavy stiff hand to hand fighting. both places counter attacked by gendarmerie with their armd cars led mostly by BELGIANS in civilian clothes. counter-attack repulsed by DOGRAS and SWEDISH armd cars. FOURTHLY due heavy mortar fire and automatic fire from gendarmerie studio completely damaged beyond repairs. FIFTHLY Irish Bn captured transmitter at College St Francois firmly in our hands. SIXTHLY Swedish Bn captured radio transmitter KILOBELOBE. SEVENTHLY. strong and automatic firing and sniping inside the town continues. EIGHTLY IRISH coy at JADOTVILLE attacked by gendarmerie. attack repulsed reinforcement of one coy and three armd cars sent to JADOTVILLE and coy directed to remain there until further orders. NINTHLY Kibwe apprehended. MUNONGO, MUTAKA, SAMALENGHE and KIMBA have disappeared. Tshombe is not traceable at present... ⁹

Hammarskjold had arrived in Leopoldville that same day and so would have been privy to the report of what happened. As the report mentioned an Irish UN Company at Jadotville was attacked by gendarmerie. Jadotville was north west of Elizabethville. Five hundred Katanganee forces had surrounded one hundred and fifty-eight Irish soldiers. The vital military base at Kamina on which the UN was dependent for supplies and reinforcements was surrounded by thousands of Baluba warriors[10]. These could have obliterated the UN forces if they had launched an all out attack. But their numerical and positional superiority demonstrated that the UN could not coerce Katanga and that the military operation undertaken by the UN was premature and exposed UN soldiers to grave danger[11].

Coincidentally the trial of five Baluba warriors held responsible for the deaths of the UN Irish at Niemba in November 1960 had been scheduled to begin at the District Court in Elizabethville on 14 September, but had to be adjourned due to the conflict begun the previous day.

The UN action had proved to be a fiasco militarily and politically. The action was condemned by the Western press, fed by local Europeans and some members of the press corps, either from Rhodesia and/or working for papers whose policy was pro-Katangan. Subsequently O'Brien attacked this press coverage as unfair and biased. He would have been very naive to expect the Western press to have supported his actions. About this time he read an article about himself in a Portuguese paper *'O Globo'*, with the text apparently supplied by the London Express Service. It was carried by several Western papers. O'Brien believed it may have derived from the British Foreign Office. It was headed:

WHO IS CONOR CRUISE O'BRIEN, THE MAN WHO BETRAYED
THE IDEALS OF THE UN?'

Part of the text ran as follows:

Mr O'Brien's lack of political ability is disastrous. He

cherishes the ambition of becoming an 'international civil servant' in New York. Hammarskjold had picked him out as a possible Under Secretary. But it is clear, we have to do with a man whose discernment does not inspire confidence.

His policy in Katanga has been a Russian policy. He is not a Communist, but in the UN he sought the company of African and Asian leaders. Here as in Dublin, he supports the admission of Communistic China to the UN. He is strongly attached to the policy of disengagement in Europe. He is a supporter of nuclear non-proliferation. Politically, if not personally, he hates the English. In this, in my view, lies the explanation of his policy in Katanga'[12].

Meanwhile Tshombe could not be located. O'Brien was forced to use the captured Kibwe as authority for a broadcast directing a ceasefire in Katanga 'in the name of President Tshombe'. Two days later Tshombe himself broadcast a call for 'all-out war' against the UN. The Indian headquarters was hit by mortar bombs and several soldiers killed. At Jadotville the situation for the Irish was critical too. The Lord Mayor proposed a ceasefire and negotiated with Commandant Quinlan of 'A' Company. Three conditions were agreed to:

1. That the water would be turned on for them.

2. That food would be made available.

3. That the Fouga jet would be grounded.

Unfortunately these conditions were not implemented. There was no UN air support and the Irish position was being bombed and strafed by the Fouga. They were very short of food and water. Finally they were forced to surrender to Munongo. Three other Irish soldiers were killed trying to locate Tshombe's secret radio transmitter[13].

The UN needed reinforcements badly but that would take

time, even if it was agreed. O'Brien was still making efforts to locate Tshombe but without success. Eventually he discovered that Tshombe was on the Rhodesian border. Tshombe offered to meet O'Brien in Rhodesia. The latter thought this would be very wrong[14]. He was also extremely annoyed that the British, via Rhodesia, seemed to be backing Tshombe against the UN. Nevertheless O'Brien informed Leopoldville and giving them his opinion, awaited instructions. By this time the Katangan situation had become of major concern in many capital cities of the Western world particularly. It could no longer be left to O'Brien or others on the ground to adjudicate. And Hammarskjold was in Leopoldville. There he was coming under intense personal pressure.

Dag Hammarskjold was born in 1905, in Sweden, where his father was later to become Prime Minister. He became Secretary-General of the UN in 1953. He sought to build up the power and authority of his office so that it could play a meaningful role in the power politics of the UN. He was being fairly successful in this. But he could not afford to be seen to be on the side of any particular bloc. Neither could he give any hostages to fortune, or else he would not last long in his powerful post. This UN action in Katanga exposed his long and painstaking efforts to great danger. On the evening the UN action began in Elizabethville, the British Ambassador in Leopoldville, Derek Riches, told him that, 'her Majesty's Government was serving notice, with the greatest emphasis at its command, that Britain would have to consider withdrawing all support from ONUC's (Organisation des Nations Unies au Congo) missions unless:

1. Hammarskjold could provide an acceptable explanation for what had happened in Katanga: or

2. Hammarskjold could provide an assurance that the fighting would be swiftly ended.' [15]

Hammarskjold knew what had happened in Elizabethville. It appears pretty certain that he had authorised it and that O'Brien had acted in total good faith. But in the aftermath, Hammarskjold had to distance himself and his office from it. O'Brien has written that if Hammarskjold had not authorised it he could have come to Elizabethville and sacked Khiary, Linner (the Officer-in-Charge in the Congo) and himself and secure an immediate ceasefire. If he had authorised it or even if he wished to support the UN action, he could have done so under the February 1961 UN Resolution. But this was not practical politics for Hammarskjold. He had to consider the macro situation of power politics and of course he did not want to become a pawn to any of the members of the Security Council or the General Assembly. The UN issued a statement on the events in Elizabethville, which did not confirm with what actually happened there.

O'Brien was feeling isolated in Elizabethville. Only General Sean McKeown came to Elizabethville from the UN Headquarters at Leopoldville. O'Brien appreciated his presence. McKeown told him of the never ending meetings going on in Leopoldville with Hammarskjold[16]. Grim messages passed between the two UN posts. According to Ian Colvin, Hammarskjold, acting through British mediators, invited Tshombe to meet him at Ndola in Northern Rhodesia, advising Tshombe that any meeting with O'Brien was cancelled[17]. Part of Hammarskjold's message read:

A Principle of the UN which is absolutely binding upon all is the maintenance of peace and, to that end in order to protect human life, they (UN) are bound to cease all hostilities and to seek solutions to the conflict by means of negotiation, mediation and conciliation. I have been informed of the message received by Mr. O'Brien from Mr Dunnett, the British Consul, inviting him to meet you at 11.30 at Bancroft in Northern Rhodesia. I suggest that I should try to meet you personally, so that together we can try to find peaceful methods of resolving the present conflict, thus opening the way to a solution of the Katanga problem within the framework of the Congo.

This must have been a very bitter message for O'Brien to have to transmit to Tshombe. It clearly cut O'Brien out of the picture, if not implying a certain blame on him for what had happened. He was being jettisoned by his boss. But O'Brien did not give up without a struggle. He sought permission to join Hammarskjold's party going to meet Tshombe, who had replied to the invitation thus: 'The President and the Katangan government agree on the principle of a ceasefire.' O'Brien wanted an opportunity to tell his version of his mission to Katanga directly to Hammarskjold. He also wished to persuade him not to see Tshombe in Rhodesia. But Hammarskjold rejected O'Brien's overtures and left for Ndola airport. There Tshombe awaited him in the company of Lord Alport, the British High Commissioner and the Marquis of Lansdowne, the special emissary of Harold MacMillan, the British Prime Minister.

Hammarskjold's aircraft, the Albertina piloted by a Swede crashed into the bush nine miles short of Ndola airport. Everybody on board was killed. The next morning Ian Colvin interrupted a press conference Tshombe was giving at Kitwe, to announce that Hammarskjold was dead. His body was later laid out in the church at Ndola, before being brought back to Sweden. He was postumosly warded the Nobel Peace Prize later in the year.

Three days later on 20 September Khiary signed a provisional ceasefire with Tshombe at Ndola. O'Brien continued to be the UN representative in Katanga. He told Ian Colvin on 29 September 'we insist on the withdrawal of foreign military men. We do not know exactly their numbers, but there are more than a hundred. I do not want to speculate on what we will do if they are not withdrawn'[18]. Georges Dumontet, who had been O'Brien's predecessor in Katanga, arrived in Leopoldville, where the press speculated he would replace O'Brien in Elizabethville. This would have been the final insult to O'Brien. Though he had made bitter enemies among Western nations, he had won some approval in Afro/Asian countries. The leader of Ghana, Dr Nkrumah, who had troops with the UN in the Congo, had sent a message of goodwill and concern for his safety to the UN during the fighting at Elizabethville.

O'Brien was bewildered and depressed due to his lost rapport with the UN headquarters at Leopoldville. He was also very eager to reinstate himself in the good offices of the UN at New York. He wrote, 'I was rather childishly anxious to reinstate myself in their good graces: a feat the impossibility of which would have been clear to my mind, had the lucidity of analysis not been rendered turbid by hope[19]. He then committed the only action of his time in Katanga of which he was ashamed. At a press conference in Elizabethville, he tried to fudge the facts and marry his own previous account of what had happened with the official UN version. He was stopped in his tracks when challenged by a journalist who had been at his earlier press conference on 13 September. 'This is not what you said', the journalist insisted much to the discomfort of O'Brien. There was an opportunity to learn, that it is a good practice for people who are in positions of power to be publicly cross-examined by the press.

An Irish reporter who met Dr O'Brien at that time said that in spite of the constant strain of his job, he was looking well and in good spirits. He exuded a spirit of confidence and assurance, though he was not inclined to speculate on the outcome of it all[20].

The final ceasefire between the UN and Tshombe was signed on 13 October by Khiary. The UN and the central government continued to build up their fighting capability. The huge refugee camp of Balubas continued to exist outside Elizabethville. Khiary advised them to remain under UN protection *pro tempore*. Katanganese gendarmerie scored some early successes against invading government troops.

In the middle of October O'Brien got a letter from a friend in Dublin saying that Dr Ralph Bunche of the UN Headquarters in New York, advised that O'Brien should seek a transfer from his present posting. On a visit to Leopoldville, O'Brien was asked by Dr Linner whether he would like to transfer to New York or Leopoldville. Feeling that the British government was behind these moves,[21] O'Brien decided that he would remain in Katanga for as long as he was permitted. His own pride and anger with Britain made him stay.

At the end of the month, O'Brien received an enormous personal boost when the lady he had been in constant communication with, and whom he loved, arrived to spend a holiday with him at Villa des Rohes. She was Maire MacEntee who also worked with the UN in New York.

Over the preceding few years Conor's private life had undergone a complete transformation. He and his first wife had moved, in a very civilised way, to a final separation, culminating in a Mexican divorce in 1961. Christine remained in the family home on Howth Head with their children. They found the separation difficult, particularly Kate, who was the youngest and at a most sensitive age. Donal was then an undergraduate student at Cambridge and away from the trauma. At that stage the British press were ranged against Conor because of his role in the Congo. Christine believed that they raided Conor's New York hotel room and discovered their marriage separation agreement. This news they proceeded to try and use against him in a sensational way. They soon came after her too, almost besieging her home. At that stage Christine had an understanding with her future husband, George Hetherington, also living in Howth. He was leaving an existing marriage and bought another house in Howth for himself and Christine. She decided to move in there with her two girls in order to avoid the British press. This strategy did not work and Christine was advised by her good friend, Douglas Gageby, the Editor of *The Irish Times*, to remain within the house and stay away from all windows. As Christine says, the photographers had their long Toms trained on every window of the house, 'like a pack of jackals'[22]. George Hetherington was the managing director of Healy's printing division until it was taken over by the Smurfit company. He also became Managing Director of *The Irish Times*. He was a highly cultured man and well known to Dr O'Brien.

Conor and Maire MacEntee had known each other for many years. They shared many common interests and gradually formed a deep attachment to each other. She was five years his junior, born in 1922. Her mother was one of the Brownes of Grangemockler in Tipperary, and her father Sean MacEntee was a native of Belfast. The latter had participated in the 1916 Rising and had his death sentence commuted. He was elected Sinn Fein MP for Monaghan in 1918. He was a founder of Fianna Fail and a TD since 1927. He had been a Minister for Finance on eleven occasions and was the current Tanaiste of the Irish Government. Maire's mother was a most impressive academic, being the only woman elected to the governing body of University College Dublin in 1932. Three of Maire's maternal uncles were distinguished Catholic clergymen: Cardinal Michael Browne OP, Monsignor Padraig de Brun and Maurice Browne PP. Maire herself took an Arts degree at University College Dublin and studied at the Sorbonne. She became a fluent Irish speaker through family holidays at Dunchaoin in the Kerry Gaeltacht. She was a noted poet in Irish. She entered the Department of External Affairs, becoming a First Secretary and a member of the Irish delegation to the United Nations in New York. So Conor had become involved with a woman of rich familial characteristics, some of which he himself did not share. But Maire, like Conor, was a formidable personality in her own right. They both needed to be, as their relationship was very soon to prove embarrassing to family and friends, on several fronts.

Maire's fortunate arrival in Elizabethville coincided with an important trip Conor was to make to North Katanga. She accompanied him to Albertville for the raising of the Congolese National flag.

The previous day, eleven Italian airmen had been murdered at Kindu in Kasai Province by contingents of the national army. Other such contingents arrived in Albertville shortly after O'Brien and his friend had left and proceeded to loot the town. O'Brien sent orders for the disarming and punishment of the offenders. It was to be his last command in Katanga.

Coincidentally two days earlier, on 13 November, judgement was given on the five Baluba warriors charged with the killing of the Irish soldiers at Niemba the previous year. They were found guilty of murder. Two got three years penal servitude. Three got two years[23].

Both O'Brien and General McKeown were summoned to New York for a debate in the Security Council on the massacres in the Congo. Ian Colvin put it thus: 'At this critical juncture O'Brien was recalled to explain himself. He never returned and the scarred face of Elizabethville remained a monument to his proconsulship'[24]. Smith Hempstone saw O'Brien as intelligent, cultured, restless and ambitious, sometimes seeming to suffer from intellectual arrogance. He believed him to have been temperamentally unsuited for service in Katanga, lacking the patience for endless discussion which is the only way anything is ever accomplished in Africa. Smith Hempstone said that O'Brien's justification for the use of force did not stand up to scrutiny. He said the Security Council only authorised the use of force, 'if necessary, in the last resort' to prevent civil war. He says it was never the intention of the Security Council to use force to remove foreign mercenaries. He further states that Dr Ralph Bunche's opinion was that Hammarskjold had never given instructions for force to be used. He adds that if, as Khiary claimed, he was in touch with Hammarskjold on the matter, there should be some documentary evidence to back it up[25]. But none was ever produced.

It may not have been without reason that O'Brien wrote, that Ian Colvin believed O'Brien's name was really Titus Oates[26].

In his commentary on my text, Dr O'Brien expresses disquiet about using material from Ian Colvin, who Dr O'Brien, writes:

...was a propagandist for the interests which Tshombe represented (and whose material) is altogether unreliable and misleading. Kamina base at the time was defended by a battalion of Jats, crack Indian regular troops who would have had no difficulty in disposing of anything that 'Katanga' could have sent against them. If there were indeed 'thousands of Baluba warriors' in the vicinity of Kamina – and I doubt this – they were there to support the garrison, not to take it. The Balubas of Katanga were hostile to Tshombe and secession and consequently supportive of the UN. The fact that Colvin didn't know this shows what a useless guide he is to the situation in Katanga. Five Baluba tribesmen actually lost their lives in an attempt to bring water to the Irish company at Jadotville. That company surrendered, not because of overwhelming Katangan military might, which did not exist, but because Belgian priests convinced the officer in charge that the UN operation was controlled by the communists. And the operation in September 1961 failed not because it was militarily impossible, but because it lacked a clear political objective once its original objectives had been disallowed by Hammarskjold... Smith Hempstone as a source is a bit better than Ian Colvin but not much. I hadn't been sent to Katanga for 'endless discussion' but to implement a particular Resolution which I found could not be implemented without the use of force. The force was used (in September as distinct from August) not to remove foreign mercenaries but to dismantle a regime which was bringing about civil war conditions by terrorising a section of its people, as witness the great refugee camps in the vicinity of the UN cantonment.

En route to New York O'Brien felt that at last he would possibly get an opportunity to put his case to the Headquarter staff. He was received very coolly. During the Security Council debate he was attacked personally by Mr Spaak of Belgium. O'Brien was sitting behind the new Secretary-General, U Thant, who, when it came to his turn to speak, left O'Brien undefended. It was clear that UN Headquarters wanted rid of their representative in Katanga. The Security Council passed a resolution demanding an end to 'secessinist activities illegally carried out by the provincial administration of Katanga'. It also sanctioned force to capture foreign mercenaries. Britain and France abstained on the vote, not using their veto. The USA and the USSR carried the other seven members with them. Smith Hempstone wrote that U Thant's only concession to Tshombe was to earlier replace O'Brien with Brian Urquhart, a Briton[27]. Unfortunately nobody had communicated this to O'Brien. When the Security Council meeting ended he booked a ticket to return to Elizabethville. This came to the notice of Linner, still in Leopoldville. He expressed surprise to Bunche in New York. Bunche then asked O'Brien to delay his return. O'Brien knew it was only a matter of time until he was put out of his misery and told the unpalatable truth. He was even being snubbed socially within UN circles in New York.

When O'Brien had left Elizabethville, his friend Maire MacEntee decided to remain on and await his return. When he discovered that he was not returning immediately, he advised her to leave. In the meantime Brian Urquhart had arrived in Elizabethville. He and George Ivan Smith, O'Brien's deputy, persuaded Maire to attend, with them, a party being given in Elizabethville for USA Senator and Mrs Dodd. All the local dignitaries including Tshombe and Kimba attended. On their way home from the party they were accosted by local soldiers. Smith and Urquhart were beaten brutally and Urquhart was taken away by the soldiers[28]. Later, after the UN staged a display of force, he was released. He had a broken nose and wrist, fractured ribs and heavy bruising. The story of his assault and kidnapping received much press coverage and the presence of Maire MacEntee at Villa des Roches was noted, much to the dismay of the UN Headquarters at New York. Dr Ralph Bunche conveyed U Thant's upset about it to O'Brien, still in New York. It was felt to be very indiscreet, to say the least, to have the lady staying there at such a sensitive period. Mr Aiken, the Irish Foreign Minister, called in O'Brien and told him that U Thant wanted O'Brien recalled to the Irish ministry. Otherwise U Thant indicated that he would call on him to resign. O'Brien agreed to request a transfer. Within days he decided to resign from the Ministry so as to be able to speak his mind. Almost simultaneously, though without consultation with O'Brien, Maire MacEntee had also resigned her post with the UN. She had been told by her father that the UN had officially questioned her presence in Elizabethville.

The Irish media reported Dr O'Brien's resignation widely, while *The Irish Times* also, quite separately, reported the resignation of Miss MacEntee. It carried a photograph of her. It described her as a Counsellor in the Department of External Affairs, who joined the Department in 1947, having been called to the Bar in 1944. She had been a member of the Irish delegation to the United Nations General Assembly for about three years[29].

Almost immediately O'Brien released a personal statement seeking to vindicate his actions in Katanga. He claimed he was doing no more than trying to implement UN resolutions. He attacked Britain and France for not backing UN resolutions, which they had not vetoed but allowed through. He attacked Britain particularly for its harrassment of himself. Lastly he admitted that though totally opposed to the UN resolution and himself, Belgium at least, acted with candour, consistency and honour. O'Brien wrote that General McKeown endorsed his statement[30] which was carried in the *New York Times* on 3 December 1961. It reads:

> On December 1st the acting Secretary-General of the UN acceded to the request of Mr Frank Aiken, the Irish Foreign Minister, to release me from the service of UN in

order to return to the Irish Foreign Service, from which I was seconded at the invitation of the late Secretary-General, six months ago. Mr Aiken's move was made at my request.

I had explained to him that, since I was regarded in some quarters as an obstacle to conciliation and negotiation in Katanga, my continued service with the UN would not be helpful to the Organisation.

I have now sent to Mr Aiken my resignation from the Irish Foreign Service.

I have done so in order to recover my freedom of speech and action. It is, therefore, now possible for me to be more explicit about the quarters which have come to regard me as an obstacle of conciliation in Katanga; about their reasons for holding that point of view, and about their methods of expressing it.

I went to Katanga in June of this year, my mission being to see to the implementation of the resolution of the Security Council, and specifically of the resolution of February 21st, which called for the immediate withdrawal and evacuation of all foreign military and para-military personnel, including mercenaries and foreign political advisers.

This resolution, though passed in February, had remained a dead letter.

There were more than 500 foreigners serving in the Katanga gendarmerie, including 200 officers of the Belgian regular army. All the key advisory posts in the Katanga service were held by Belgians.

Months of negotiation had failed to modify this situation. My instructions from the late Secretary-General were to effect a break-through and end the situation in which a Security Council resolution was being openly flouted.

When I got down to this task I found myself increasingly exposed, both inside and outside the Organisation, to mounting criticism. This criticism came not only from Belgium but from two permanent members of the Security Council, Britain and France.

If either of these countries had frankly opposed the resolution it could not have been carried. They did not oppose its passage, but they did most bitterly oppose its implementation.

One form their opposition took, especially after August 28th – the date on which a large number of mercenaries were apprehended and expelled – was a demand for my removal.

After September 13th, when the UN was obliged to take counter-measures against a hate campaign launched by Tshombe with the more or less open support of these same members of the Security Council, the demand for my removal turned into active and heavy pressure.

The British delegation at the UN was particularly active in this respect and not unduly fastidious about the methods it employed.

The immediate end pursued and eventually obtained was to make my continued presence in the Organisation a burden both to the Secretariat and to myself. The remoter end was to bring home to all servants the Organisation that, whatever resolutions the Security Council may say, it is unwise to apply them if these powers do not wish them to be applied.

The point of principle involved here is exceedingly important for the Organisation.

The Soviet Union has been accused of excessive use of the veto, that is, of voting against resolutions it does not like.

There is no doubt that excessive use of the veto power by a permanent member of the Security Council is a danger to the Organisation, but a danger not less great and much less known is failure by a permanent member to vote against – and thereby veto – resolutions which it is, in fact, radically opposed to. In this way the Organisation becomes committed to tasks the fulfilment of which is obstructed by very powerful members of the Organisation.

Servants of the Organisation trying to carry out these tasks on behalf of the Security Council are squeezed out by members of the Council itself. I am not the first and I am very far from being the most distinguished victim of this process.

My predecessors have usually kept silent, no doubt because they judged silence to be in the best interests of the UN.

I cannot share this view but feel on the contrary that the UN can only gain by having public attention brought to bear on the real source of many of its present troubles in the Congo.

This is not the place for a detailed narration or discussion, but one point is worth making. On November 24th, the Security Council passed a resolution which was even stronger than that of February as regards Katanga, Britain and France once more abstained.

If my resignation and consequent publicity make it even a little harder for these members of the Council to obstruct the implementation of the Council's new resolution also, thereby wrecking the UN operation in the Congo, then my resignation will have been worth while.

In conclusion, as M Spaak has said some hard things about me, I have pleasure in saying something nice about M Spaak. M Spaak's country openly opposed the resolution and M Spaak openly attacked me at the Security Council for applying it. M Spaak, therefore, has the distinction of having acted in this matter with candour, consistency and honour[31].

The British government issued a response to O'Brien's accusations on 4 December stating: 'It is not the practice of Her Majesty's government to enter into matters of public controversy with individuals acting in a private capacity'[32].

The debacle in the Congo had been of enormous seriousness for the Irish government of Sean Lemass, as it faced the possibility of further loss of Irish soldiers lives, particularly at Jadotville. The personal involvement of Dr O'Brien in Katanga brought additional pressures, particularly after the military action at Elizabethville. Many Irish expatriates wrote to the Taoiseach and the President condemning O'Brien and his actions. They and others failed to understand that Dr O'Brien was not acting as an agent of the Irish government. On 22 September 1961 the Government Information Bureau prepared a statement for the Taoiseach's office on the matter. It was quite supportive of O'Brien, so much so that a pencil insertion on the margin posed the question, 'Does it commit us to action?' The statement says:

The Government do not consider that he (Dr O'Brien) acted otherwise than in accordance with his instructions from his superiors in the United Nations service. Indeed, the Government would be likely to take a serious view of any attempt to place on Dr O'Brien personally any responsibility for the United Nations policy[33].

But the official attitude to Dr O'Brien was to change subsequent to his resignation and his outspokenness in placing blame particularly on the British. In the Dail on 6 December a major row broke out when the Opposition tried to get the Taoiseach to comment on O'Brien's accusations.

During the debate the Labour Party Leader William Norton said, 'It is important that the people of this country should know the Government's view on the rationality or otherwise of Dr O'Brien's statements... why should we desert him now without giving the reason?' The Taoiseach, Sean Lemass retorted, 'I reject completely that we have deserted Dr O'Brien... He left the public service to recover his freedom of speech and action'. The National Progressive Democratic Party, a splinter party of Clann na Poblachta, composed of Noel Browne TD and Jack McQuillan TD, had supported the murdered Congolese Prime Minister Patrice Lumumba. They proceeded to stage a walkout of the Dail over what they claimed was the Government's failure to support O'Brien.[34] Mr Aiken, whom Conor said took a rather paternal interest in both himself and Maire, later expressed regret at the resignation. Aiken was to be hurt by the subsequent publication of Conor's apologia *To Katanga and Back* in 1962. But Taoiseach Sean Lemass expressed no such regrets[35]. What the Tanaiste, Sean MacEntee, thought of it all is unrecorded.

The next day saw Con Cremin, the secretary of the Department of External Affairs, write in a confidential memo to his Minister, Frank Aiken, expressing 'the Taoiseach's, everybody else's and the Department of Defence's surprise at General McKeown's statement supporting O'Brien. On 8 December the Government Information Service sent a copy of a note to Con Cremin, which the Taoiseach had handed to the British Ambassador that same afternoon. It read:

> The statements made by Dr O'Brien, both in certain organs of the press on Sunday last and in a press conference he gave in New York on Monday, have occasioned me much concern because of the risk of misunderstanding of their status. I was particularly disturbed that, in allocating blame in his press conference for the evolution of the events in Katanga in September, he should have mentioned the British Prime Minister personally.

Since he was seconded to the United Nations in May, Dr O'Brien no longer exercised any function in our administration and was not entitled to speak for this country ... Mr MacMillan will be aware of the position and will have realised that Dr O'Brien's statements since his resignation (on Saturday, 2 December 1961) from the public service are solely his own responsibility and in no sense whatever represent the views of the Government...

Insofar as General McKeown, the United Nations commander in the Congo, may appear, from declarations attributed to him by the press, to have endorsed the views expressed by Dr O'Brien about the attitude of the British Government in relation to affairs in the Congo, it is important to note that he, also, is not in any sense a spokesman for the Government[36].

The file of the Taoiseach's department of the period also contains voluminous press cuttings of Dr O'Brien's publicity campaign. There is also a letter therein which showed confusion in official circles about whether in fact Maire MacEntee had also resigned.

In the meantime Dr O'Brien had left New York to launch a major publicity drive in Britain against the role of that government in Katanga. He travelled first to Dublin, where he was met at the airport by his three children, Donal, Fedelma and Kate. He was also met by a group of well-wishers organised by Owen Sheehy-Skeffington. This party included three TDs, Maurice Dockrell, Lionel Booth and Noel Browne. Owen had feared what kind of a reception Conor would get at the airport, so he prepared the welcoming group which also included Paddy Lynch[37]. Even at that stage Owen continued to be an example and influence on Conor. Owen was an academic with a concern for the political and social problems of society. He had been elected to the Administrative Council of the Labour Party in 1941, but expelled in 1943 on a trumped up charge. When his mother, Hanna, died in 1946 he refused all Christian obsequies, according to her wishes. His republicanism, with which he always differed from Conor, still flourished as he supported the IRA hunger striker Sean McCaughey in 1946. Owen was gleeful to see de Valera defeated in 1948 and glad to see a peaceful departure from the British Commonwealth. He became a champion of 'the Liberal Ethic' in Irish society, becoming a prolific letter writer and public speaker. This brought him into conflict with the conservative powers of Church and State. Though he opposed the Stormont regime, he saw the Anti-Partition Campaign as misguided and crude. He became a Trinity College Senator in 1954 and a frequent contributor to its deliberations. He became involved in many major controversies, e.g. corporal punishment, the Irish language, censorship, State connivance at IRA activity. In 1961 he said, quoting Thomas Davis, 'Ireland's dead and Ireland herself was betrayed, not by those who died, but by those who survived'. His views were often shared by his cousin, though they did differ publicly on the proposed merger of the two Dublin Universities in 1967. Conor said that Owen was for many years the most articulate and courageous – and at times virtually the sole – voice of liberal and secular values in this country.

From Dublin Airport Conor travelled with his children, escorted by the Gardai, to Christine's new home in Howth. This was still surrounded by the Press. Conor remained there all that day. At midnight he went to his own house at the top of Howth. The next day he flew to London, accompanied by Donal. At Heathrow, he cut short a press briefing after sixty seconds, saying he was 'under strain'. He told the reporters:

> You are a decent and reasonable people, but some of you have the misfortune to work for people who are not so decent and who are engaged in blackening me. I am telling the truth and telling it has been a strain. I am a witness of the truth and there is more to tell. I shall tell the truth in my own way[38].

In London Dr O'Brien was widely interviewed and was most forthright in giving his own version of what happened in Katanga which was not to the credit of the British government. He claimed that both he and the Secretary-General of the United Nations only had the support of one member of the Security Council, namely the USA, while trying to implement the United Nations mandate. Despite the constant propaganda that had gone on in Britain over the previous year, Dr O'Brien was quite successful in countering this. The *Observer* wrote in a leading article that same weekend, 10 December:

> Many people in this country believe that Katanga is the innocent victim of the United Nations aggression, and that Dr Conor Cruise O'Brien... is a wild Irish militarist who provoked the present fighting. This notion is so ludicrously at variance with the facts that it could only be entertained by a nation that had been systematically and deliberately misinformed[39].

The *Observer* and Dr O'Brien would be at one mind on many future occasions and form a fruitful relationship for both parties.

The United Nations forces and the Katanganese army remained locked in fighting until, on 14 December, another ceasefire was agreed. But Dr O'Brien remained far away, recovering from his personal six month ordeal of field service and the snubbing by his erstwhile colleagues in New York. He had shown himself a poor practitioner of the art of real politique, where theory and logic often have to give way to the art of the possible.

The aftermath of the debacle in the Congo for Dr O'Brien though, showed that he was made of stern stuff. He could have easily succumbed to the pressures emanating from so many different sources, and simply retired to his desk at the Department of Foreign Affairs in Dublin. But he had such a high opinion of his potential and that of the United Nations, that he could not bow out tamely from the public arena. The Congo had made his name a household word internationally and he intended to trade on that. Firstly he would defend his role in the Congo by writing his own account and then he believed he would be in demand for a variety of roles. But more immediately he had private and personal business to attend to with a person who had given him total support in these difficult times.

That same UN session in New York in which U Thant did not endorse O'Brien, had a motion before it again on the admission of Communist China. The latter had earlier said it did not recognise the Charter of the UN or the validity of any of its decisions. That year a vote was to be taken on admissions. The Irish would have to take a stand. Mr Aiken demanded that China guarantee to end its aggression against Formosa and withdraw from Korea as well as respecting the basic freedoms of its own people. China of course would give no such guarantees. Ireland then voted against the admission of China. This was seen as a shift in Irish foreign policy. Some linked it to the departure of O'Brien from the service, but this would be to overstate his role.

In his commentary on the text Dr O'Brien elucidates what precisely occurred at this UN session. He also feels that Aiken's speech would not have been made, had he himself been still a member of the Irish delegation. He writes:

> The Chinese government had in fact fallen into a carefully constructed American trap. In the circumstances of 1960/61, with a large new African entry priding itself on its newly acquired independence, the Americans knew that the old formula of 'not discussing the representation of China' would no longer serve. Instead Adlai Stevenson proposed a new formula which sounded sweetly reasonable; 'to ask the Peking government whether it supported the Charter of the United Nations and the validity of its decisions'. This sounded sweetly reasonable. In practice it was a new formula for exclusion, since the decisions included several which loudly denounced Peking as an aggressor

regime. The Americans knew – as the Africans probably did not – that the question would evoke an angry and contemptuous reply from Peking, which it duly did. The Americans and others interpreted the reply as a refusal to recognise the Charter of the United Nations as well as the decisions, and of course no country could be admitted which rejected the Charter itself. If I had been still a member of the Irish delegation, Aiken would certainly have consulted me about what to say. I would have advised him that if he wished to maintain the substance of his earlier independent position in relation to the question of Chinese representation, he would suggest that a further question be put to Peking. This question would be whether the Chinese reply to the previous question should be interpreted as meaning that Peking rejected the Charter itself or only certain previous decisions affecting China? This approach, if adopted, would probably have evoked a relatively conciliatory reply from Peking and would therefore have reopened the question of the representation of China. It would have been fully consistent with Aiken's original approach as was certainly not the case with this Cold War speech. I don't think that speech would have been made if I had been still a member of the Irish delegation. The remaining senior advisors had both been strongly opposed to Aiken's original position. They knew perfectly well what the Americans were up to with that question. They would not have opened Aiken's eyes on that matter, as I would have done. I don't want either to over-estimate or under-estimate my influence in the delegation, but it was certainly significant in relation to China.

But already Ireland was having to reassess its role in world affairs and think seriously about its economic development and future. It saw this as within the European Economic Community. This naturally meant more consideration would have to be given to taking into account the interests of those countries already forming the European Economic Community.

During 1961 Dr O'Brien's marriage to Christine Foster was terminated by a Mexican divorce. Conor and Maire MacEntee prepared to be married in New York on 9 January. Because his first marriage was a civil one, he was free as a baptised Catholic to get married again in a Catholic ceremony. His first marriage would not have been recognised as a marriage by the Catholic Church. This was a sensitive issue, particularly in Ireland, but the rules of the Catholic Church were clearly stated and Dr O'Brien received no special treatment from that body. The wedding took place at the Carmelite Church of Our Lady of the Scapular on East Twenty-Eighth Street. The celebrant was Fr Donal O'Callaghan who was a missionary priest[40]. For the wedding Maire wore a dress of Irish oatmeal brocade and a fur piece of grey beaver. Her model hat was white and coffee, and her shoes cigar brown. She had a two-tone bag and gloves to match and carried a spray of small pink orchids. Mr James Kirwan, Irish Deputy Consul-General in New York gave the bride away in the absence through illness of Mr Joseph F Shields, the Consul-General. The couple were married from the home of Mr and Mrs William Lescaze, a well-known New York architect. Mr Sean O Criadain was Best Man, with Mrs Marie Paul, wife of a New York banker, Matron of Honour. Mr O Criadain was a poet from County Cork who knew the couple for many years. He was a director of publicity for Simon & Schuster, the firm which intended to publish Conor's forthcoming book on Katanga. Mrs Paul was a native of Tipperary and a cousin of the bride. A reception was held later at the Manhattan apartment of Miss Dorothy Iyre, a friend of the couple and the Best Man. About one hundred people were invited, including several United Nations Under-Secretaries. Afterwards the couple left for a honeymoon in Trinidad.

Chapter Six

---◆---

GHANA: VICE CHANCELLOR OF UNIVERSITY

---◆---

Kwame Nkrumah of Ghana was a leader who had taken note of Conor Cruise O'Brien's career at the UN, and approved highly of it. He now sought to entice O'Brien to transfer his services to Ghana. O'Brien had met Nkrumah in Dublin in May 1960 when the latter had spoken on South Africa and apartheid. He had met him again in September when Nkrumah spoke at the UN on the Congo crisis. O'Brien was impressed by Nkrumah's analysis of the situation causing O'Brien to review his own thinking on the matter. Nkrumah was not without political problems in Ghana. In October 1961 he arrested fifty opposition leaders believing they were plotting against him. In August 1962 he escaped an assassination attempt.

Ghana had contributed soldiers to the UN mission in the Congo and Nkrumah was intimately involved in that process, believing that the UN could solve the problem satisfactorily from an African viewpoint. Even when he came under pressure from more militant African states, Nkrumah did not withdraw his troops from UN service. He wrote an account of this episode in 1967[1]. During the fighting at Elizabethville he sent a message to the UN in New York expressing 'good wishes and concern for my safety' O'Brien wrote[2].

The Gold Coast in West Africa, on the Gulf of Guinea, was a British colony from 1874. In 1957, known as Ghana and almost as big as Britain, it got its independence. Kwame Nkrumah was its first Prime Minister. He had studied in the UK and the USA. In 1949 he had set up the Convention People's Party which pushed for independence. He intended to transform Ghana into a modern democratic state on the lines of the Western industrial countries. For historical reasons the British always resented him.

Even before its independence many people from the Gold Coast came to Ireland for third level education. So it was natural that Nkrumah would also look to Ireland for specialist help when he assumed power and decided to move his country towards a republic within the Commonwealth in 1960. Vincent Grogan, Director of Statute Law in Ireland, went to Ghana, as did John Hearne who drew up the Irish Constitution and was an ex-Ambassador to the USA. Several articles of the Ghanian Constitution come from the Irish Constitution[3]. Geoffrey Bing, who also had strong Irish connections, was Attorney General in Ghana from 1957 to 1961. He admired what Nkrumah was trying to achieve in the twentieth century, what Western nations had done in the nineteenth, but without the exploitation and misery of those experiences. But the forces lined up against Nkrumah were formidable and vast. It was a third world country trying to join the industrial west, on its own terms. The economics of trade with the west were insurmountable.

One of the institutions in Ghana which was causing Nkrumah great difficulty was the University of Ghana. It was modelled on the old, almost medieval, model of Cambridge University. The government, though covering all the costs, had no real say in how it was run. The government felt the University was out of touch and out of sympathy with what the requirements of the country were. In 1957 the old Principal had left and Nkrumah had hoped to get someone completely different. Geoffrey Bing was sent abroad to seek suitable candidates. He wrote, 'even then he (Nkrumah) was thinking of someone of the type of Conor Cruise O'Brien'[4]. In the event a Dr Stoughton of Reading University got the job. He outlined the problems to the government: 'So far as the school leaver is concerned, it is a degree or nothing. From the national point of view the most significant feature of this situation is the serious wastage of talent[5]. The University refused to change its ways, citing academic freedom as essential. No African or Arabic language was on its syllabus, yet the Classics were. Its entry standards were linked to those of the University of London. Ten per cent of the University's budget went in air fares to London for its Staffs' annual leave.

In December 1960 Nkrumah set up an International Commission to study the problem of the university. It had representatives from the USA, Britain, the USSR and local educationalists. In the end very few changes were effected in the university. The main result was the offer of the Vice Chancellorship to Conor Cruise O'Brien in December 1961. Conor knew that there were major difficulties between the university and the government, but he was interested in doing something different in his career. He arranged to go to Ghana in February with his wife, to assess the situation. There he was impressed with what he saw. He also found that the staff at the university were favourably disposed towards him accepting the job, lest somebody worse than he be offered it[6]. Conor accepted the offer and went to live in Ghana. Robert Collis, another emigree Irishman then working in Africa, wrote:

> I often stayed in the university which, built on a hill outside the capital, rose tier upon tier towards the sky and was by far the most inspiring campus of any university I have ever known. There I used to stay with Conor Cruise O'Brien who was elected Vice-Chancellor of the university, after becoming famous in the Congo. The story of his time in Ghana gives a vivid personal picture of what happened during these years which I was able to understand through my friendship with him and his wife[7].

Collis adds that to begin with Nkrumah appeared to be a splendid statesman but he was corrupted by power and surrounded by sycophants.

Conor got his first opportunity to outline his ideas on Ghana and the university when he addressed the Academic Board on 12 October 1962. He said he believed that the university was rather slow to adapt itself to the independence of the country. He believed it must do this, as universities had historically changed with differing circumstances. He recognised that some of the audience distrusted politics and wanted to concentrate on academic matters. He accepted this could be valid. But he held that the university could not reject the new independence of Ghana. He believed in African independence. He hoped that non-nationals and Ghanians would see their duty to the new state. He vowed to defend the academic freedom of the university. He did not think it was under attack then or likely to become so in the future. He said that the State had the right to put forward its views on various matters, like the number of students and the type of graduate the country required. He did not see this as being contrary to academic freedom. Nor did he believe that academics should in any way be treated differently, by the laws of the land, from other people. He noted that Ghana was spending an unusually large proportion of its income on education and therefore its *bona fides* should be accepted and regarded as a challenge by those who delivered the educational services.

Matters went quite smoothly for a couple of years and the long holidays back in Ireland kept Conor in close touch with home. He was satisfied with his tenure. But early in 1964 the political situation in Ghana deteriorated. An attempt was made on Nkrumah's life in January. This was followed by a state of emergency with two of Nkrumah's closest ministers being arrested. Terrorist bombing started in Accra and many people were killed and wounded. Damafio, Nkrumah's chief minister along with several associates, were found not guilty by the courts. This was a major surprise and one of which Nkrumah had not been notified. Nkrumah set the verdict aside, thereby losing support from many influential figures he had depended on for retaining power. He also decided to seek major changes in the constitution by way of referendum. This led to a militant campaign with the government demanding loyalty from various state institutions. The newspapers went on the offensive against people and places they considered disloyal. The University of Ghana was one of these.

A fortnight after the assassination attempt on Nkrumah the government ordered a temporary close down of the university. It was raided by the police and two senior lecturers were arrested. This led to a demonstration by hundreds of students. Conor, aware of great danger, intervened and persuaded the protesting students to disperse. Many students decided not to obey the government order closing the university, intending to remain in residence until forced out. Again Conor saw the danger, fearing that such action would play into the hands of those who criticised the university as a hotbed of subversion. He warned the assembled body of students and they heeded him. Conor also appealed to Nkrumah to release the two arrested lecturers, one of whom was British. Conor saw Nkrumah himself and discussed the whole situation with him. The Briton was released into Conor's custody on condition that he would be available to the security forces and would stay away from all Ghanians. He was later allowed to leave the country. The other lecturer, who was a member of Nkrumah's own Convention People's Party, was not released.

That same month of January, police returned to the university and alleged to Conor that four more senior members of staff were involved in subversion against the State. He replied that he could not take any action against the men without evidence. The police told him they had the evidence but could not divulge it. The next day deportation orders were served on the four (three Americans and one French) to leave Ghana within twenty-four hours. Conor sought a meeting with Nkrumah, without success. He did

74

see the Minister of the Interior who postponed the deportations for one week. In the meantime Conor succeeded in seeing Nkrumah, but he confirmed the deportations.

The university resumed classes early in February with the returning students in an angry mood. Once more O'Brien was in the middle of a maelstorm not of his making. The press continued to attack the university. The deportation of the senior staff was due within days. The students planned a big demonstration for that same day. This fact came to Nkrumah's notice. O'Brien feared this could be the opportunity for the government to move decisively against the university and close it down, until it could be reopened and managed by trusted people. Conor assembled all the students on the morning of the planned demonstration. At the same time he was told that a large outside march was on its way to the university. This was three thousand strong and led by a Mr Welbeck, secretary of the Convention People's Party. Their aim, it emerged, was to dissuade the proposed student demonstration. The march entered the university and demanded access to the students. In the meantime Conor left the university to see government officials to explain what was happening and to try to get the march called back. He later returned to the university and met Mr Welbeck. He told Welbeck that under the circumstances, it was not possible for him to address the students. The march later left the university fairly peacefully.

The *Ghanian Times* said that the universities, 'have become the fountain heads of reaction and fertile ground for imperialist and neo-colonialist subversion and counter-revolution'. Geoffrey Bing says that this charge was untrue. Rather, he says, the harm it did was to give, 'nothing directly or indirectly to the solving of the basic problem of changing the nature of Ghanian education generally, so as to provide the skilled personnel necessary for development. Worse still its influence on the secondary schools produced there too, the idea of an elite trained in the classics.'[8]

During January and February, politically trusted people were put into key parts at the university with the intention of ending its independence. On this point Dr O'Brien states: 'We were ordered to appoint these people but I explained that the University of Ghana Act and the Constitution of the University required us to follow certain procedures. These were followed and we were not in fact forced to accept anybody.' O'Brien adds though that 'other influential sections of opinion in and close to the government regarded these developments with apprehension and displeasure'[9]. This statement itself gives an inkling of the intrigue involved.

In March O'Brien addressed the Congregation of the University in a major speech. He noted that the country was in a national emergency with intense security measures in operation. He welcomed the proposed changes in external dress and formalities among students and staff, as in line with a socialist society. But he emphasised that fidelity to the values of teachers and scholars was vital i.e. the process of learning. He praised the secondary school system which allowed the university to keep high standards for entry. He praised the government which paid for all students who met that standard. He praised the quality of the teaching staff. He thanked the government for its funds to run the university. He said the university was not, as its critics said, indifferent to the sacrifices of the manual workers of the country who produced the wealth. The university wanted to produce graduates who would be able to contribute to the Seven Year Plan. He denied that it was really colonialist or neo-colonialist, behind a concern for academic freedom. Respect for the truth and the moral courage to tell it, were what the university was about. These were universal values, not colonial ones. He quoted the Chancellor of the University, Nkrumah, speaking earlier about academic freedom:

We know that the objectives of a university cannot be achieved without scrupulous respect for academic freedom, for without academic freedom there can be no university. Teachers must be free to teach their subjects without any other concern than to convey to their students the truth as faithfully as they know it. Scholars must be free to pursue the truth and to publish the results of their researches without fear, for true scholarship fears nothing. It can even challenge the dead learning which has come to us from the cloistral and monastic schools of the Middle Ages. We know that without respect for academic freedom, in this sense, there can be no higher education worthy of the name, and, therefore, no intellectual progress, no flowering of the nation's mind. The genius of the people is stultified. We therefore cherish and shall continue to cherish academic freedom at our universities[10].

Dr O'Brien's commentary states: 'Nkrumah had indeed delivered these words but he took them all with the exception of one sentence from a draft prepared for him by me in the first year of my term when I was still in favour with him. The one sentence which comes from another source is that beginning: "it can even challenge...". From internal evidence I judge that it was clearly by Geoffrey Bing'.

O'Brien maintained that the university had to be a place of independent and critical thought. He believed that if Nkrumah's words prevailed, the future of the university was secure and would flourish. He adverted to the fact that university staffs were dismissed in varying political systems worldwide. He said coercion was tried in Ghana by some people and he did not know how successful it might be. But the university must retain its freedom, its values, and hopefully it would.

Geoffrey Bing says O'Brien's appointment came too late to effect a major change within the University of Ghana. He also believes that:

Dr O'Brien's mistake was that he did not see that the academic freedom of the university which he defended with such skill, courage and pertinacity, was not intended by most of those who most vigorously proclaimed it, to be a license for the free expression of opinion in academic circles. It was merely the modern version of the ancient claim of the academic clerics to be the sole arbitrators of truth and to have the sole right to punish and expel the heretics from their midst[11].

In the event, as scheduled, the following year O'Brien left Ghana to take up a position at New York University. The next year saw the deposing of Nkrumah by a military coup. Among those who found themselves in jail there was Geoffrey Bing. Within a month O'Brien was invited back to attend the Congregation of the University as an honoured guest. He spoke and said, 'This occasion will perhaps go down in history, that is if history is properly nursed, as the greatest day in the life of this university'. He told them that the university never had the chance to develop academic freedom. He went on:

There may still be members of staff whose intellectual faith in Kwame Nkrumah, his ways and his manners has not suffered a change in spite of recent events. Such men if they exist may not find the new going easy or congenial. On the assumption that such people are sincere in their faith and will hold on to their faith as all believers do, I say to them with all due respect to be patriotic and leave the campus for the good of the campus[12].

Writing in 1985 O'Brien said of his experience there: 'I went to Ghana... partly because I had just recently been politically clobbered by certain colonialists while I was on a UN mission in Katanga, Congo (which was mainly why Nkrumah had invited me)'.

He says that socialism in African countries is a fraud or a decoration. He instanced the first time he attended the spectacular opening of parliament in Accra. When Nkrumah spoke about honesty and penalising people who held foreign currency abroad, the whole of parliament laughed loudly. Even Nkrumah himself smiled. 'Nkrumah's State was one huge rip-off,' he writes. O'Brien attended two more of these openings of parliament and each time the same sentiments were repeated and treated with equal hilarity. The tragedy of the country, he felt, was that honest people were side-lined to make way for the supposedly socialist colleagues of Nkrumah, to plunder and ruin the country [13].

Chapter Seven

VIETNAM PROTESTS IN NEW YORK

CONOR AND MAIRE ASSAULTED

ARTICLE ON 1916 COMMEMORATION

◆

Conor Cruise O'Brien was Albert Schweitzer Professor of Humanities at New York University from 1965 to 1969. He has written about Albert Schweitzer that, to educated Africans, Schweitzer represented the paternalism, condescension, resistance to change by the white man in Africa. Whites had thought of him as altruistic and living a life of dedication to blacks[1].

O'Brien's period in New York saw the escalation of the war in Vietnam. In February 1965 American planes bombed the perimeter of Dan Nang Airbase to oust Vietcong attackers. In March Lyndon Johnston sent in the marines to protect the Airbase, while the Vietcong blew up the American Embassy in Saigon, killing twenty-one people. By June American troops were in combat against the Vietcong[2]. In July fifty thousand American troops went to Vietnam. That same month, Martin Luther King called for an end to the war. In May 1966, eight thousand war protesters encircled the White House for two hours. In April 1967, two hundred thousand people protested in New York and San Francisco[3]. The Vietnam War was gradually sucking in more and more Americans, causing the nation, especially the young, to question the validity of the war.

It was only natural that young people, especially those who were called up in the ever widening net of the army draft laws, would protest and question their elders. Turmoil was created across America as people split on the issue. Universities were often the focal points for dissent and protest. Young people began to flee abroad to escape being drafted into the army. Draft dodgers became commonplace as did the ritual burning of the call up cards[4].

Dr O'Brien was caught up in this maelstorm in New York and played a significant part in the anti-war protests. He saw the American campaign as imperial aggression against a rural people thousands of miles away. Very many famous people turned against the war taking on the authorities who responded with all the vigour of the law.

In December of 1967 'Stop the Draft Week' came to Manhattan and two thousand demonstrators assembled to picket the conscription centre in Whitehall Street. Three thousand police were in the immediate area. Ten husky policemen stood on the main steps of the Armed Forces Induction Centre, while a three deep line of police at the front entrance kept the protesters back as the latter tried to climb through to commit a civil disobedience. The surrounding streets were lined with double and triple barricades as Mayor John Lindsay surveyed the scene. The majority of the demonstrators staged a sit-down at the nearest intersection. After five hours of protest, among the two hundred and sixty-four people arrested were Dr Benjamin Spock, Mr Allen Ginsberg, Miss Susan Sontag, Dr Conor Cruise O'Brien and his wife Maire MacEntee. Dr Spock had told the gathering, 'We have massacred Vietnamese and we have lost fifteen thousand young Americans. All this has happened mainly because Lyndon Johnston is incapable of admitting that he has made a mistake'[5]. The protesters chanted in vain, 'Don't Go, Don't Go', as the conscripts entered the building. The police then were ordered to break up the demonstration. Among those taken to hospital with injuries after a confrontation with police was Dr O'Brien. His wife described the scene as mounted police drove their horses into the sitting group and her husband was assaulted by police who followed on foot. 'They kicked Conor around quite a bit'[6], she said. Conor insisted that he and Maire be taken to hospital. They spent nine hours at the Bellevue Hospital, where Conor was treated for bruising. The next day Conor, in his inimitable way, described what had happened. 'The Officer started to drag me away, which was fair enough, but I'm a little heavier than the average man, and it was difficult for him. He gave me a sharp kick in the right lumbar region, as a result of which I cannot walk now. Another Officer came by on a horse and asked "Do you want more?" I didn't want more, as a matter of fact, so I dodged behind a car'[7].

One of the perks of Conor's position in the university was that his children were eligible for free tuition there. He was adamant that all his children should have a university education. Kate, his youngest daughter had not been to university in Ireland, so he prevailed on her to come out to New York and enroll there as a student. But she did not like New York and got homesick. Her father was annoyed that she should decide to pass up the opportunity. They had a very serious row before she returned home. In retrospect he said of this episode, 'I missed the opportunity of understanding her better, of understanding her homesickness. I was too bossy and I was rebutted'[8].

Dr O'Brien was a very serious-minded person who was very proud of his achievements as a writer, a United Nations official and a university teacher. Because of the controversy that had followed him since Katanga, he was always on guard lest his reputation be unjustly besmirched. In August 1966 the intellectual English magazine *Encounter* carried a very critical article which attacked him on all three fronts mentioned above. He decided to sue the publication and instituted proceedings in the High Court in Dublin, where Ronan Keane acted for him. Conor claimed that the words used in the article 'meant that he had prostituted and perverted his literary talents in the service of a political cause; that he for political reasons was willing in his writings to abandon the virtues of objectivity, intellectual detachment and scrupulous regard for the truth'. He claimed that he had been gravely injured in his credit and reputation as a writer and teacher. The offending article had criticised part of his recently published book, *Writers and Politics* and also an article he had written in *Washington Post's* Book Week and an expanded version of the article given as a lecture by him at New York University. It called into question his role in Katanga, using such words as subterfuges, stratagems, mendacities, betrayals, duplicities. Conor had once used the term 'a Machiavelli of Peace' to describe his own political activities on behalf of the United Nations in Katanga; the article's use of this term also offended Dr O'Brien. He complained that *inter alia* these words meant that he was obsessed to an absurd degree with those with whom he disagreed. *Encounter* also made reference to his alleged acceptance of the *New York Times'* assertion that it was backed by the Central Intelligence Agency. Dr O'Brien claimed that that passage meant that in his writings he was guilty of smears, of making false accusations which he knew to be untrue and that he conducted deliberate campaigns to injure the reputations of other persons by making unfounded assertions with the object of securing his own personal advancement.

Encounter did not enter a defence to the High Court and Ronan Keane said that he was asking for the reliefs sought in the statement of claim and damages. The damages would have to be assessed by a jury. Mr Keane said that in view of the fact that there was no appearance entered, the jury would be asked to proceed on the assumption that the statements complained of were published, untrue and bore the meanings alleged in the statement of claim. Mr Justice Murnaghan gave judgement in default in favour of Dr O'Brien[9].

The major focus of events in Ireland during these years was the fiftieth anniversary of the 1916 Rising at Easter 1966. All sorts of elaborate preparations were in train to mark the occasion in a note of triumph. The resources of the State were funnelled towards recalling the glorious men and women of 1916. Among the special events was the publication by each of the national newspapers of a supplement to commemorate the occasion.

The Irish Times called its supplement '*A Historical Review of the Men and the Politics of the Easter Rising*'. It invited Dr O'Brien to contribute a major article. Among the other contributors were well-known academic figures, FSL Lyons, Nicholas Manseragh, Owen Sheehy-Skeffington, Basil Chubb, Roger McHugh, Owen and Ruth Dudley Edwards, Donal McCartney.

Owen Sheehy-Skeffington wrote a portrait of his father. He concluded saying, 'Tributes to Frank Sheehy-Skeffington came from many quarters: Sean O'Casey, Tom Kettle, Robert Lynd...'

Dr O'Brien saw this as a major opportunity for him to address the Irish people on the 1916 Rising and on how the State measured up to the ideals of Pearse and Connolly. It also gave him the opportunity to settle a few old scores with people whom, he felt, had not measured up to the historical challenge. His article was called *The Embers of 1916*.

As was already known to many, Dr O'Brien felt that there had been no real need for the 1916 Rising. But if it had to happen then it was premature. It would have been better timed in 1918, when the whole country was opposed to the British extending conscription to Ireland. He posed the question: 'If Pearse and Connolly could have had a foresight of the Ireland of 1966, would they have gone with that high courage to certain death?' In answering it he wrote:

> There would be some positive elements, people are better fed, better dressed, better housed, healthier. But the fact that this partition is accepted, the fact that nobody anywhere, by any means, is seriously trying to bring about political unification of the country would be disappointing. Of course it was safe to raise it at the Council of Europe, because no one there would pay attention. But at the UN such a matter could run the risk of attracting support. So the Government had to decide,

it had to put up or shut up on partition, so it shut up. This end of official pretence on partition was painful, for it was a betrayal in terms of the revolutionary tradition of Tone, Pearse and Connolly. That the Republic was not attainable caused a blight of cynicism and disgust in 'Free Ireland'. The Anti-Partition Campaign was officially a correct way of proceeding. It gave the Government the moral authority to lock up those of the IRA who raided barracks in Ulster, as a way of ending partition. Lemass' solution was to wait until O'Neill's people would accept the Irish Constitution. Pearse's Gaelic state was a fantasy. In Dublin this year, [O'Brien wrote,] were held the funeral ceremonies of the Republic proclaimed fifty years ago.

O'Brien continued:

Connolly's Worker's Republic is as far off as ever. The *Irish Independent*, which in 1916 continued to call for more executions until it got Connolly, remained the paper of the Catholic bourgeoisie. No significant Labour movement exists North or South. The Labour Party has been dominated by dismal poltroons on the lines of O'Casey's Uncle Payther. The economic progress which has occurred was mainly due to external forces. The same educational system which Pearse condemned survives, controlled by the bishops. There is no cause in this anniversary year for self congratulation.

As a former civil servant, he accepted his own share of the blame, but said many others in government and the Church are also blameworthy.

He concluded by saying that 1916 was a challenge. Pearse challenged us on education and culture. Connolly challenged us on social objectives. For a time at the UN, Ireland measured up against imperialism, but since 1965 it had acquiesced. Connolly's writings and the record of his action are examples of what Ireland requires today[10].

The article was a devastating critique, typical of the man, when only praise and triumphalism was being showered on the populace. Little did it appear that the critic would soon, in the clothes of those he criticised most, put himself forward as a liberator of his people.

Chapter Eight

---◆---

---◆---

In January 1956 the Government had received an Aide-Memoire from the British Government pressing strongly for the cooperation of the Gardai. It alleged 'a total unwillingness on the part of the Civic Guard to assist the RUC with information or to cooperate in identifying the raiders. (on Roslea RUC Barracks)'. The Memoire refers to the fact that in March 1955, training activities were going on at Scotstown, Co. Monaghan. This information was given to the Civic Guard and the Irish Government, 'yet it appears that the men were allowed to continue with their illegal activities without interference'.

A February 1956 Department of External Affairs Aide-Memoire replying to the British says starkly, that the British could expect little cooperation from the Irish on subversive activity. It said: 'Briefly, the attitude is that the Government could not allow information to be furnished about Irishmen already apprehended, or being actively sought in connection with armed political activities and could not accept any responsibility or commitment, in regard to the intentions of unlawful organisations which are, of their nature, secret'[1].

Writing of this Aide-Memoire to the British in the *Irish Independent* 1/2 January 1990 Conor Cruise O'Brien states: 'This document was issued under the Second Inter-Party Government, and it clearly reflects the influence of the late Sean MacBride, on whom that Government depended for its continued existence. It represents what was to remain the high water mark (until 1969-70) of Irish Government collusion with the IRA. This policy was dropped by the de Valera - Lemass Government when it came back to power in 1957'[2].

Conor recalls telling Northern politicians, from the nationalist persuasion, that they should integrate more within the public life of Northern Ireland. He was acting on the orders of his Minister, Mr Aiken. The politicians listened politely but took little positive action. The Nationalist Party refused to act as an official opposition party in Stormont as participation in the State apparatus was frowned upon within the nationalist community. Dr O'Brien regarded the Catholics of Northern Ireland as the main victims of the Home Rule debacle. They became a permanent minority, ruled by a majority of Protestants who in their turn felt besieged by Catholics in all of Ireland. The Catholics of Northern Ireland were discriminated against in housing and jobs and local government voting. They were also humiliated by certain ritual commemorative ceremonies and in other ways[3]. Dr O'Brien writes disturbingly, that in 1960-61, the official mood in Dublin was impatience and even aversion for Northern Catholics. It was felt that they had brought most of their troubles on themselves and should accept the reality of their situation.[4]

Yet even in the larger mentality of Northern Ireland, change was inevitable. In 1963 the long time and virulently anti-Catholic Prime Minister, Lord Brookeborough, resigned due to sudden illness[5]. Terence O'Neill, the Minister for Finance, was selected to succeed him. O'Neill had made no real political impact and had no obvious political base. He had a close relationship with Dr Ken Whittaker of Dublin through attending meetings of the World Bank[6]. Northern Ireland was part of the Welfare State under which Education Act many Catholics had benefited from third level education for the first time. O'Neill realised that change was essential to preserve a peaceful state. He set up new Ministries for Development and Health and Social Services. He even recognised the Northern Ireland Committee of the Irish Congress of Trade Unions. He made several public gestures towards the Catholics of Northern Ireland by visiting their schools. In January 1965 Sean Lemass visited O'Neill at Stormont and the next month O'Neill returned the visit at Dublin. Many Unionists bitterly resented these initiatives, including O'Neill's cabinet colleagues, who were not consulted.[7] They also gave the Reverend Ian Paisley, at that time emerging as a politico-religious demagogue, an easy issue to exploit. In April 1965 O'Neill won a vote of confidence from his parliamentary party and in November 1965 the Unionist gained three seats in the General Election.

Easter 1966 was potentially a dangerous time in Northern Ireland but the only real violence occurred when Gardai in Dublin's Parnell Square attacked a march of Northerners to remove an IRA emblem. Parades and celebrations were held in Northern Ireland. The nationalists there believed, in a sense, they were the forgotten people of Irish history. The last IRA campaign had ended in 1962 due to a lack of nationalist community support for violence. But 1916 was their heritage too and they celebrated accordingly. This led to a heightening of tension within a state which discriminated so widely against its second class citizens. But the celebrations there passed off without serious trouble.

But after Easter, in May and June of 1966, the Ulster Volunteer Force, an extremist Protestant body murdered two Catholics in Belfast[8].

O'Neill's reaction was to declare it an illegal organisation under the Special Powers Act. This came as a shock to hard line Unionists who thought the Act was only for use against Catholics, as had always been the case hitherto. Moves were made to try to oust O'Neill within the parliamentary party, but were unsuccessful. He still held majority Protestant support and Catholics were well disposed to him. But the latter were demanding action on ending discrimination.

In early 1967 the Northern Ireland Civil Rights Association (NICRA) was formed to push for various reforms including: 'one man one vote' in local elections; the end of gerrymandering of constituencies; fairer allocation of public housing; repeal of the Special Powers Act; disbanding of the B-Specials and a complaints procedure against local councils. There was also a group called Campaign for Social Justice. Both these groups staged a march from Coalisland to Dungannon to protest against a blatant sectarian housing allocation decision. The era of the protest marches and counter marches had arrived. Mass action, with the security authorities taking the side of the Protestant counter protesters, led to the radicalisation of the Catholic population.

This new movement reached a high point on 5 October 1968 when a march in Derry was attacked by the police in full view of the television cameras of the world. This was followed by vicious sectarian battles when Protestant civilians came to support the police. Public opinion was outraged that people (many prominent politicians among them) marching for basic civil rights could be so abused by the guardians of law and order. Among the people drawn to Northern Ireland later that month was Conor Cruise O'Brien, home from New York. With his experience of the protest campaign against the Vietnam War, he spoke in Queens University Belfast on 'Civil Disobedience'. Like with the march in Derry, the authorities in the university were urged to ban this meeting, to be addressed by the radical from Dublin and New York. Unlike the Minister for Home Affairs, the Vice-Chancellor of Queens University had more sense. He allowed it to proceed, minus the media circus which was then building up in Northern Ireland. Like in America the university was a focal point for protest. Dr O'Brien spoke of the experience of protest in the USA where blacks forced the central government in Washington to intervene locally, ending its collusion with Southern States which practiced discrimination. Dr O'Brien predicted that a campaign of civil disobedience in Northern Ireland would force the central government in London to discharge its responsibilities to the underprivileged citizens there[9].

Around this time also Terence O'Neill made a famous speech saying, 'Ulster is at the Crosswards'. O'Neill called for a breathing space for the whole community. His Home Affairs Minister, William Craig, was forced to resign when he criticised government policy on the matter.

In January 1969 another example of police collusion with Protestant violence against civil rights marchers occurred at Burntollet Bridge near Derry city. A left wing offshoot of the Civil Rights movement named People's Democracy, which did not regard themselves as being sectarian and for whom the unity of Ireland was not a burning issue, organised a march to Derry which was ambushed by Protestants at Burntollet Bridge. The security forces allowed the Protestants to assault the marchers at will. The People's Democracy were as critical of the Republic of Ireland as they were of the North. They endeavoured to get cross community support. Dr O'Brien saw great difficulty ahead for them in this. He wrote of them: 'Now I think it is likely that these young people will find as the civil rights struggle develops, that religion is more important than they thought it was, and that historically formed suspicions and animosities are not quite so easy to dispel – even in themselves – as they now assume'[10].

The Protestant people saw the Civil Rights Movement as a threat to them and their way of life. Dr O'Brien wrote that when Tricolours began to appear in the wake of mass-participation by Catholics, the Protestants read the movement as Dublin and Rome orientated and automatically injurious to them[11]. The Unionist party was in a state of turmoil. It was a situation ready made for extremists. After another Civil Rights march and disturbance in Newry, Brian Faulkner resigned from O'Neill's government because it was increasingly refusing to face realities and was losing control of the situation[12]. O'Neill had recently set up the Cameron Commission to inquire into the civil disturbances since 5 October 1968. This led to a backbench revolt in his party. O'Neill called a General Election and the Unionists divided into pro-O'Neill and anti-O'Neill candidates. O'Neill hoped for support from Catholics to protect him from his own hardliners. This did not materialise and the results left him vulnerable. He only barely held off Ian Paisley in the Bannside constituency. The next month Paisley was jailed for offences in Armagh. Bombs exploded at electricity stations. The Unionist Party voted by twenty-eight to twenty-two votes to allow 'one man one vote' in local elections. The next day the Minister for Agriculture, Chichester-Clark resigned saying it was too soon for such a move[13]. Five days later O'Neill felt he could not continue any longer and resigned. Chichester-Clarke defeated Faulkner by one vote for O'Neill's job. Dr O'Brien wrote that the new government lacked any clear direction. It mistakenly released Paisley from prison and dropped pending charges against Bernadette Devlin MP. Thus it showed itself to be weak. The annual marching season of the Protestant ascendency was fast approaching in July and August.

Chapter Nine

In 1966 Conor Cruise O'Brien had described the Irish Labour Party as one which had been 'dominated for years by dismal poltroons, on the lines of O'Casey's Uncle Payther'[1]. It had been founded by the ICTU in 1914. It contested its first general election in 1922, winning seventeen seats and twenty-one per cent of votes. In 1933 this was reduced to eight seats and five per cent of votes. But by 1943 Labour held seventeen seats again. The Labour Party formed part of the two Coalition governments of 1948-1951 and 1954-1957. It was a conservative party in a conservative country with little taste for radical socialist policies. But the 1960s saw a major change when the party began to develop towards socialism. Even Noel Browne, a renowned radical in Irish politics, decided to join the party in 1963. Fine Gael itself began to develop a type of Christian socialist policy in these years, which was called *The Just Society*. In the General Election of 1965, Labour made most gains getting twenty-two seats. It was a close runner-up in five others. Barry Desmond became Party Chairman with Noel Browne Vice-Chairman. Socialism became the byword for a major push towards power at the next election, though rural Labour TDs were not so sure about the wisdom of this trend. The party began to attract many new members, among them several with a very high public profile.

In December 1968 Dr O'Brien announced that he was rejoining the Labour Party. This must have caused much heartsearching by the older members, but the price of power is never cheap. He gave his reasons for such a move at a specially convened meeting to honour the occasion.

The six hundred capacity auditorium of Liberty Hall was full as the meeting organised by the Dublin Regional Council of the Labour Party gave a minute's standing ovation to Conor Cruise O'Brien as he was introduced. Mr Dan Browne, Vice-Chairman of the party welcomed him into the party. Mr Corish said that his reputation, both nationally and internationally, as a scholar and writer and politician stood high. His decision to join the Labour Party 'is warmly welcomed by us' he added. Corish said that it was no surprise that O'Brien had joined, for he had seen the party produce policies and also had seen some of the most brilliant young men from the universities, the secondary schools and the primary schools join the party in recent years. His contribution to a nation, that could ill afford to reject his talents, would be immense. Mr Corish adverted to past difficulties and lack of policies but felt the future was theirs. Michael O'Leary and Barry Desmond also welcomed Dr O'Brien. The scene was set then for the star of the evening to address the expectant multitude.

After a few preliminaries, questioning whether a new recruit should be really listened to by so many experienced party members, he said he did so at the request of the Chairman. He said that in politics the Irish people had only seldom changed its mind but that when it did, it was apt to change with decisive effect. He instanced the three major shifts since modern electoral party politics came to Ireland. These were: in 1880 when the people voted in part for the New Departure of Parnell and Davitt and away from the Home Rule Party of the landlords; the second was in 1918 when the Irish Parliamentary Party was swept away by Sinn Fein; the third was in 1932 when de Valera was put in power.

Dr O'Brien saw hopeful signs that the current situation in Ireland might lend itself to another decisive change. He instanced the era of free speech when taboo subjects like sex and Church authority were debated openly. He believed that there were new conditions for the Labour Party to advocate social and political change. He said that the influence of the Catholic Church on politics had often been exaggerated but that it had been extensive and generally favourable to the social and economic *status quo*. It was sometimes exploited by conservative laymen.

The more frozen a social and political situation is, he said, the more startling the effects of thaw when it·sets in. He compared the Unionist Party's unbroken period of power to that of the Communist Party of the USSR. The civil rights activists in Northern Ireland had a long and tough struggle ahead. There was very little we here could do to help them. Fianna Fail had been the dominant regional party here for almost as long as the Unionist Party and there was no more real antagonism between the two than there was between Northern Republicans and Southern Democrats in the USA. In theory they are separated by a gulf of history and of principle: in practice they understand one another quite well. Each knew that the other was speaking the same basic language of the social and economic *status quo*, through a peculiar religious and political dialect, appropriate to the traditions of its own particular region.

On foreign policy, he continued, Ireland through MacBride or Cosgrave had been pro-British and pro-American. Mr Aiken could get credit for breaking that policy but then, for whatever reasons, perhaps simply through old age, his independence sagged and finally collapsed. Now Ireland's voice is heard with the same kind of attention paid to Belorussia or Bulgaria. Irish Labour should never abandon control over External Affairs as it did in the Inter-Party government, or else it should retain the right to criticise it. James Connolly was the great enemy of Imperialism.

Dr O'Brien did acknowledge that within Fianna Fail and Fine Gael there were elements which wanted social change. The untimely death of Donagh O'Malley dashed any hopes that Fianna Fail might travel that road. But he did think that the supporters of the *Just Society* document within Fine Gael could find common ground with Labour.

Dr O'Brien defended the right and role of intellectuals like himself to play a meaningful role in politics. He did not accept the idea that workers distrust intellectuals more than the bourgeoisie. Nobody distrusts an intellectual more than another intellectual.

The Irish Labour Party was in the process of change as the policy documents which would be put to the January 1969 party conference would show. He invited all progressive thinkers to pay attention to that conference, where a well articulated modern Socialist policy would emerge. He believed that only Labour could mobilise the young and frame new policies. That was why he joined the Labour Party.

During this speech there were frequent interruptions for applause. He sat down to a long standing ovation. Despite his words of less than two years earlier which had insulted and mocked the party, here was the mountain not just forgiving Mahomet, but coming to meet him with open arms. The drive for political power was on. *The Irish Times* saw the event of some significance, by giving it extensive front page coverage and carrying the speech in an inside page[2].

Basil Chubb later wrote of anti-intellectualism in Irish politics, saying it began to change in the 1960s. He added:

> Nevertheless, it cannot be said that the traditional distrust of intellectuals in politics has been wholly dissipated, as witness the innate hostility of many politicians to the mass media in general and their distrust of 'pundits', or the general reactions in the 1970s to the intellectual pyrotechnics of Conor Cruise O'Brien[3].

Labour's new policies were soon attacked as left wing and communistic. It was said they wanted Ireland to be run like Russia, Cuba, or the Eastern European totalitarian regimes. Dr O'Brien made an unfortunate point at a Labour conference, that Ireland might consider establishing diplomatic missions with left wing countries like Cuba, rather than right wing dictatorships like Portugal. He and Labour were pilloried for this by their political opponents. The Catholic card was still a very powerful one and any political party ignored it at its peril.

Early in 1969 there was a public reminder that Dr O'Brien was no ordinary political aspirant, but an intellectual, a writer and a person with a past that had been controversial and a future that might be no less so. He had written a play entitled *Murderous Angels*, based on his experiences in the Congo. The play gave the impression that Dag Hammarskjold connived in the murder of Patrice Lumumba, who had been Prime Minister. It was published in the USA, where plans were proceeding to have it staged in New York and Los Angeles. It was submitted to the Abbey Theatre in Dublin and the National Theatre in London. The controversy arose when both these theatres refused to stage the play. Phil O'Kelly spoke for the Board of the Abbey saying:

> It was found not to be suitable. One of the reasons was it required quite a number of negro actors. That would be alright if the play was being put on as a special production by a theatre, but we are a repertory company and it would be difficult to meet the requirements[4].

A General Election was announced for June 1969. Conor was selected as a Labour Party candidate in Dublin. He resigned his New York University post and returned to Ireland. This was against the advice of his son, Donal, who was then a political scientist. Donal advised his father, very sensibly as Conor later admitted, to hold on to his nice tenured academic post and not take this leap in the dark. His father countered, saying that it would be an interesting experience. 'Paw', the son replied with not a hint of exasperation, 'don't you have enough experience already?'[5.]

Despite all the trouble going on in Northern Ireland, Conor was surprised to discover that the North did not figure as an issue in the election. He stood in the same constituency as the Minister for Finance, and son-in-law of Sean Lemass, Charles J Haughey,

Dublin North East. O'Brien came under much personal attack and innuendo about his private life and his service abroad. He proved a pugnacious opponent and hit back by raising the sale of land by Haughey to builders for £204,000 as unethical[6]. This proved to be the start of bitter personal animosity between the two men. O'Brien came in second to Haughey in the four seat constituency, which was a great achievement. Fianna Fail, then under Jack Lynch, won the election well. Labour did not achieve the expected breakthrough, getting eighteen seats from seventeen per cent of the vote. It was strongest in Dublin with ten seats there. The party was disappointed but O'Brien defended the party policies from those who wished to see a change. He argued that the party had to work harder to get their message across more clearly to the people. Jack Lynch, he believed, played the Catholic card very successfully in the election, being photographed often visiting convents.

After the General Election, Conor was appointed Labour Party spokesman on Foreign Affairs. Michael Gallagher says that it was not then 'forseen that Northern Ireland would be by far the most important area covered by his portfolio.' Gallagher also says that O'Brien's lack of sympathy with traditional nationalism was not fully realised though he was on public record since at least 1966[7].

Dr O'Brien's first speech in the Dail was on 2 July 1969 on the nomination of members of the Government. It was obvious from the outset of the first session that the Labour Party intended to make the running against Fianna Fail in that Parliament. Conor took up his position on the second row of the Chamber. He looked around the galleries with mild disinterest, fingering his chin now, then his forehead. He made his maiden speech on a point of order as Tom O'Higgins of Fine Gael was speaking. He said:

'On a point of order Ceann Comhairle, I am not a member of the Government...', at which point O'Higgins interjected, 'No, and you never will be'. When Conor got the floor he made, as expected, the sharpest of the Labour speeches, launching an immediate attack on Fine Gael and its style of opposition. He said that Fianna Fail and Fine Gael existed in a 'kind of symbiotic relationship'. He declared the list of Government nominees as a 'rather depressing little list the Taoiseach has laid before us... representing essentially an attempt at self-perpetuating Government... in a kind of semi-hereditary succession'. Luckily for him, his father-in-law, Sean MacEntee, had retired from the Dail four years earlier. Conor accused Fianna Fail of winning the election by conning the electorate that their rightful entitlements were 'a gift from Fianna Fail'. He noted how Deputy Childers had boasted how Fianna Fail had provided the longest existing Government in Western Europe. Conor reminded the House that there was another Government at Stormont, which was in power even longer, and 'even more effective in the use of patronage for self-perpetuation'. He then went on to criticise in particular the nomination of his constituency colleague, Charles J Haughey, whom 'as we know, personally benefited from a situation – the free market in building land – which ought, in the public interest, to be regulated'. He said that Deputy Haughey was publicly known to be associated with people who have been seen to violate the law with impunity, with people who have gone ahead with buildings without planning permission. He noted that Deputy Haughey had been exonerated of a charge of failing to disclose a conflict of interest when introducing a taxation change.

Dr O'Brien, as expected, commented on his old stamping ground, saying that the Department of External Affairs had in recent years departed entirely from any attempt to sustain independence in foreign policy. He wondered 'whether in fact the Government had abandoned the idea of neutrality'. He commented on the current situation in Nigeria-Biafra, which the London *Times* had said was the greatest crime committed by the British Government since the Irish Famine. He requested the Irish Government to speak on the matter.

In conclusion, he indicated that Fine Gael provided little real opposition but the Labour Party would 'supply a flow of critical opposition, genuine opposition... to show the people how and why the Labour Party policy of democratic socialism is the best way forward for the country'[8].

In August 1969 the Northern Ireland troubles impinged on the politics of the Republic in no uncertain terms, as the marching season reached its climax in Derry as the Apprentice Boys celebrated the raising of the siege of Derry in 1690. A vicious confrontation between local nationalists and the police went on for days and was flashed on television screens around the world. Pressure mounted on the southern Government to do something to protect the Northern Ireland Catholics under siege by the police. Jack Lynch made a speech saying that 'We will not stand idly by'. He said the Government had asked the UN to send in peacekeeping troops. He also said that recognising, however, that the reunification of the national territory can provide the only permanent solution of the problem, it is our intention to request the British government to enter into real negotiations with the Irish Government to review the present constitutional position of the Six Counties of Northern Ireland.

Patrick Hillery, who was only three weeks in office as Minister for Foreign Affairs, got the task of going to the UN. From his earlier discussion with Sean Lemass he fully realised the danger of taking the Northern Ireland problem to the UN. As he put it himself later, 'Here I am needing to make a speech and yet trying to avoid a vote'. The French and the Russians were valuable allies, Hillery said. He feared that his speech would be interrupted by the British Ambassador, Lord Caradon. But as Hillery said, 'We got the ideal situation and got to make a statement. Caradon was a bit annoyed, with me. He said: "You went further than we thought you'd go". But he didn't interrupt. The British said they would talk to us (on the North) after that. Before that, they would not talk to us. Northern Ireland was an internal problem and not our business, but after that, they talked to us and that was a good result'[9].

Jack Lynch's call and statement about national territory, O'Brien contests, 'was later to combine with the deployment of British troops into an acceptable Republican tableau[10]', which the IRA took up. He believes that Protestants saw Lynch's statement as calling on Northern Ireland Catholics to revolt.

Jack Lynch moved Irish Army units to the border. There, field hospitals to deal with refugees from the North were opened as violence spread throughout. A police station on the Falls Road in Belfast was attacked to minimise Royal Ulster Constabulary reinforcements going to Derry. The Northern Ireland government called out the para-military B-Specials. Mayhem ruled in Belfast with inter communal violence on a wide scale. The Northern Ireland government sounded out the British government about army assistance, but was told that if the army went in, 'the relationship between Stormont and Westminster would be fundamentally changed'[11]. But the continuing civil disorder led to the British Army arriving in Derry on 14 August and Belfast the next day. It was welcomed by the Catholics of both cities as protecting them from the local security forces, which then came under the control of the British Commander. The B-Specials were ordered to hand over all their weapons. In September the Cameron Report indicted Northern Ireland discrimination. Sir John Hunt headed an inquiry into security. As Dr O'Brien had forecast at Queens University, London intended to see that United Kingdom standards in public affairs would be met in Northern Ireland. In October Hunt recommended disarming the RUC and disbanding the B-Specials, to be replaced by an Ulster Defence Regiment within the British Army.

The British and Irish governments believed that fair play would satisfy the Civil Rights movement which had no plans for further protest. But as Dr O'Brien has noted the humiliation of the Protestants and their anger was deep and bitter[12]. Some nationalists meant to go on fighting. As Bernadette Devlin wrote:

'For half a century now, it (Unionist Party Government) has misgoverned us. Now we are witnessing its dying convulsions and with traditional Irish mercy, when we've got it down, we will kick it into the ground.'[13]

The Government decided to hold a debate on the 'Situation in the Six Counties' in October 1969. The debate which was a calculated risk, paid exceptionally heavy dividends: it dispelled many myths and demonstrated not merely an unexpected awareness of the realities of political life, but more important a willingness to state them publicly. Dr O'Brien, who was winding up the debate for his party, surrendered some of his allotted time so that the other deputies could participate in the proceedings. One of these was Billy Fox of Fine Gael who detailed the campaign mounted against him in his constituency by Fianna Fail, accusing him of being a B-Special. His religion had been raised saying that he didn't worship in a Catholic Church like a true Irishman. Mr Fox noted that Erskine Childers, a Protestant and fellow constituency candidate, saw these things happen and would not stand up and be counted.

In his contribution, Dr O'Brien began his parliamentary campaign of seeking to open minds in relation to the North. He chided a Fianna Fail Deputy who appeared to suggest that a Belfast Protestant came from 'an alien background'. Unless such thoughts were banished, the idea of 'conciliating or persuading these people' should be forgotten about, he said. Agreeing that there was a strong and generous vein of tolerance in this society, he adverted to the existence of intolerance. He referred to the contribution of Billy Fox and noted the hostility he drew from Fianna Fail benches. He believed that it was vital to reach the Protestants of the North with a friendly worded and unanimous message, that we have no intention of trying to coerce them or get others to coerce them into an Irish State. It was time to drop altogether, all forms of anti-partition propaganda, while continuing to publicise the real and serious grievances of the minority in the North, he said.

Dr O'Brien said that certain symbolic matters are important, noting that we say 'Six Counties', avoiding the term 'Northern Ireland', though the latter term is favoured by the majority of that entity. He asked could there be political unity unless it was desired. The abolition of Article 44 of the Constitution was symbolic but also urgent. He said that children were still being brought up, as older people had been, to believe that the North was part of 'occupied Ireland'. He said that the terrible troubles and partition were both off-growths of the deep historical division between the two main religious communities. He ended by quoting Eamon de Valera who said in the Dail on 1 March 1933, 'The only policy for abolishing partition that I can see, is for us in this part of Ireland, to secure such conditions as we will make the people in the other part of Ireland, wish to belong to this part'[14].

The Fianna Fail cabinet of Taoiseach Jack Lynch contained several Ministers who had close family connections with republicanism. This was not surprising, though when they expressed themselves in public in old fashioned rhetoric, it did not help the cause of peaceful coexistence, which Jack Lynch was trying to achieve. The foremost of these Ministers was Neil Blaney of Donegal, who regularly passed through the North on his way to Dail Eireann. Dr O'Brien began to criticise Blaney directly, fearing that the legitimate demands for civil rights were being subsumed into sterile and dangerous anti-partitionism.

Dr O'Brien believed that Republicans in the North still saw the British Army as the real enemy. He believed that Jack Lynch sought to play down that situation, but that some of his cabinet were not content to 'win the agreement of a sufficient number of people in the North to an acceptable form of re-unification'. He quoted Neil Blaney, Minister of Agriculture speaking in Letterkenny as saying: 'The ideal way of ending partition is by peaceful means... No one has the right to assert that force is ruled out'. O'Brien was in Belfast when Blaney made that speech and called unsuccessfully for his dismissal. That month too saw a split in Sinn Fein and the IRA which gave birth to the Provisional IRA. It had few guns but set out to get them. Things had been so bad then that 'IRA' was colloquially taken to mean 'I ran away' in 1969 on the Falls Road. The IRA had almost become non-existent since 1962, when the last military campaign had ended. Around this time the Provisionals were dedicated simply to the forceful reunification of Ireland. O'Brien wrote that they did not even regard the Ulster Protestants as a major player or see the danger of civil war. O'Brien speculates that members of Lynch's cabinet may have been instrumental in the coming into being of the Provisionals. He quotes a Penguin Special by the *Sunday Times Insight* Group which published a book in 1972 on the matter. This group were relying on information supplied by the opposing wing of the Official IRA[15].

Unfortunately the British Army played into the hands of the Provisionals, when in July 1970, it effected a thirty-four hour curfew on the Falls Road, while it searched, with little success, for arms. This episode alienated the general Catholic population, which one year earlier welcomed the same army. Then the only protector of the Catholic people seemed to be the Provisional IRA, whose membership swelled accordingly.

During that summer Dr O'Brien, as Labour Party spokesman, visited the North constantly. In June he was in Newry for the inaugural meeting of the Movement for Peace, which was trying to bring Protestants and Catholics together. There he was accompanied by his daughter, Fedelma and her husband, Nicholas, who was the son of the Church of Ireland Archbishop of Armagh, Dr George Otto Simms. The same night he spoke in Downpatrick with a Labour Party colleague, Michael O'Leary, at an election meeting of a 'Unity' candidate, in the forthcoming British General Election. This pattern continued giving him a first hand account of how the situation was deteriorating all the time into further violence. He had meetings with many of the main figures involved on either side, including Fr Patrick Murphy, Tom Conaty, Maurice

Hayes, Tom Mitchell, Ruairi O Bradaigh, John Taylor, Gerry Fitt, Paddy Devlin (who warned Conor against being too moderate, 'Our people need guns', he was told) and Fr Des Wilson[16]. On 28 June Dr O'Brien witnessed the defence of St Mathews Church on the Newtownards Road when a pitched battle took place.

Subsequently Conor had a long meeting in Dublin with Ruairi O'Bradaigh who was believed to be the leader of the Provisionals. He gave Conor contacts for his forthcoming trip to Derry. On one trip to Belfast Conor and Michael O'Leary encountered an army roadblock where cars were being searched. They had a bundle of the Republican paper, *An Phoblacht*, with them. O'Leary managed to dump them out of the car without being noticed by the army. On that trip they heard directly from the people of the Falls how the army curfew had just ended after terrorising the people. On 12 July Conor attended the Orangemen's march to Finaghy. On 12 August he was in Derry for the Apprentice Boys march, as a Labour Party observer.

He was accompanied by his brother-in-law, Seamus MacEntee, a psychiatrist. As they approached the city their car was checked by the Royal Ulster Constabulary who gave them an entry pass permitting them to travel across the fortified Craigavon Bridge to the west of the city. The march had been banned by the government, which closed all public houses and erected barricades all over the city, guarded by the police and army personnel. Conor and his companion therefore succeeded in reaching the Catholic Bogside, which itself was almost under siege. Conor's face was well known and accepted there and he signed autographs for young boys. He later returned to the inner city where some dignitaries of the Apprentice Boys were laying a wreath as the band played 'God Save the Queen'. He was also recognised there, as one RUC Constable told him that he had read some of his books and approved of his speeches in the Dail. Shortly after this friendly encounter the atmosphere changed for the worse as Conor was told by a burly Apprentice Boy that he had been 'spotted', and advised him to leave town. Conor was never one to run away, so he decided to proceed to St Columb's Park for the afternoon Apprentice Boys Rally. He did not anticipate any danger, as the previous month he had attended the great Twelfth of July Orange March to Finaghy Field in Belfast. Though he had been recognised there by many, there had been no incident. But the mood of the Apprentice Boys in Derry was different. They were angry that their march had been banned. William Craig, a leading Unionist hardliner, was the main speaker at St. Columb's Park. It was a miserable afternoon with the rain pouring down. Soon Conor was recognised and he began to be jostled and harassed. When asked why he wasn't clapping Mr Craig's speech, Conor replied that he did not agree with a lot the speaker had said. His interlocuter then ordered him to clap. Conor did not oblige, realising that he was probably going to be hit anyway, he did not want to compound the unpleasantness of it all by doing what he knew to be wrong. Several young men, not Apprentice Boys, surrounded Conor and his companion and began to accost them, kicking at their legs. Retreat appeared the most sensible action, which was adopted, but in the process Conor got a bloody nose and lip. Apprentice Boys then offered them protection and escorted them away through a meadow. But their attackers followed behind intent on 'getting O'Brien'. As Conor reports the incident, 'They hit me several times and I fell down, then they started kicking me. An Apprentice Boy said: "Is it murder ye want?" After a short while they stopped kicking and went away. I was shaken and sore but not badly hurt; Seamus – who had been trying to pull back my main assailants but who had not been attacked by them this time – said that the long grass got in the way of their boots'. Still escorted by the Apprentice Boys, they walked for about a quarter of a mile, until they reached the end of the meadow and the relative safety of a police car. There, a small crowd noticed the commotion and one man shouted, 'Ye didn't get half enough'. As they were driven away by the police, the car was hit with fists and umbrellas on the roof and windows[17].

106

Chapter Ten

◆

THE ARMS CRISIS

◆

The eruption of violence in Derry and Belfast in 1969 led to the Taoiseach taking some limited measures to support Northern Ireland Catholics. Subsequently it emerged that much stronger measures were being urged on him from within his own cabinet. Two ministers, Neil Blaney and Kevin Boland wanted the Irish Army to occupy Derry city[1]. Lynch set up a cabinet subcommittee to deal with the crisis. Neil Blaney, Kevin Boland, Charles Haughey, Jim Gibbons, the Minister for Defence, were its members. Lynch himself did not sit on the subcommittee. Dr O'Brien wrote that if Lynch did not know what his actions meant, his ignorance was deliberate. O'Brien contends that the composition of this subcommittee by Lynch 'reassured those who favoured a war of liberation' while through his speeches Lynch was 'reassuring those who feared and rejected the idea of such a war'[2]. In March 1970 the Dail voted, without debate, in the supplementary estimates, a Grant-in-Aid for Northern Ireland relief the sum of £100,000. This, as O'Brien saw it, was the southern government getting involved with the Catholics of Northern Ireland in a way that had not happened since 1922. Part of this money was spent to purchase arms for defensive purposes in Northern Ireland. A scheme to train Northerners in the use of arms was organised by the Irish Army.

Mr Liam Cosgrave, leader of the Opposition spoke in Dail Eireann on May 1970 of 'a situation of such gravity for the nation that it is without parallel in this country since the foundation of the State... an alleged attempt to import arms from the continent'. The next day Jack Lynch dismissed Charles Haughey and Neil

Blaney from Government. Another minister, Mr O'Morain, Minister for Justice, had already resigned. Kevin Boland later resigned in sympathy with the dismissed ministers. A debate followed in Dail Eireann lasting for thirty-seven and a half hours.

Dr O'Brien at first praised Deputy Blaney's remarkable theatrical performance, which he said, ended up on a skilful and successful appeal to unity which earned the applause of the Fianna Fail benches. Blaney, he said, 'touched the chords of the emotions of an old civil war, the emotions of nearly fifty years ago'. Conor said that it was rather hard in the present tense and dangerous summer to forgive such language. He quoted Blaney as saying, 'I cannot stand idly by while the nationalist people are subjected to murderous assaults'. Dr O'Brien wondered what exactly these words meant, what was Mr Blaney saying? He noted that Deputy Boland was a straighter man, indicating that he was opposed to illegal organisations of a military character in the Twenty-Six Counties, that arms importation into the Six Counties should not be illegal.

Dr O'Brien then noted that these speeches had already been heard in the North, falling on attentive and fanatical ears. He said that he had been in Belfast the previous night and found the atmosphere electric: he saw mobs in the streets, their faces contorted with hatred and fear. He added that the hatred and fear was being carried along by people like Mr Paisley and Deputies Blaney and Boland, who play into each others hands, confirming one another's prophecies of woe. He appealed to the Taoiseach to see the danger of the island drifting to the very edge of civil war through the words and actions of members of his party. He urged him to withdraw from them the Fianna Fail Whip, though he doubted the ability of Mr Lynch to do this, because, 'I fear he may have become the prisoner of these men. Fianna Fail is a sick party... It is incubating the germs of a possible future civil war'.

Conor's general psychological approach had been to the effect that Fianna Fail had mauled itself so much that there was no need to hack the pieces into mince meat. He would display sympathy towards them in the hope that some of them would do the right thing and expose the charade that was taking place. But the name of the game was survival in the Dail. After a week of political bombshells, sensational revelations, charges of criminal conspiracy, Jack Lynch's Cabinet decimated and battered, Fianna Fail survived, though about forty of them clapped Boland's contribution. The vote of confidence in Lynch's Government was passed, with the four departed ministers among those voting such confidence. Owen Sheehy-Skeffington wrote an article for *The Irish Times* on the departing Ministers under the heading, 'they'll none of them be missed'. Speaking on RTE's *'This Week'* programme the next day, Dr O'Brien was less sanguine, saying almost prophetically:

> These men are not eliminated. They are out of the Government, which is a different thing. They remain very powerful forces in Fianna Fail policy, they speak for powerful and confused people in the party, they can touch latent emotions which could be extremely destructive and dynamic – unfortunately for Mr Lynch and for other people[3].

Three weeks later Mr Haughey and Mr Blaney were arrested and charged with conspiring to import arms and ammunition. In the following July, Mr Blaney was acquitted on the charge of conspiracy. In September Haughey and three others were tried but the judge ended the case when he was accused of conducting the trial unfairly. The second trial was held in October and all the accused were acquitted. Haughey called for Lynch's resignation. Lynch, who was in New York, said there was 'no doubt of an attempt to smuggle arms and that those dismissed were involved'[4].

Dr O'Brien argues that the Arms Trial showed that the Minister for Defence, who was the star prosecution witness, knew about the importation of arms as did Lynch himself. He also argues convincingly that the trial showed that the Government was unfit to cope with the Northern Ireland crisis. It was content to make gestures of intent without any substance but with the realisation that the same gestures would cost lives in Northern Ireland. Democracy was seen to be very puerile. O'Brien believes the Irish Army officers in the trial, Colonel Heffernan and Captain James Kelly, 'had clearly been doing what they took to be their duty' and emerged with their honour intact. Dr O'Brien has most respect for John Kelly of Belfast who spoke with the voice of the Provisional IRA. O'Brien calls him the real hero of the Arms Trial. John Kelly made a speech in court explaining and defending his role in the operation of the Citizens Defence committee of Belfast. He claimed that they and he were 'acting on foot of' speeches by people, political figures of authority in this part of Ireland, speeches which had led the Six County minority to believe sincerely that a new era was dawning in Irish life. He said that Dr Hillery, the Minister for External Affairs, had gone to the UN and asserted there that the breakdown of law and order in Northern Ireland and the plight of the minority community was due to the partition of Ireland, brought about by an Act of the British Parliament, in which not a single Irish vote had been cast. Kelly then quoted Hillery: 'The claim of Ireland, the claim of the Irish nation to control the totality of Ireland has been asserted over the centuries by successive generations of Irishmen and women and it is one which no spokesman for the Irish nation could ever renounce'.

Kelly then attempted to quote Taoiseach Lynch, in what has become known as his 'We will not stand idly by' speech. But he passed on reluctantly as the Judge Aindrias O Cuiv insisted he should not quote speeches. Kelly continued:

We did not ask for blankets or feeding bottles. We asked for guns and no one from Taoiseach Lynch down refused that request or told us that this was contrary to government policy...

I think it is, as far as I am concerned, only right that I should point out that throughout the period from August of last year until the first time that I was arrested in Dublin, everything that happened within that time leaves me in no doubt whatsoever but that what was being done was being done with the full knowledge and consent not only of Mr Gibbons, but of the Government as a whole. And it is my conviction, whether I be right or whether I be wrong, I am only speaking from knowledge that I have, it is my conviction that what Mr McKenna said at the beginning, that this trial is an exercise in democracy or a case of the people of Ireland versus the accused, and many things have been done in the name of the people of Ireland, it is my conviction that I stand here and those who stand with me, that we are here as a matter of political expediency, and not from any desire that the course of justice be impartially administered.

My Lord, I find it a very sad occasion indeed, that these institutions for which so much was sacrificed, which had been gained by such nobility, should be abused in this manner. There is no victory for anyone in these proceedings, my Lord. There is only an echo of sadness from the graves of the dead generations. I thank you, gentlemen, I thank you, my Lord[5].

Dr O'Brien said that through the deficiencies of our democratic system the Provisional IRA gained respect due to the State.

After the Arms Trial Jack Lynch had little choice but to seek a vote of confidence in himself and his Government. It was a situation without parallel in the history of the State. Mr Jim Gibbons attacked Dr O'Brien directly in his contribution and drew hostile responses from that gentleman. Mr Gibbons reminded the Dail that if he had wished to cooperate with the illegal importation of arms, by virtue of his Office, he could have done it and nobody would be any the wiser. He continued the debate:

> As I said, I do not propose to go back over the evidence I gave on oath in court except to say that it was evidence given on oath. Deputy Conor Cruise O'Brien said in this house that I was a convicted liar. Upon what basis he makes that charge I do not know. I do not know what code of ethics Deputy Conor Cruise O'Brien observes. I do not know whether or not he is a Christian at all, but I want to tell Deputy Conor Cruise O'Brien that when I take the book in my hands it means something to me although it may mean nothing to him.

Dr Cruise O'Brien:	Does this mean that without the Book you can lie like a trooper?
Mr Gibbons:	I am inviting the Deputy or any of his colleagues, whether they come from Accra, Moscow or Havana, to demonstrate here or elsewhere that the charge that the Deputy has made against me has any substance. I am inviting the Deputy to substantiate the foul charge he made against me.
Mr Desmond:	Deputy Boland has also made it.
Dr Cruise O'Brien:	The Minister's colleague has also made it.
Mr Gibbons:	The Deputy is getting angry now because he is ashamed of himself and he is very right to be ashamed of himself. I am a countryman.
Dr Cruise O'Brien:	... and look like one.

112

Dr O'Connell:	The Minister is under severe mental strain.
Leas-Cheann Comhairle:	
	Order. Deputies must cease interrupting.
Mr T J Fitzpatrick:	All of this is only a smokescreen.
Leas-Cheann Comhairle:	
	The Chair wants to point out —
Mr J Lenehan:	You should all shut up —
Dr O'Connell:	Is it in order for the Deputy to tell the Chair to shut up? ...
Leas-Cheann Comhairle:	
	... Personalities and casting aspersions should be avoided...
Mr Gibbons:	I was dealing with the assertion that Deputy O'Brien made in this House the other night that I was a convicted liar. I was going on from there to compare our different backgrounds and to compare the sources from which we draw our different ethics because obviously they are different.
Dr Cruise O'Brien:	Hear, hear. I thank the Minister.
Mr J Gibbons:	I have said I am a countryman and I learned my first bit of ethics from the penny catechism —
Dr Cruise O'Brien:	The Minister should learn to tell the truth.
Mr J Gibbons:	I do not know whether Karl Marx, Che Guevara or Kwame Nkrumah —

113

Mr Desmond:	The Minister is indulging in personalities now.
Dr Cruise O'Brien:	The Minister is being abusive now.
Dr O'Connell:	He is putting up a very poor defence.
Mr J Gibbons:	I am not nearly as abusive as the Deputy was the other night. Neither Deputy Cruise O'Brien nor any other Deputy in the House has any grounds to call me a convicted liar.
Dr Cruise O'Brien:	The same grounds as every other Deputy – it is what you have put on the record.
Mr J Gibbons:	I am on the records and I am inviting you today, as I invited you then, to destroy my credibility if you can.
Dr Cruise O'Brien:	It does not need to be destroyed; it is gone forever.
Mr B Lenihan:	Is Deputy Cruise O'Brien to be allowed to continue in this way?
Dr Cruise O'Brien:	Am I supposed to put up with all those attacks?
Leas-Cheann Comhairle:	
	The Chair has already pointed out that interruptions from any side are disorderly. The Minister must be allowed to make his speech.
Mr J Gibbons:	We will leave Dr Cruise O'Brien alone because the country in general understands by now where he stands –
Dr Cruise O'Brien:	If you want to know, why not go to

114

Falls Hotel, Ennistymon, family home of Francis Cruise O'Brien, father of Conor.

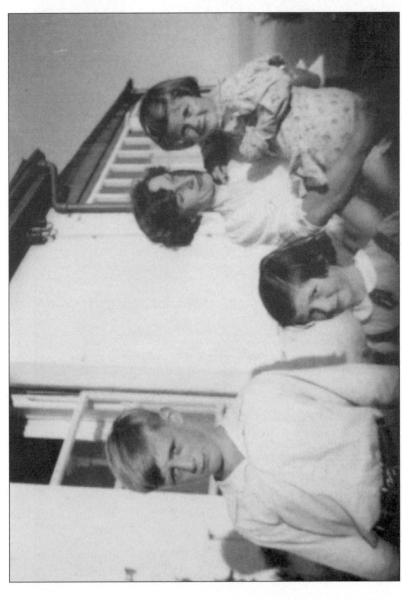

Conor's first wife, Christine, with children Donal, Fedelma and Kate in 1952 . (*Christine Hetherington*)

Fedelma at her graduation from TCD in 1966. *(Christine Hetherington)*

Kate's graduation from TCD in 1970. *(Christine Hetherington)*

Christine and Dr George Otto Simms, Archbishop of Armagh at the wedding of his son Nicholas to Fedelma, 1968. *(Christine Hetherington)*

The family man — Conor with his second wife, Máire, and their children, Patrick and Margaret. *(Colman Doyle, Irish Press)*

Brendan Corish, Conor and Dr John O'Connell. (*Colman Doyle, Irish Press*)

1973 Cabinet — Fine Gael/Labour Coalition

Back Row (L/R): TJ Fitzpatrick, Michael O'Leary, Tom O'Donnell, Garret FitzGerald, Conor Cruise O'Brien, Dick Burke, Peter Barry, Justin Keating, Paddy Cooney, Declan Costello

Front Row (L/R): Jimmy Tully, Paddy Donegan, Liam Cosgrave, President Eamon de Valera, Brendan Corish, Richie Ryan, Mark Clinton. *(Irish Times)*

Conor in puckish mood, with Donal Ó Moráin. (*Colman Doyle, Irish Press*)

Conor in typical "Waiting to pounce" pose. (*Colman Doyle, Irish Press*)

Conor with his adopted son Patrick at Dublin Airport in 1986 . *(Eamonn Farrell, Photocall)*

Conor at an anti-Provo demonstration in Dublin in 1990. *(Eamonn Farrell, Photocall)*

Conor and Máire at John A Costello's funeral. (*Colman Doyle, Irish Press*)

Conor and Máire MacEntee with Garret FitzGerald at the funeral of Séan MacEntee (Eamonn Farell, Photocall)

Conor at home in Howth. (*Colman Doyle, Irish Press*)

President Mary Robinson with Conor in September 1992 at the launch of
his book on Edmund Burke. *(The Irish Times)*

	the country?
Deputies:	Hear, hear.
Mr J Gibbons:	Any time you like.
Dr Cruise O'Brien:	All right, tonight then.
Mr J Gibbons:	I was speaking earlier about the strength of the Fianna Fail Party and the source from which it derives. We will give the Opposition a demonstration of that any time they like.
Dr Cruise O'Brien:	Do it tonight then[6].

The bitterness of these exchanges illustrated clearly how Fianna Fail sought to isolate and cast aspersions on Dr O'Brien. They also demonstrated his unwillingness to accept such treatment and his ability to retort with cutting remarks. When Mr Boland's resignation from the Dail was dramatically announced, Mr Lynch moved the writ for the by-election to cheers from all sides. When O'Brien made himself heard, he asked if Fianna Fail would not have the decency to have a parting word for Mr Boland, he was shouted down by Fianna Fail.

Dr O'Brien made a very lengthy contribution to the debate. His tactic was to cut out individual and vulnerable members of the Fianna Fail Party, flatter them with having a semblance of integrity, after which he went on to point out where their duty lay in the vote. He opened by expressing astonishment that the Taoiseach had said that the rectitude or otherwise of individual activities or actions, was not the important point in the ministerial changes. The Taoiseach wanted agreement to consign his previous government to history, O'Brien said, with Deputy Blaney taking his place with Eoghan Roe O'Neill, Deputy Haughey with Silken Thomas and Deputy O'Morain with the Firbolg. At that point Deputy Davern interjected to ask, 'What about Nkrumah?'. O'Brien said that there was so much that was sordid in yesterday's

115

debate, that Kevin Boland's statement shone out as a kind of honour to his integrity, because it was the speech of a man taking a transparently honest stand and sacrificing his interest for that stand. He referred to the difficulty of voting confidence in a Government containing the Minister for Agriculture. He challenged the Tanaiste, Erskine Childers, whom he believed to be genuinely sensitive on this kind of issue, to speak in the debate. He recalled that Deputy George Colley had spoken about low standards in high places, suggesting that this was precisely what Fianna Fail were about to vote for.

Dr O'Brien said that in the recent series of crises, 'many people didn't know whether to laugh or to weep and many did both'. He drew the picture where the Minister for Agriculture ordered the Minister for Defence to send five hundred rifles to Dundalk, with the latter obeying, explaining that if he had not done so, his colleague might have done something worse. This is government by the Keystone Cops, O'Brien said, asking what was the Taoiseach doing at the time? He described Lynch as the missing man in the Arms Trial. He asked was Lynch standing idly by, invisibly by? He argued that for the Taoiseach to have allowed Blaney and Haughey sit on the committee about the North, without himself, was an abdication of responsibility. Lynch made conciliatory speeches while Blaney made bellicose ones, intensifying Protestant fears. He accused Lynch of absurd smugness, knowing his majority was safe because Fianna Fail Deputies, like Pavlov's famous dogs, were conditioned to salivate in a particular way at the sound of a given bell. They are wise, the guys, who may do anything, say anything, sign anything in order to get into power and hold on to power. He asserted that when Deputy Haughey voted confidence in the Taoiseach and Deputy Gibbons that night, he would be saying to the public, 'I am a phony', as loud and clear as if he were bearing a placard with that legend. He recalled that the judge in the Arms Trial found a total conflict between the evidence of Deputy Haughey and Deputy Gibbons: one or other was a perjurer according to the judge.

Dr O'Brien concluded, showing that he could be a pragmatist, stating, 'If the people of this country in the next general election show that they demand an alternative to Fianna Fail, then it becomes the duty of the present Opposition to furnish that alternative'[7]. This speech was widely regarded as one of the most brilliant of the historic debate.

In 1969 thirteen people had lost their lives violently in Northern Ireland. In 1970 it was twenty-five.

In August 1970 the Social and Democratic Labour Party was founded in Northern Ireland. It was a new nationalist grouping with a socialist wing. It accepted that there could be no unity without the consent of the majority within Northern Ireland.

The Parliamentary Labour Party, still smarting after its hurt in the 1969 election, began to indulge in internal disputes, some of which had Dr O'Brien as a target. Two Labour TDs introduced a Bill to liberalise the law on availability of contraceptives. In the Dail three rural Labour TDs joined with Fianna Fail in defeating it. Noel Browne continued to attack clerical influence within the State. Steve Coughlan TD, in referring to a money-lending scandal, compared the situation to that in Limerick in 1904, 'When the people were in dire straits, thanks largely to the Jews of Limerick'. At an Administrative Council meeting of the Labour Party in 1970, it was proposed that Coughlan be expelled. In reacting to this move, David Thornley TD proposed that Noel Browne be also expelled for his statements. Thornley also asked for Conor Cruise O'Brien to be 'disciplined' because of his questioning the practice of Radio Telefis Eireann broadcasting the Angelus[8].

During the latter period of 1970 the Fianna Fail government sought to introduce amendments to the Offences Against the State Act. The Labour Party objected vociferously. Their leader, Brendan Corish, tried to raise the matter on the Order of Business in the Dail. He was ruled out of order and when he continued to object, he was expelled from the Chamber on a vote of sixty-nine

117

votes to twenty-four, several Fine Gael members voting for Corish. Conor was furious and berated the Ceann Comhairle saying, 'Your scandalous ruling that this is not a matter of urgent public importance is probably the most scandalous ruling ever made in a sovereign, democratic State'. The matter was then pursued by both Steve Coughlan and Noel Browne, who were both expelled. The next day, 10 December, Conor again raised the matter demanding that the Ceann Comhairle justify his ruling that Conor's question on an impending derogation from the European Convention on Human Rights be out of order. When he would not accept the Ceann Comhairle's ruling on the matter, Conor was expelled from the Chamber on a vote of sixty-five votes to twelve.

One week later Dr O'Brien made a statement which like most of his utterances, was perfectly rational, but in hindsight turned out to be mere wishful thinking on his part, and totally underestimating the staying powers of the person referred to. He said in the Dail, 'Deputy Haughey, for example, is politically dead and everyone knows it except Deputy Haughey apparently'.

Chapter Eleven

LABOUR PARTY SPOKESMAN ON NORTHERN IRELAND

Within the North the violence got worse as the IRA attacked the security forces. In March 1971 Chichester-Clark sought extra army support from Lord Carrington, the British Minister for Defence. This was refused and Chichester-Clark resigned to be replaced by Brian Faulkner. Faulkner spoke by phone to Lynch who congratulated him and was pleased for his success[1]. Dr O'Brien believed that the IRA felt they forced the resignation and that by escalating it further they could topple Faulkner also, thus destroying the structure of the Northern Ireland government[2]. It was at this period that O'Brien began to realise fully that almost the totality of people in the South were in a real sense through 'words, assumptions, silences, evasions, inciting the IRA to continue their campaign: a campaign in which they would again look to the South for help which would not materialise: a campaign which would be hopeless and lead to innumerable Catholics in exposed parts of Northern Ireland being killed'[3].

Political life in the Republic continued on local and EEC issues as if Northern Ireland was far away. Dr O'Brien participated at length in Dail Eireann where the Forcible Entry Bill took up much time. But he was determined to take a stand on the drift to anarchy in the North. In June at the ITGWU conference in Galway, which had a motion for the release of all political prisoners, he saw an opportunity. Though realising it was foolish from a party political stance, Conor intervened after the motion had been formally proposed and seconded without speeches. He went to the podium to define what a political prisoner was, believing that the motion really was a pro-IRA message to Northern Ireland. He asked were people who killed innocent civilians, even children, political prisoners? His short but lucid intervention was listened to in silence but won some nervous support. Subsequent speakers attacked him for asking such questions. The motion was passed with a large majority. But O'Brien was satisfied as he had really been addressing the whole nation as the debate was televised. Judging by the reaction he got in Galway, he had an uphill struggle to get people to think about these difficult questions. But as often with him, he believed he was being rational and would pursue his position logically, expecting reason to win out in the end.

Jack Lynch made a speech in the Garden of Remembrance in July, trying to be conciliatory, but which drew this response from Brian Faulkner: 'He can develop with us a relationship of mutual respect in which, while acknowledging our fundamental differences, we can do business on practical issues: or he can switch to a hard-line anti-partition stance, addressing himself to London as if this Government and the people who elected it do not exist'[4]. In Derry two men were shot dead by the army. The SDLP demanded an inquiry from London and threatened to withdraw from Stormont. This they did, determined to set up an alternative assembly. IRA violence continued to grow. Fifty-five people had been killed by July: there had been three hundred explosions and three hundred and twenty shootings.

Almost inevitably internment without trial was introduced in August. Despite the British Home Secretary Maudling's advice to Faulkner to 'lift some Protestants if you can',[5] only Catholics were taken. Many of these were totally innocent. The operation began at four o'clock in the morning. A description of the events goes:

> The terrifying circumstances of that morning were never to be forgotten. Whole areas were sealed off. Paratroopers smashing down doors and literally dragging men from their homes in front of hysterical wives and

terrified children, the brutal knock in the middle of the night reeking of totalitarianism about its dirty work. The random brutality, the abuse of rights, the uncertainty, the spread of rumours and counter-rumours, the callous indifference of the army to inquiries as to the whereabouts or the fates of internees, and the holding of a small number at secret locations for interrogation in depth transformed the psychology of the conflict[6].

Internment was a shocking political mistake. It totally alienated Catholics and made it impossible for Jack Lynch not to condemn it and the Northern Ireland authorities. The immediate resulting violence was widespread. The SDLP vowed never to return to Stormont. Dr O'Brien saw the IRA having, through violence, a veto over all meaningful political initiatives and dialogue within Northern Ireland[7].

That same summer Dr O'Brien decided that the cycle of annual commemorations was of no help in the Irish context, rather it was divisive, despite the best efforts of some people to be generous in their words to Northern Ireland Protestants. In his own local area of Howth, one such event commemorated Erskine Childers, who, though an English born Protestant, had been an Irish patriot. He had brought guns into Howth for the Volunteers in 1914. O'Brien wrote a letter to the local organising committee explaining his absence: 'In the present time ...commemorations of this kind are liable to be exploited for purposes disruptive of peace in this country ...Let us have a truce on commemorations until we can find something which Irishmen of both the main political and religious groupings can commemorate in peace together'.

By this time the Parliamentary Labour Party and other organs within the party, were becoming very restless with the statements of their party spokesman on Northern Ireland. David Thornley criticised Conor because of his IRA condemnations because Thornley believed force could not be ruled out. The Dublin

Regional Council said that the views expressed by O'Brien did not reflect those of ordinary members[8]. In Dail Eireann in October the party was completely split on Northern Ireland. Three members spoke for traditional nationalism while five others opposed it. These latter included the leader, Brendan Corish, Barry Desmond, Noel Browne, Michael O'Leary and Conor Cruise O'Brien.

The special two day debate on the Northern Ireland situation could be characterised as a declaration of verbal war on Britain and Northern Ireland. Almost every speech was a tirade against Britain. The debate did the opposite of cooling the situation. At one point Paddy Kennedy MP burst down the steps of the Dail chamber and asked the Ceann Comhairle for permission to speak on behalf of his people. Three ushers hustled him back up the steps and out of the lobby. Neither the Taoiseach nor the Minister for External Affairs turned in their seats to witness the spectacle.

In his contribution Dr O'Brien said that Mr Lynch had in the past made model speeches about a peaceful solution to the Northern situation, but he regretted that because of his need to keep the Fianna Fail party together, Mr Lynch's speeches have become 'vague and woolly', as he dodged so many thorny issues on the subject. He named Paddy Harte TD as one who understood the problem and added wisdom to his knowledge. He said Mr Blaney had first-hand contact with the problem and a commitment to a certain passionate mythology. His morning speech was 'chilling, ominous and sinister', raising the possibility of whether he is helping when he said, 'We have a right to bring about the end of partition by any way we can'. He found Patrick Hillery's UN speech on 7 October as lamentable.

Conor felt that the claim in Article 3 of the Constitution to legal right to govern all of the North, was at the heart of the difficulty. The IRA violence also contributed. He agreed that fifty years of discrimination and misrule in the North also aggravated the matter. But he maintained that the whole style of the Southern

122

approach to the Northern majority, was what their style had been to their Catholic minority. He said, 'There is only one logical conclusion to that way of proceeding and that is civil war, on the brink of which this whole island now stands. It seemed as if we lived, as Yeats once said, where motley was worn and we did not have to mean what we said'. Mr Charles Haughey interrupted O'Brien at that point to insist, 'Finish the quotation'. Dr O'Brien desisted replying, 'I will not trouble the House', to which Mr Haughey again insisted, 'Finish the quotation'. Mr Michael O'Leary interjected, 'A terrible jinx has fallen on the Deputy's party anyway', after which the Ceann Comhairle had to restore order. Mr Haughey then apologised, 'I apologise for my interruption, but I do not like to hear the words of Yeats prostituted'. Nearly twenty years after this exchange Dr O'Brien recalled that Haughey wanted him to speak a line about the terrible beauty, although he didn't say so. Conor declined, leaving it to Haughey to do so. He refrained, for reasons that Conor could guess at. 'The unspoken line:... "All changed, changed utterly:/A terrible beauty is born."...sort of hung there, in the air between us'.

Conor had the impression, rightly or wrongly, that Mr Haughey understood that line as validating the 'armed struggle' then underway in the North. Conor understood the line in very much the same way himself, which was why he did not comply with Haughey's directive. Conor recalled it, 'as an odd little scene, and the nearest I ever came to a meeting of minds with Mr Haughey'. Dr O'Brien continued his speech saying that under Sean Lemass' Taoiseachship, the constitutional claim did not seem to matter. But after August 1969 and the IRA revival of 1970/71, it became a very grave matter. He felt that the Government was becoming more and more locked into the campaign of violence, with a failure to educate the public mind. He asserted that the *Irish Press* was running a pro-Provisional campaign. Lynch's speech could have sought to tackle those problems but he 'chose the road of appeasement of the Blaneys in his own party'. He acknowledged that 'perhaps every party has, if not Blaneys, at least sub-Blaneys, semi-Blaneys or pseudo-Blaneys, who are active at various levels. either you appease them or you do not'. He noted that if such persons existed within the Labour Party, Brendan Corish dealt with them by ignoring them[9].

David Thornley described O'Brien as 'the so-called spokesman on Northern Ireland' and said 'since Article 2 of the Constitution was in Labour's own Constitution the abandonment of party policy automatically disqualifies O'Brien from membership of the party, let alone being a spokesman for it'. Fianna Fail launched an all out attack on O'Brien alleging his 'abandonment of the national position'.

Subsequently, various attempts were made within the parliamentary party, without success, to remove O'Brien from speaking on Northern Ireland. The party leadership realised that such public division would not help politically. Efforts were made to try to secure unanimous agreement on a policy. Finally at a meeting of the parliamentary party and the Administrative Council, a policy statement was carried by twenty-seven votes to three[10]. This policy sought 'the voluntary reunion of all Irish people and territory... the sectarian Unionist regime in the North must be brought to an end... the withdrawal of British troops as soon as a political solution permits'. The use of force was rejected. In Northern Ireland that year one hundred and seventy-four people had been killed.

On an amendment to the Constitution Bill 1971, taken on 12 January 1972, Dr O'Brien took the opportunity of spelling out how unsatisfactory Articles 2 and 3 were. He claimed that there was a great deal of intellectual dishonesty in relation to the whole question. He noted that Article 3 said, 'Pending the re-integration of the national territory, and without prejudice to the right of the parliament and government established by this constitution to exercise jurisdiction over the whole of that territory, the laws exacted by that parliament shall have the like area and extent of application as the laws of Saorstat Eireann and the like extra-territorial effect'. He said it was questionable to seek to exert such jurisdiction over the whole of the thirty-two counties. He agreed about the right of the Irish people to self-determination for the whole of the island. But he said this parliament and government were Twenty-Six County institutions. While he would like to see the people of this island in one state, he asserted that Articles 2 and 3 were barriers to unity with the Ulster Protestants.

Chapter Twelve

On 30 January 1972, in Derry city, soldiers of the First Battalion of the Parachute Regiment shot dead thirteen civilians, none of whom was a known terrorist and none of whom was found with a weapon. This happened at the end of an illegal anti-internment march while people were dispersing. This was followed immediately by a total sense of shock and disbelief all over Ireland. Bernadette Devlin physically attacked Reginald Maudling on the floor of the House of Commons. Protests took place throughout the country. The British Embassy in Dublin's Merrion Square was burned out. Only a week earlier the British and Irish Governments had together signed the Treaties of Accession to the EEC. Now the mood was black as the Irish Ambassador was withdrawn from London. Many people seemed to believe that the time was ripe for a United Ireland to be achieved: Britain should withdraw its troops.

Conor Cruise O'Brien believed that the actions in Derry were murder, but he feared the exploitation of this by the IRA to involve the Republic in a war. He spent three days in London after 30 January. Though unwell, he saw as many politicians as possible to emphasise to them the mood of the Republic at the wholesale slaughter. He too was feeling highly emotional about what had happened. Though he had previously said that a withdrawal of British troops would precipitate a civil war, he now found himself telling Maudling, Harold Wilson and Jeremy Thorpe that the continuing presence of the same troops could also be disastrous. He feared that a repetition by the British troops of such murderous activity would result in cross border retaliation. He also believed that the Catholics in Northern Ireland would never reject the IRA while British troops remained. He advised the British to name a future date for withdrawal of the army. In retrospect, he realised that in this, he was acting as a member of his own community and forgetting about the other community.

The night the Embassy was burned, Conor phoned his wife from London. She told him that she felt he was overreacting and that the people of the South, though shocked and traumatised would hold their nerve. They would not want any hostilities with Britain for which they would have to pay economically. She said that the burning of the Embassy would not help the IRA[1].

In a Dail debate on 4 February several Labour TDs, including Conor Cruise O'Brien, Michael O'Leary and Frank Cluskey, called for a withdrawal of British troops. This was a highly charged debate. Dr O'Brien said that the debate was being held under the shadow of death, most immediately under the shadow of the deaths of thirteen young men, criminally shot down by British paratroopers in Derry last Sunday. He had told the British political leaders in London, the previous day, that the action of their troops on Sunday had created a situation that their continued presence, with no date for their removal, made the working out of political structures impossible. Deputy Loughnane interrupted to say that the speaker had asked last week for British troops to be retained. O'Brien said he recognised the inherent dangers in asking for a date to be set for the beginning of troop withdrawal, but the presence of the British troops would do nothing to avert the danger of civil war on their withdrawal, which was inevitable. He argued that an announced withdrawal would force the Northern and Southern leaders to work out structures within which Irish people could live together on the island. Quoting Jonathan Swift, he pointed out that all government required consent. The Unionists had ignored that principle for fifty years and he denounced them for it. Real dialogue between Unionists and

Nationalists had never taken place due to the intervening British presence. Though the British had pulled out of Palestine without notice, he did not foresee a Conservative government leaving the North. He foresaw the whole island on the verge of a catastrophe comparable to the great Famine, as the economies were affected by violence and relations with England suffered. He said that Enoch Powell's idea of making the Irish foreigners could become practical politics in Britain.

Dr O'Brien commended the fair-minded and balanced speech of the Tanaiste, Erskine Childers but called for a tone which recognised the note of a national emergency. The whole country was seriously ill and ill founded noises from the Taoiseach were dangerous. Talk of sending troops across the border was dangerous and misleading, as there was no way the Irish Army could take on the British Army. He believed in the decency of the mass of the British people, who should be addressed on what happened in Derry. Dr O'Brien had earlier said on RTE that there should be an international inquiry, as happened with American Officers and men responsible for similar actions at My Lai in Vietnam. He cautioned that reprisals for the deaths would not bring the dead to life, would not console those who mourned and would in their results, bring on more innocent deaths. He ended his Dail speech by asking for calm at Sunday's Civil Rights March at Newry[2].

In the West Galway constituency several members of the Labour Party resigned over Dr O'Brien's continuing attacks on the IRA[3]. At the Labour Party Annual Conference in February there was again a motion urging the dropping of O'Brien as Northern Ireland spokesman[4]. Sean Tracey TD proposed the motion saying O'Brien had denigrated James Connolly, betrayed Labour's Constitution and given comfort and solace to the Stormont regime.

Dr O'Brien denied the accusations including 'peddling any so-called two nations theory'[5]. Gerry Fitt, the Leader of the SDLP and a fraternal delegate, said that no Labour member should give any support to either wing of the IRA. Paddy Devlin, another fraternal delegate from the SDLP, urged the withdrawal of the motion for the sake of party unity. Dr O'Brien remained as party spokesman.

Within the North the violence escalated with the IRA shooting and bombing indiscriminately. But in March it suddenly called a three day truce. Harold Wilson came to Dublin where O'Brien was among a Labour Party delegation consisting of Brendan Corish and Brendan Halligan, who saw him at Leinster House. Earlier in the summer Wilson, in his capacity as Chancellor of Bradford University, had conferred an Honorary Doctorate of Letters on Conor, so they had something to reminisce about. Wilson also said that as Labour MP for Huyton in Liverpool, he represented more Irish voters than any of the TDs. Conor was reminded of a Red Indian powwow, as Wilson ritualistically set about preparing his pipe for a smoke. Eventually Conor briefed Wilson on the situation, stressing that it would be unwise to enter into negotiations with the IRA just then. He said it might make them think that their violence would work. The next day it became clear that Wilson had seen the IRA that very same evening. This meeting was arranged by another Labour Party TD, Dr John O'Connell in whose house the meeting occurred. This was very embarrassing for the Labour Party spokesman.

Dr O'Brien has referred to this meeting as the 'Inchicore Summit' as John O'Connell lived in that Dublin suburb.

But despite Wilson's request, the IRA refused to extend their truce. Later in March the British Prime Minister, Edward Heath, prorogued Stormont for one year and introduced Direct Rule from Westminster, with William Whitelaw as Secretary of State for Northern Ireland.

Dr O'Brien contended that it was the Civil Rights Association which had brought down Stormont, not the IRA. This process began to occur inevitably when Westminster took over the control of security. But both the IRA and the Unionists saw the Heath action as the result of IRA activity. O'Brien maintained that the IRA made a major mistake by announcing just then that the war would continue. Catholics, North and South, were tired of the violence. Mr Whitelaw created an immediate good impression on Catholic opinion by releasing all the internees. Security forces were given a low profile and expected to do nothing provocative[6]. The Protestants dubbed him 'Willie Whitewash'. But there was a feeling of hope in Northern Ireland.

In the South political eyes were on Ireland's bid to enter the EEC. A White Paper on *The Accession of Ireland to the EEC* presented the Government's case which was being handled by Foreign Affairs. Both of the major parties, Fianna Fail and Fine Gael, were in favour of entry. Against were Labour, Official Sinn Fein, Provisional Sinn Fein and the ICTU. A direct contest between the two opposing groups took place, as entry demanded a constitutional amendment by way of referendum. This placed Labour in a rather embarrassing position from several points of view. It was most reluctant to be seen as an ally of Sinn Fein on any issue. It also feared that Fianna Fail might shortly call a general election, where its natural ally would be Fine Gael. Nevertheless, Labour opposed EEC entry on economic grounds, arguing that it would raise food prices and cause a loss of jobs in industry and fisheries. But, as often was the case, the party was not fully united. Some TDs did not campaign very vigorously. Among those was Dr O'Brien. He was a committed internationalist and the idea of being on the same side as Sinn Fein displeased him. He felt embarrassed that he had quite recently considered a left wing alliance a good idea. He did campaign but insisted on the separateness of Labour's efforts to secure a 'No' vote. Eighty-three per cent of those who did vote, voted 'Yes'.

So despite their differences over Northern Ireland, both Britain and Ireland joined the EEC and proceeded to work harmoniously together there. This was quite a contrast with

Ireland's refusal to join NATO because of partition. Ireland had realised that its economic future could not be put at risk because of the continuing problem of partition. This became the continuing practice of future Irish governments.

The Government then made several moves against the IRA in the South. A Prison Bill allowed the Minister for Justice to move some prisoners to military prisons after rioting in Mountjoy Jail in Dublin. On a free vote for the Labour Party, Dr O'Brien voted with the Government. Special courts, without juries, were set up to try terrorist cases. On 30 May, O'Brien took part in a television debate with Ruairi O Bradaigh. The next day the latter was arrested. Blaming O'Brien for inciting such a government move, O Bradaigh's successor in Sinn Fein, Daithi O Conaill, made an immediate personal attack on O'Brien:

> The British government can be well pleased with the action of Lynch and O'Malley. Their official mouthpiece in Ireland and abroad, Conor Cruise O'Brien, has long agitated for a policy of violence against Sinn Fein. Violence is nothing new to O'Brien; his legacy to the Irish people is a mass grave of young Irish soldiers in Glasnevin Cemetery and a denigration of the character of one of the world's greatest diplomats – Dag Hammarsjkold.
>
> O'Brien's pathological hatred of republicanism found an outlet in personal vicious attacks on Joe Cahill. It is ironic that Joe Cahill should have been arrested while making arrangements to meet the Evangelist, Mr Billy Graham, who requested a meeting with Republican leaders for Wednesday night. No doubt, Mr Cruise O'Brien is now pleased that Joe Cahill did not meet Billy Graham. It shocked O'Brien last March that Harold Wilson would express pleasure at meeting any of Ireland's most dedicated sons[7].

In 1972 Dr O'Brien did not believe that any of the main sections

131

of the total Irish people wanted unity: the Ulster Protestants did not and he believed people in the Republic were very doubtful about it. He believed that the Catholics of Northern Ireland were more interested in equality than unity. He foresaw two possible outcomes:

1. The end of the IRA violence and the return of the British Army to barracks; Administrative reform in policing and jobs; the Irish Government, while still aspiring to unity by consent, cooperating with Northern Ireland.

2. Violence continues; British agree to Irish Unity and withdraw; Catholics driven out of eastern Northern Ireland; Irish Army occupies Catholic areas; Irish Government seeks UN military aid which is not forthcoming; eventual repartition occurs.

The latter scenario he regarded as a nightmare though one which could become a reality. He was concerned because he was of the Catholic community. He feared it may destroy itself and him with it. It must, like himself, try to understand the Ulster Protestants, and confront its own mythology[8].

The SDLP, of course, had become the chief party representing the Catholics of Northern Ireland. It had some very able people within it who believed, not unreasonably, that they were the main ones to develop a strategy for the way forward. In late 1972 the SDLP issued its policy document – *Towards A New Ireland*. It called for Irish-British sovereignty in Northern Ireland. It said that the British government should declare that eventual Irish unity would be best for all concerned. The Irish Labour Party did not react enthusiastically to the document. Dr O'Brien believed that to be looking for Irish unity then, was counter-productive and was 'unwittingly and unintentionally a formula for civil war'[9]. This led to a public disagreement on radio between the redoubtable John Hume, Deputy Leader of the SDLP and O'Brien. This division proved a fundamental one. Paddy Devlin said relations with the Labour Party would never be the same again. At a meeting of the Labour Parliamentary Party, a motion supporting the SDLP document was tabled. If this was carried then O'Brien's position as party spokesman would have been untenable. But Brendan Corish, as he so often did, tried to defuse the situation and protect O'Brien. He suggested that the two parties meet and thrash out the matter. His parliamentary group agreed to this. But the next day the Administrative Council of the party passed the original motion. Austin Currie of the SDLP commented that the Parliamentary Labour Party's lack of support for their document was a 'face saving charade' for Dr O'Brien[10]. The Parliamentary Labour Party held firm for Dr O'Brien and his position as spokesman was not seriously challenged again[11].

On 7 December a referendum in the South voted to drop the reference in the constitution to the Special Position of the Catholic Church. Four hundred and sixty-seven people were killed in Northern Ireland that year.

Writing about this period in 1991, Dr O'Brien said:

My trouble was that I had published a book, at just the wrong time. *States of Ireland* had come out in 1972 and was immediately reviewed by John Hume in *The Irish Times*. John said that it was the ablest statement of the Unionist case that had ever been made. Coming from John, this was not exactly a compliment. Few of my Labour Party colleagues ever read that book, I believe, but all of them read John Hume's review. The late David Thornley put down a resolution calling for my resignation as spokesman on Foreign Affairs and Northern Ireland. The resolution was debated in the Parliamentary Labour Party. It was defeated, but not resoundingly. There was one surprise, and not a pleasant one. Justin Keating, whom I had up to then regarded as a friend, joined in the call for my resignation. He did so without warning and from a chair positioned immediately behind me. So I could feel what it was like to be stabbed in the back, politically speaking[12].

Chapter Thirteen

In 1969 Conor Cruise O'Brien had said that Labour should oppose any government proposed in Dail Eireann, so as to force a merger between Fianna Fail and Fine Gael[1]. Speaking in the Dail in July 1969 he said that Fine Gael, 'is, as it has been for almost forty years, not an alternative to Fianna Fail but an auxiliary to it'[2]. After the Arms Crisis O'Brien began to realise and propound that the opposition parties had an obligation to offer the electorate an alternative government. Labour front benchers wanted to exercise power[3]. Conor himself called the effort by the Parliamentary Party to get out of its former anti-coalition stance, 'Operation Houdini'. But the Labour annual conference gave the leader and the Parliamentary Party a free hand to seek partnership in Government. Of course there were some dissenters.

When the General Election was called in 1973, Fine Gael and Labour agreed a fourteen point manifesto. Fianna Fail and Fine Gael both increased their percentage of votes, but Labour declined from 17 per cent to 13.7 per cent. But because the voters of Fine Gael and Labour transferred their votes to each others candidates, under proportional representation, Labour won nineteen seats, a gain of one. Fine Gael won fifty-four seats, while Fianna Fail won sixty-nine, a loss of six. The National Coalition government was born. Labour got five ministries and two Parliamentary secretaries. The allocation of Dr O'Brien to the Ministry of Posts and Telegraphs was, 'probably a case of picking a ministry for the man rather than a man for the ministry'[4]. But Foreign Affairs or Education, where he continually castigated the Catholic Church for its role would have been too dangerous to give him. But his sphere of control did include authority over broadcasting, in which he was very interested. As Joe Lee has written, 'The appointment... was a cute ploy in turning poacher into gamekeeper'[5]. He also got responsibility for public relations for the Government. Bruce Arnold has written, 'He was the Government's only first class brain'[6]. Liam Cosgrave became Taoiseach with Brendan Corish Tanaiste.

There had been much speculation about the composition of the cabinet and about Conor's expected position. John Healy wrote in *The Irish Times* of 3 March 1973:

> Naturally the berth for O'Brien is one which absorbs most of the cabinet-makers this weekend. In Leinster House yesterday evening, it came in for a lot of mock arguments: 'There is only one Ministry for Conor – he'd make a great Minister for Lands'; 'Not at all, Conor would be happy nowhere else but in the Gaeltacht; he could open Dunquin and spend his holiday in the Blaskets'; 'What this country needs is a strong Minister for Defence – and no better man than O'Brien. Look at all the experience he had in Katanga'; 'What's wrong with the Board of Works? Conor is the only man who could drain the Shannon.'

Shortly after the election Dr O'Brien received news of his appointment on a Sunday morning in a public house in Coolock. The Sheaf of Wheat was a meeting place for many of his constituents and, while in their company, he received a phone call from his party leader. As Conor recalled it, Brendan Corish offered him the Posts and Telegraphs portfolio and Conor replied, 'I said I would and that was that.'

When O'Brien's cabinet position was announced in the Dail, there were gasps of derision from the Fianna Fail benches. Perhaps they assumed that such office would not be to his liking, as it would not afford him the facility of continuing his crusade about educating nationalists about the folly of their ways. But as they and others were to discover, that was not to be the case at all. O'Brien was to outmanoeuvre his party and coalition colleagues in this important sphere.

Dr O'Brien would have loved to have been made Minister for Foreign Affairs. As he later wrote:

> I had served seventeen years in the Department of External Affairs quite successfully. I was certainly better qualified for that post than I was for any other in the cabinet. I didn't however expect to get it, so I was not disappointed. Mr Cosgrave didn't veto such an appointment and I don't think he would have. He would have vetoed me as Minister for Education because that might have meant trouble with the Church. But he wouldn't have vetoed an appointment that would have kept me out of the country for a lot of the time. No, the reason why I didn't get it was that the leader of my own party did not ask for that post. Brendan Corish got all the posts he asked for, for the people he named. I understand why he didn't ask for Foreign Affairs. If that post was to go to a Labour member, my claims on it were strong. But if it had gone to me, that would have meant serious trouble inside the party, and with the SDLP.
>
> In the circumstances Brendan Corish did well by me in nominating me to a cabinet post at all. I was in no position to ask for the one I wanted. Corish also allowed me to remain as Labour spokesman on Foreign Affairs and Northern Ireland and to exercise those functions during the lifetime of the Coalition. Garret FitzGerald naturally resented this, though probably not as much as I would have done, had I been in his shoes.[7]

In his autobiography Garret FitzGerald writes:

> In the 1973-77 government a new element was added to the complex equation (Inter Departmental and Government Press Relations) however, in the form of Conor Cruise O'Brien, Minister for Posts and Telegraphs

and *de facto* Minister for Information, for at the very outset Cosgrave had delegated to him operational control of the Government Information Service.

FitzGerald recounts several occasions when this caused conflict between himself and O'Brien. The latter regarded FitzGerald's 'frank and open disposition' might lead him to say too much to journalists. He feared that he might even talk to reporters in his sleep. On one occasion when FitzGerald made a statement which seemed to be critical of the Minister in charge of Fisheries, O'Brien was... 'furious. He (O'Brien) never had been happy about my informal contacts with the press'[8].

Two major problems haunted the lifespan of the new Government: security and economics. The quadrupling of oil prices at the end of 1973 sent economic shock waves through Western countries. Unemployment and prices and inflation rose alarmingly. The elimination of poverty and the ending of social injustice, which the Coalition Manifesto had spoken of, was difficult to achieve. O'Brien's own departmental work was very mundane, as he tried to grapple with poor industrial relations and outdated technology in the Posts and Telegraphs areas. But the really contentious area for his tenure there proved to be broadcasting, especially as it affected the Northern Ireland situation.

A very strange action occurred early in the life of the Government which could have created an air of permanent mistrust in cabinet. A 1935 Act made the importation and sale of contraceptives illegal. In December 1973 the Supreme Court ruled in the McGee Case, that such a ban on importation was unconstitutional. Reform of the law proved necessary. The Minister for Justice introduced legislation in 1974 to permit chemists to sell contraceptives to married people only. This was a highly charged moral issue, since the Catholic Church held that their use was wrong. The Church also said this did not mean the State had to follow its teaching. Fianna Fail opposed the Bill.

Dr O'Brien said, 'If the (Contraceptive) Bill is defeated, Northern Ireland will point to it as final proof that Home Rule does indeed mean Rome Rule... Few things have done more damage to the cause of better relations between the two communities on this island than the atmosphere of pussy-footing or hugger-mugging that has prevailed in the Republic on such an issue'.[9]

The Government parties allowed their members a free vote on the Bill. When the members of the Dail were going through the voting gate, consternation occurred when the Taoiseach walked through the gate for voting against the Government Bill. He was quickly followed by the Minister for Education, Dick Burke and five other Fine Gael TDs. One Labour TD, Dan Spring, did not vote at all. Cosgrave had never once at cabinet given any indication of his intentions, but it made a mockery of collective cabinet responsibility.

FitzGerald reports that at the relevant Government meeting, 'Three times at this meeting Conor Cruise O'Brien endeavoured to extract from the Taoiseach a reaction to the proposed Bill, but each time he failed. We left the meeting no wiser about his attitude'.[10]

His colleagues, though, decided to keep their heads down and press on with Government work, as the Contraceptive Bill was defeated by seventy-five votes to sixty-one.

Speaking about this episode on RTE in 1977, Conor, rather magnanimously, said that he wished that Mr Cosgrave had told his cabinet colleagues beforehand, what way he was going to vote but he didn't, said O'Brien, and he saw his reasons for so doing. The Taoiseach felt that he would be exerting pressure on others if he were to do so. Perhaps he was wrong politically, but he believed that Mr Cosgrave did not see the vote as a political matter, but one of personal morality. Dr O'Brien said that he would not attack any man for acting sincerely on what he believed to be right.

Another area of social legislation the Government failed to

deliver on was that of criminal conversation and divorce. O'Brien and Garret FitzGerald, the Minister for Foreign Affairs, did raise the issues, but Cosgrave was very conservative here too and stymied efforts at legislative reform. The only movement allowed was to allow the Attorney General to propose an extension of the very narrow grounds for granting state decrees of nullity.

Later in the life of the Government O'Brien got into a public debate with Bishop Newman of Limerick, who like Conor, was not adverse to putting his own point of view very forceably. Conor had questioned the wisdom of not making available to young people, 'effective means of limiting families and the knowledge of how to limit them'. The Bishop replied that:

> It shows he appears to be committed to the idea of a secular state in which the moral standards of the majority of the people, insofar as they are rooted in their religious persuasions, would be of no concern whatsoever to the State... It is surely a monstrosity for anybody to imply that the moral attitudes of the generality of Irish Catholics – whether North or South – based as they are on a code that is reflective of their traditional faith, are in any way sectarian.[11]

In 1972 a Fianna Fail Government had dismissed the Radio Telefis Eireann (RTE) Authority because of an interview RTE had carried with an IRA man. This the Government said was in breach of Section 31 of the Broadcasting Act which said:

> The Minister may direct the Authority in writing to refrain from broadcasting any particular matter or matters of any particular class and the Authority shall comply with that direction.

The Minister of the day, Gerry Collins, had issued a directive under the Act which could set out any particular matter which RTE might not transmit, which could be calculated to promote the activities of any organisation engaging in or supporting the attainment of any particular objective by violent means.

Sean Lemass, as Taoiseach, had set down the Government view of RTE in 1966 when he said:

> The Government have overall responsibility for its conduct and especially the obligation to ensure that its programmes do not offend against the public interest... To this extent the Government reject the view that RTE should be, either generally or in regard to its current affairs and news programmes, completely independent of government supervision.[12]

John Healy, an astute political observer, saw Liam Cosgrave's adroit positioning of the liberal Dr Conor Cruise O'Brien in Posts and Telegraphs, as a ploy to get him to ride herd on, what was called in Leinster House as 'the Provo Station'. The liberals in RTE expected that Conor would repeal Section 31 overnight. Conor dampened this expectation by promising, in June 1973, to abolish it in the following year. But, as Healy observed, despite O'Brien talking in his 1973 Estimates Speech about future developments in open-window broadcasting, he remained sceptical about any deletion of Section 31. Healy saw O'Brien as having been very gloomy about the North while out of office. He had chided Healy and others who had suggested that the game was up in the North, accusing them of being cruelly optimistic and peddling false dawns. Healy held that, as far back as 1970, Jack Lynch had read the European Community situation as linking the common destinies of the two islands, and that the ancient anti-British sentiments were out of date. For this he had been referred to as 'Union Jack'. Healy had tried to unscramble Jack's 'Lynchspeak' for Dr O'Brien at the time and had gently chided him for his inability or perverseness in that deciphering operation. But now that Dr O'Brien was in office, with access to official files, Healy hoped that he could understand what Jack Lynch had been saying.

Dr O'Brien, in office, would certainly agree with the general thrust of Sean Lemass' 1966 sentiments, though he would also be aware of the difficulties these posed for the journalists on the ground. But he was adamant, as a first principle, that no subversives should get access to the airwaves. As John Healy had forecast, there was no early rush to repeal the restricting legislation. Conor took his time but did eventually take decisive action on the matter. In 1976 he introduced an Amendment to Section 31, which prohibited any interview or report of an interview with a spokesman... for any one or more of the following organisations. These included Sinn Fein and the IRA. He explained his thinking thus:

> Since membership of a private army is a crime, propaganda in favour of such an army is incitement to crime, and therefore is itself a crime. That much is clear. But whether given words and images constitute propaganda or incitement is endlessly debatable – or rather would be endlessly debatable if, in practice, somebody did not have to decide. But who should that somebody be, in relation to broadcasting..? I could have left that decision to the authority itself. In the circumstances... I thought it safer to act myself[13].

Conor slightly modified the Minister's power as well as curtailing the Government right to dismiss members of the Authority. Both these powers were made subject to Oireachtas approval and annulment[14]. *The Irish Times* editorialised saying, 'Dr O'Brien in his more rational moments is perfectly aware of the irrationality of his decision[15].

A case was taken by the members of the National Union of Journalists and the Services Industrial Professional Technical Union (SIPTU), working at RTE, to the European Court of Human Rights in 1991. The case wished to challenge Section 31 under the European Convention on Human Rights. In April 1991, the European Commission of Human Rights refused to admit the case to a full hearing, so closing off any further challenge to the broadcasting ban in Europe. Over the years RTE had introduced

141

guidelines for its staff to assist them in the compliance of Section 31. In practice this developed into a situation where members of Sinn Fein were prohibited from access to the airwaves in any capacity whatsoever. In August 1992 the High Court found in favour of a member of Sinn Fein who had been denied access to broadcasting in his capacity as a member of the national executive of the Baker's Union and chairman of the strike committee at his place of work. Mr Justice O'Hanlon found that the Act prohibited broadcasting by 'spokesmen' of certain organisations which the Minister and his successors were empowered to designate. Dr O'Brien caused consternation in media circles, at least, by agreeing with the judgement. He wrote that the word 'spokesmen' was used designedly. If they had meant 'members' they would have used that word. He wrote that the Act did not prevent a member of Sinn Fein, who is not a spokesman nor attempting to broadcast as such as a spokesman, from broadcasting. Dr O'Brien added that he had expected that RTE would have interpreted the Act liberally, but it had not done so. He thought it possible that RTE acted thus to discredit the Act itself. He wrote that the Act was primarily intended to protect RTE from possible abuses of power by any Government, such as had occurred in 1972 when 'my predecessor Mr Gerry Collins had sacked an entire authority without stated reason, under powers conferred on him by the basic statute, the Broadcasting Act of 1960... The Act of 1976 needs no amendment. Its provisions should now be respected, without either extension or reduction by RTE'[16]. This contribution by Dr O'Brien brought a furious riposte from RTE staff and ex-staff. Mr Wesley Boyd, Director of Broadcasting Developments in RTE said, 'Conor Cruise O'Brien, who indicated when he took office as Minister for Posts and Telegraphs in 1973 that he would abolish Section 31, but a couple of years later reinforced it in the Dail, has been sounding off in the papers and on the radio in the liberal way that only a politician out of office feels free to do'[17]. Mr Colum Kenny, a lecturer in Broadcast Journalism at Dublin City University, and a former 'father of the chapel' of the National

Union of Journalists at RTE wrote:

> I find the reported statements of Conor Cruise O'Brien to be particularly bizarre. His period as Minister for Communications was not one which I recall, as a journalist then working for RTE, as one of great liberalism. He was fully aware of RTE's internal practices in connection with Section 31 and was widely believed to support them. Then and later, those suspected of not sharing a simplistic revisionist analysis of Northern Ireland politics felt under threat within RTE, in terms of their professional deployment and promotion[18].

It was reported that in 1987, 'The RTE authority formally approached the Government and requested that the Ministerial Order under Section 31 be allowed to lapse. RTE said it would then amend its own guidelines to ensure that certain views and opinions were not broadcast. The Government turned down the proposals'[19].

In August 1992 RTE announced that it intended to appeal Justice O'Hanlon's decision on Section 31 to the Supreme Court. On Tuesday, 30 March 1993, the Supreme Court delivered its judgement ruling that RTE was wrong to ban all members of Sinn Fein from the airwaves. In a discussion on this judgement and subsequent RTE reaction Dr O'Brien spoke. On an RTE programme called *Questions and Answers* on 5 April he was critical of RTE's advice to its news staff not to use the word murder in relation to paramilitary killings or to describe the perpetrators as terrorists. He said 'RTE is slanted in favour of the Provos, to put it brutally'.

It was left to the Coalition Government of Fianna Fail and Labour to finally suspend Section 31 early in 1994. The Minister, Michael D Higgins of Labour, so advised the cabinet during the aftermath of the Downing Street Declaration between Albert Reynolds and John Major.

But, as Minister for Posts and Telegraphs in 1973, Conor wanted to do more than fulfill his ministerial duty on the security

143

front. As another Labour TD of the period wrote:

> O'Brien became almost a national symbol, idolised and
> reviled in proportions that were always difficult to
> establish... his enemies labelled him as not only anti-IRA
> but anti-republican, an enemy of the Constitution itself.
> As Minister for Posts and Telegraphs his appetite for
> attacking the IRA and those he perceived as fellow-
> travellers grew apace, to the point where it became an
> obsession difficult to understand from the outside. Like
> all government ministers during this period, his home
> and family were subjected to continuous threat, usually
> by anonymous telephone callers, to a degree that would
> possibly have broken people of lesser strength[20].

The danger to elected parliamentarians became very real as a Fine
Gael Senator, Billy Fox, was murdered by the IRA in 1974. That
same year saw violence come South in a major way, when in May,
massive loyalist car bombs exploded in Dublin and Monaghan
killing twenty-eight people and causing shocking injuries to over
one hundred others. Dr O'Brien was one of the first people on the
scene at one of the Dublin explosions, that on Parnell Street. He
was appalled by the carnage and reinforced in his belief that the
whole country was in grave danger. No person was ever prosecuted
for these atrocities. An IRA hunger strike at Portlaoise Jail led to
threats on the Government that if one hunger striker died, two
Ministers would be assassinated. The homes of two Labour TDs
were attacked by IRA supporters. Dr O'Brien and his family were
particularly at risk as they lived in a very isolated and exposed site
on Howth Head.

In 1975 the security situation did not improve. A Dutch
industrialist, Tiede Herrema, was kidnapped. The ransom
demanded the release of the IRA prisoners in Portlaoise Jail.
Dr O'Brien later recalled that, to the best of his recollection, the
Government did discuss this demand only once, right at the
beginning of the case and properly and unanimously decided to
make no concessions. The Ministers in fact took an oath that there

would be no giving in to the kidnappers, even if one of themselves became a victim or was threatened with death[21]. The country was combed by the security forces until the location of the kidnappers and their victim was discovered. Then a long siege developed with Dr Herrema being eventually released unharmed.

The funerals of two Mayo-born IRA hunger strikers who had died in English jails, Frank Stagg and Michael Gaughan, caused major security operations as their remains were returned to Mayo for burial. The Cabinet appointed a subcommittee on security which took day-to-day decisions. This was probably the most powerful committee of the Government, and its recommendations, when unanimous, were often passed by the full Cabinet virtually without discussion. Dr O'Brien was a member[22].

Conor was interviewed by Ludovic Kennedy on British television in October of that year. He was asked if he had been frightened by the death threat. He replied that, 'It did not please me very much'. He said that the hideous acts of the IRA had made many people recoil against them and an act like the kidnapping of Dr Herrema only increased the general revulsion against acts of violence. He denied that the IRA had brought down Stormont rather was it the Civil Rights movement in 1969 and 1970. The IRA offensive did not commence until 1971. The only achievement of the IRA, he said, was to widen the gap between the two communities in Northern Ireland and to create counter guerilla forces that carried out even more violent acts than themselves. He said that those who wanted to force an All-Ireland Republic were guilty of colonialism. When asked how he would like to be remembered as a politician and writer, he replied, 'I would like to be remembered primarily as a person, even in politics, who tried though he did not always succeed'. He said he would fight the next election with the present Government. He hoped that they would win the election – 'It is very important, I believe, that we win,' he said[23].

Chapter Fourteen

————◆————

A SECOND FAMILY

————◆————

Given the hectic nature of Conor's life, often lived in the public domain, it would be easy to forget that he continued to have a private domestic life of a most satisfying dimension. Maire MacEntee was well used to a household where the male was engaged in a public life, which gave little scope for him to devote much time to his family. She has recalled how her own father was often a stranger to his family. Maire was keen that she and Conor would avoid that thorny path, as far as possible.

As we have already seen Conor and Maire came from very different backgrounds. Yet they combined together to form a loving and stable marriage. In the traditional Irish family, children are seen as a blessing from God, which help to bring a marriage to fruition. Maire would have been steeped in this tradition, her husband only less so. But Conor had his three children from his first marriage and remained on excellent terms with them, their mother and her new husband. Maire needed the fulfilment of motherhood. Together, she and Conor decided to adopt a family. They came to this decision in New York, and in 1968 they adopted a baby boy of Ghanian background, whom they christened Patrick. That summer as was usual they spent their holidays in the MacEntee holiday house, in the Kerry Gaeltacht of Dunchaoin. Later as they were preparing to return to New York, they ran into legal difficulties barring the movement out of the country of Patrick, then still under six months old. This delay in fact, was to give them the welcome opportunity of accepting an invitation from President de Valera to visit him, *en famille*, at Aras an Uachtarain[1].

146

A couple of years after their permanent return to Ireland, Maire was to become personally involved in a controversy which was to last several years. The Department of Education had been pursuing a policy of closing down small National Schools and amalgamating them with larger schools. After the summer holidays of 1970, it transpired that this policy had been implemented at Dunchaoin in Kerry, which was the spiritual home of the Brownes, MacEntees and latterly the Cruise O'Briens. The local Principal Teacher had been transferred to Ballyferriter, four miles away, and the school's twenty-six pupils were expected to do likewise on the first of September. This reorganisation would have taken place in consultation with the local school authorities, Bishop Eamon Casey and Fr Kissane PP. But the local people were outraged at this attack on their community and were having none of it. As Maire Cruise O'Brien later said, a second, fail-safe key to the school always hung in the nearby Post Office. This key was used by the locals to reopen their school, and most pupils returned there on 21 September, to be taught by two temporary voluntary teachers. Meantime the news of the official closure, had become of national importance, despite the Arms Trial currently in progress. Outrage was expressed by a wide selection of academic figures, including Maire MacEntee and others interested in the Gaeltacht.

Dunchaoin was no mere country parish but one of the locations of the cultural soul of Gaelic Ireland. Many famous literary figures came from there and the nearby Blasket Islands. The revival of the Irish language, one of the mythologies Fianna Fail was founded upon, was seen as under threat by a Fianna Fail government. One resident of Dingle asked, 'Three prominent politicians holiday annually in Dunchaoin: one of them has a rest home there. Have they nothing to say about this final solution?'[2].

The annual Cumann Merriman Summer School met in Kilkee on the weekend of 19 September. A proposal calling on the government to reconsider its decision to close Dunchaoin School

147

was seconded by Dr Conor Cruise O'Brien TD. He said that he had been in touch with the local parents and they were unanimously in favour of keeping their school open. They had asked him to enlist the help of the Merriman School. He made the point that while the Department of Education implemented the closure decision the Government was collectively responsible. The next day, a Sunday, hundreds of people assembled at the school in Dunchaoin for a public meeting. Dr O'Brien attended. Maire, who was highly emotionally committed, was one of the main speakers. When she had first heard of the school closure, she said, 'My reaction was the most contemporary one to most bereavement: to try to pretend it hadn't happened and to close my mind to what it meant to me. Then the conviction that if I didn't take my two year old to the Gaeltacht before winter this year, I would be depriving him of a whole world of pleasure and excitement, forced me to face up to the situation'. She then volunteered to teach in the school 'to teach reading, writing and sums rather than Irish, which these children could teach me',[3] she said in impeccable Irish. Thereafter Maire remained living in the MacEntee family house and taught in the school. She was always at pains to make clear that she was not attempting to direct the people's affairs for them, but that she was willing to help their local committee, which was in control. One local man repaired the roof, another supplied turf. Later a mass meeting was held in the Mansion House in Dublin to raise funds. A Kildare man, Michael O Dubhshlainte, a qualified National Teacher, volunteered to teach in Dunchaoin. He and Maire taught for the whole of the first term to Christmas when another qualified teacher became available. He confessed to being a little in awe of Maire when he arrived in Dunchaoin but found her to be a wonderful person to work with. He recalls several visits during the term from Dr O'Brien, whose Irish he found to his surprise, was also excellent. Maire was always anxious to make clear, that there was no battle involved with local Ballyferriter, 'but the closing of the school and the blow to the people's self-esteem which that constituted, must prove a near-mortal wound to the morale of the entire Irish-speaking area'[4].

Despite the public protests and the local feeling, the Fianna Fail Government surprisingly, refused to alter its stance on the school closure. Various schemes were put in hand to finance the school, including the issuing of a record by Maire, reciting her poetry. The record was named *In Omos do Dhunchaoin* – In Honour of Dunchaoin. The school pupils themselves performed at many functions, even travelling to Dublin, where on one occasion they were all guests of Maire at her home in Howth[5]. Eventually the matter was only resolved, when in 1973 the new Government, which included Dr O'Brien as a Minister, granted official recognition to the school again. The new Minister for Education, Dick Burke, had been a keen supporter of the school over the difficult years and took great pleasure in confirming Mr O Dubhshlainte as Principal when answering Dail questions from Fianna Fail.

It was not surprising that when Patrick came of school going age, he was enrolled at an all Irish school – Scoil Nessain in Raheny. There he spoke Gaelic and was called Padraig, after his maternal uncle. Of course Conor could also feel that in involving his children so intimately in Irish, he was being faithful not only to his own wife, but also to the memory of his mother, Kathleen, whom he often felt he had so misunderstood during her life. Maire herself was one of a family of three children, two girls and a boy. In 1974 the couple decided to adopt again. This time, it was a baby girl of Ghanian background, whom they christened Margaret, after Maire's mother. She too followed her brother to Scoil Nessain, where she was known as Mairead. At Scoil Nessain, both the Cruise O'Briens were prepared for the reception of First Holy Communion and Confirmation, following the tradition of both their parents. The latter were assiduous attenders at school functions and parental meetings while the children attended Scoil Nessain. While there, Margaret became a member of the junior girl guides, called the Brownies. Her mother was to coin a Gaelic word, na Suaircini, for the Brownies. After primary school both children transferred to Mount Temple Comprehensive School in

149

Clontarf, which would not have had a Catholic ethos, though many of its pupils would have been Catholic. This in a way was a parallel of their father's own education. Conor tells an amusing story about the occasion he discovered how quick-witted his son Patrick was. Conor had stumbled on Patrick in the act of cuffing his sister Margaret. The young boy was suitably told off and made to understand how annoyed his father was, with that sort of unacceptable behaviour. Patrick did not enjoy his father's angry tone and was not looking forward to a continuation of it. He obviously knew his father very well, as he decided to take outrageous diversionary action brazenly telling Conor, 'Daddy, you are biased, over-protective, and sexist'. Conor realised exactly what was happening but he could not restrain himself, as he burst out laughing at the nerve of his son. He was reassured of the sharpness of the boy's wits[6].

Against this background of continuing family life, Conor's hardline approach to the IRA and its fellow-travellers was all the more brave and praiseworthy. Their house was literally only a stone's throw from a public car park which was frequented by scores of cars, especially during the summer months.

Like Conor, Maire was a formidable intellectual. Her main field of interest was the Gaelic language. She spent quite a long time working with Professor Tomas de Bhaldraithe of University College Dublin, working on the production of a famous Irish-English dictionary. The English language she found useful for logical and intellectual thinking. But in the sphere of emotions and feelings, the spirituality and descriptive nature of Irish appealed to her most. Her own particular artistic expertise lay in the writing of poetry, exclusively in Irish, at which she gradually acquired a reputation as one of the foremost poets of her generation. She was an academic and critic and like her husuband was not afraid of being controversial. She went on the record for disliking the poetry of two of the foremost Gaelic poets, Sean

O'Riordain and Sean O'Tuama. This was because she found their poetry too much like English poetry. She was keener on European influences in Gaelic poetry[7]. But for Maire these years were filled with child rearing, involving all the domestic chores that entails. In all this, her husband was closely involved, as he took immense pride and pleasure in his new family, more of which we shall see at a later stage.

Chapter Fifteen

Government responsibility in 1973 for Northern Ireland was held by the Taoiseach and Garret FitzGerald. Dr O'Brien remained the Labour Party spokesman for Northern Ireland throughout the lifetime of the Government. This was in line with his address to the Labour Party in December 1968, when he argued that the party, when next in government, must not repeat the mistake of previous occasions by handing over External Affairs to another party, without retaining the right to criticise any particular policy it disagreed with, on a party basis. This was the only such position Labour had. O'Brien spoke on the subject of Northern Ireland more often than any of his Government colleagues. As usual he pursued an individualistic role. In 1974 he announced that Irish unity was not a practical goal and he was not working actively for it. [1] This provoked disagreement within the Labour Party. Some of those who felt his policy was misguided prepared a document calling on the Government to give vocal encouragement to the minority in Northern Ireland and to demand a declaration of intent by Britain to withdraw economically and militarily.

Subsequently Conor himself put a paper to the Administrative Council of the Labour Party which argued that the Government should keep a low profile on Northern Ireland as, in the event of civil war, the State would not be able to cope. He hoped that within Northern Ireland more moderate politicians might be elected by the Protestant community.

Dr O'Brien's memorandum on the Government's policy on Northern Ireland presented to the Administrative Council of the

Labour Party was in part as follows:

It is generally agreed that there is a serious danger that:

(a) The projected Convention may have a Loyalist majority.

(b) That such a majority might disregard the parameters of the White Paper and might establish, by majority vote in the Convention, an entirely Loyalist executive which would proclaim itself the Provisional government of Northern Ireland.

(c) That the Loyalist paramilitary groups would be recognised by the 'provisional government' as security forces of the Northern Ireland State.

(d) That a British Government might either acquiesce *de facto* in this state of affairs or be drawn into military confrontation with Loyalist groups.

(e) That the further development of the situation would pit the British Army against both the Catholic and Protestant sides.

(f) That the British Army command would then inform the British government that its position was untenable and recommend withdrawal.

(g) That in these circumstances and facing a worsening economic situation, the British would disengage altogether from Northern Ireland.

(h) If this decision were taken, it is virtually certain to be carried out speedily. It is known that no military staffs would favourably envisage the kind of gradual 'phased withdrawal' which journalists and others discuss in this context.

(i) In the event of a British withdrawal under such circumstances it is virtually certain that civil war would break out in Northern Ireland.

(j) The precise outcome of such a conflict is unpredictable but it is certain that they would include heavy civilian casualties in Northern Ireland, especially among exposed minorities, and most especially among the Catholics of the Belfast region, serious casualties also in the Republic as a result of 'retaliatory raids and bombings by Loyalist forces into our territory', massive disruption of the economy and of social life, both North and South, total elimination of the tourism industry, suspension of foreign investment, widespread and lasting unemployment, and a vast refugee problem in the Republic.

Dr O'Brien said SDLP members estimate that in the event of such a 'doomsday' situation the number of refugees from the North we might expect here would be in the order of sixty to seventy thousand families – not less than a quarter of a million people. It was obvious that such an incursion could not be sustained without a very severe drop in the standard of living in the Republic. Northern observers have also warned us that any such incursion would necessarily include large numbers of teenagers who, by reason of the conditions in which they have grown up, are tough, violent and virtually ungovernable.

The Document went on to disabuse people that the situation outcome could be controlled either by the Irish Army or by any United Nations force. 'As far as the Irish Army is concerned,' he wrote, 'it is reliably estimated that, with its present effective size, it could, if called upon, hold one Border town, e.g. Newry.'

For all of these reasons he concluded that, 'It is our view that a relatively low profile by Dublin is that best calculated to allow the emergence of a non-Loyalist Protestant vote'. On the other hand he argued that a 'noisy and threatening posture' by Dublin would help to make a Loyalist victory certain.[2]

Unfortunately for Dr O'Brien, the document appeared on the front page of *The Irish Times* on 25 September under the headline:

LOW PROFILE BY DUBLIN

'BEST WAY' TO THWART LOYALIST TAKEOVER –

CRUISE O'BRIEN CITES POLICY IN CONFIDENTIAL

REPORT TO LABOUR.

The strategy of the document outraged Unionists. It shocked southern nationalists. It drew odium from most quarters including the SDLP and especially Fianna Fail who saw it as anti-national. The latter party came to almost automatically oppose any idea O'Brien proposed. The point was also eventually reached where it was felt that he was politically more of a liability than an asset to the Government. He had become obsessed with Northern Ireland. He was such a polished and persuasive public performer that the media gave him constant exposure. It came to be felt that he was actually losing support for his cause by being so vociferous in his exposition. It has been suggested that, but for the support Brendan Corish gave him within the Coalition, Cosgrave would have insisted on O'Brien adopting a lower profile.[3] Though it could also be argued that he deflected much opprobrium from Fine Gael and on to himself and the Labour Party.

The fact that so much of what Dr O'Brien said about nationalism in Ireland held merit, made him all the more insufferable. He brought a cold dispassionate reasoning to much which was enshrouded in webs of deceit, delusion and mythology. He mocked popular beliefs. 'Any mature culture could take pride in its ability to produce a critic of O'Brien's calibre and courage,

155

despite his occasional eccentricities'. But there is little doubt he went overboard in his eagerness to serve. He dispensed too much logic. His full scale attack, on the view of a people of itself, was bound to be counter-productive. His hectoring approach began to turn people off, rather than persuade them to his view. The style with which he performed continued to mesmerise his audience, particularly foreign ones. But more and more, nationalist people, North and South, began to resent him and what he said. Senator John A Murphy wrote that such resentment, 'may have been linked with an intuitive popular feeling that he had begun to challenge the basis of Irish nationality itself'.[4] Yet his contribution to the clarification for nationalist Southerners of Northern Protestants has been recognised by the poet, Seamus Heaney. It created 'some kind of clarity in Southerners thinking about the Protestant community in the North. And it is not enough for people to simply say "Ah, they're all Irishmen", when some Northerners actually spit at the word Irishmen. There is in O'Brien a kind of obstinate insistence on facing up to this kind of reality, which I think is his contribution'[5]. Professor Seamus Deane of University College Dublin, in a May 1977 issue of *Crane Bag* in a conversation with Seamus Heaney, felt that the clarity of O'Brien's position was what was most objectionable. He saw it as giving a rational clarity to the Northern position which was untrue to the reality. He saw O'Brien's humanism being used as an excuse to rid Ireland of the atavisms which give it life, even though the life itself may be in some way brutal. He regarded O'Brien's humanism as a very bourgeois form of humanism. But Heaney again defended what Conor had done. He believed that Conor had performed an utterly necessary job in rebuking all easy thoughts about the Protestant community in the North. Heaney argued that seven or eight years ago, there was a tremendous sentiment for Catholics in the North, among intellectuals, politicians and ordinary people. Because of O'Brien's sentiments, those same people still revile O'Brien, though they themselves now harbour sentiments which mirror O'Brien's thinking, Heaney added. Furthermore, he concluded, those people

156

will not cede the clarity or validity of O'Brien's position.

Senator John A Murphy also wrote that O'Brien had performed a very great public service, 'because he compelled people to make uncomfortable reappraisals of emotions cosily and lazily cherished. He masterfully exposed the woolliness of Southern attitudes towards Northern Ireland and in particular the ambivalence of Southern thinking – or more accurately, feeling – about the Provisional IRA.' [6]

Conor himself realised that there would be people he could not hope to influence. He wrote:

> To minds that are possessed by that idea of sacrifice it is irrelevant to prove that a campaign like the current IRA campaign, for example, cannot possibly accomplish any desirable political objective. That can be demonstrated, it can be quite logically and clearly demonstrated, but it doesn't matter. The objective is to become part of 'history' in the abstract or mythological sense, to achieve immortality by getting oneself killed for Ireland's sake. That the actual people of Ireland, in their overwhelming humdrum majority want no such sacrifice is also irrelevant, having no other effect than to cause the people in question to disappear from 'Irish history' which in every generation consists of the doings and sayings of martyrs.[7]

But there were more than those above whom Conor would not influence. Terence Brown of TCD wrote:

> As a Government minister Cruise O'Brien set his face against all those aspects of Irish popular culture which carried an infection which presented itself as an 'unhealthy intersection' between literature and politics. The patriotic ballad, the commemorative speech, the public veneration of the nationalist dead all seemed to fall under his increasingly intemperate interdict. As a result, even those who were willing to grant the substance of his views on the Northern question

found it impossible to stomach his iconoclastic handling of national sentiment. [8]

Dr O'Brien had written in 1972 of Articles 2 and 3 of the Irish Constitution which claimed *de jure* jurisdiction over Northern Ireland: 'It would be hard to think of a combination of propositions more likely to sustain and stiffen the siege mentality of Protestant Ulster'.[9] Now in Government, he suggested removing or amending the said Articles. [10] This drew violent criticism from Fianna Fail and the SDLP. The other members of the Cabinet remained silent in public, realising that all party agreement would be necessary for any such move. Desmond O'Malley of Fianna Fail spoke of the 'anti-national semantics of Conor Cruise O'Brien'. [11]

Introducing Dr O'Brien in his autobiography, Garret FitzGerald wrote:

> He had been an exponent of the prevailing sterile anti-partition propaganda line... By 1973 Conor had swung to a very different position: he had become highly sensitive to Unionist concerns, not, as some of his many enemies contend, because he agreed with their views but because he believed, with reason, that insensitivity towards the genuine fears of Unionists was dangerously counterproductive. In propounding this position with what has seemed to me at times to be the fervour of a convert he has courageously challenged cherished nationalist myths.

> What I found, and still find, myself in disagreement with him is, in relation to his single-minded concentration on one of two dangers in Northern Ireland, and what I regard as his unwillingness to take adequate account of the other danger, namely that exclusive attention to legitimate Unionist concerns, may dangerously exacerbate tensions on the Nationalist side, thus abandoning mainstream moderate nationalism to the IRA. In that way too there is a serious risk of provoking violence. [12]

Chapter Sixteen

---◆---

EMERGENCY POWERS BILL 1976

RESIGNATION OF THE PRESIDENT

---◆---

After the assassination in Dublin by the IRA on 23 July 1976 of Christopher Ewart-Biggs, the new British Ambassador, the Government felt almost under siege. It reacted somewhat unwisely by declaring a state of emergency. It then let quite a long period intervene until the measure was formally declared in the Dail on 1 September, under an Emergency Powers Bill. By this time the public sense of emergency had abated and the situation appeared a little unreal, making the task of the Government more difficult in the Dail.

When the Minister for Posts and Telegraphs first spoke in the debate, he felt constrained to regret some of the opinions he had expressed in 1972, when Fianna Fail introduced the Offences Against the State Act. He said, 'I was wrong. I did not allow adequately for the forces in that party, that sincerely intended to uphold the law and order and protect the security of the citizens'. The current Emergency, as he saw it, lay in the existence of a core of hardened terrorists; very dangerous men of different persuasions, who were capable of striking terrible blows. He argued that law and order constituted the basic essential part of the Government's Northern Ireland policy.

Some days later Dr O'Brien gave an interview to Bernard Nossiter of the *Washington Post* newspaper on the situation in Ireland. Reaction to the Nossiter article created a furore. Conor had spoken about the powers which the new measure before the

Dail would give the Government. He appeared to hint that some of those powers might be used against Irish newspapers. The *Irish Press*, which had a mutual feeling of hostility with Conor, carried its reaction to the Nossiter article under the headline:

'O'BRIEN CHIEF CENSOR', HISTORIAN TELLS MEETING

The Irish Times headlined:

FIANNA FAIL OPPOSITION HARDENS AFTER O'BRIEN

CENSORSHIP THREAT

Mr Haughey told RTE, 'There is a militaristic Fascist mentality behind all this, and the Minister for Posts and Telegraphs has given perhaps inadvertent expression to that'. Pressure mounted on Conor to clarify what exactly he had said to Mr Nossiter in connection with the Emergency Powers Bill. As he again offered to speak in the Dail, *The Irish Times* editorialised on 6 September, 'All ears will be bent expectantly towards Conor Cruise O'Brien, when he makes his promised statement in the Dail, about the press and the new legislation'.

The House was treated to the unusual spectacle of Dr O'Brien in a mood of reconciliation – a mood one might almost recklessly have thought, of contrition. He rejected the accusation that the Emergency was a window dressing operation, designed to take people's minds off the economic situation. He referred 'to the discovery of the very important arms cache in this city... enough incendiaries to destroy the whole centre of Dublin'. He compared the current situation to that of the 'Lebanon a few years ago'. He said that Fianna Fail and the IRA shared a common aim to see the British withdraw from the North. He feared this could lead to a Lebanon scale sectarian civil war. He regarded a five year jail sentence for IRA membership as too low. At that stage many felt that they wanted him to come to his reason for participating again in the debate. Mr Haughey began to interrupt and the spleen between the two prima donnas got a full, though rare, public ventilation, to the high entertainment of all those present.

160

The following exchanges occurred:

Mr Haughey:	The Minister should come back to the question of censorship. That is what we want to hear.
Dr O'Brien:	I appreciate Deputy Haughey's intervention. He has commented recently on our being Fascists and militarists, perhaps, unintentionally. I do not want to lower this debate by any *tu quoque*. However this, this is an old challenge and Deputy Haughey knows it well: if he wishes to debate these matters with me on any public platform in this country, not by interruption here because the Chair would not permit me.
Mr Haughey:	What about here?
Dr O'Brien:	If the Deputy wishes to debate with me on any public platform, I will do it.
Mr Haughey:	I understand the Minister is not permitted to meet us in debates on radio.
Dr O'Brien:	Who said that?
Mr Haughey:	That is what the Radio Eireann people tell our Whips.
Dr O'Brien:	The Deputy had a go at me the other day when I was not there. He is not available when I want him.
Mr Haughey:	I was there last Sunday morning.
Dr O'Brien:	All right. If the Deputy wants to meet me next Sunday morning, I shall be available.

Mr Haughey:	I recognise that the Minister is not at the top of his form.
Mr Tunney:	The Minister attacked Michael O'Morain for attacking the *Irish Press*.
Dr O'Brien:	I always think it is a good sign when the Deputies opposite start interrupting. When I am being conciliatory it seems to annoy them more than anything else.
Leas-Cheann Comhairle:	
	The Minister must be allowed to make his speech.
Mr Haughey:	Let him get back to the question of censorship.
Dr O'Brien:	I should rather not get back to Mr O'Morain and all that area. I notice that Deputy Haughey is equally anxious to avoid that subject.
Mr Haughey:	Let us get back to censorship.

Dr O'Brien then went on to refer to a collection of clippings from the *Irish Press* that he had been keeping, and which the *Irish Press* had referred editorially to as 'the infamous file'. Mr Haughey again interrupted, referring to Conor's practice, saying, 'It can hardly be regarded as ministerial activity'. This led to another period of interruption.

Mr Donegan:	Neither can some of Deputy Haughey's deeds in 1970 be regarded as ministerial activity.
Mr Haughey:	If I were the Minister, I should keep quiet.

Dr O'Brien:	The Deputy who ought to keep quiet in that area is not exactly Deputy Donegan.
Mr Donegan:	I did not run guns.
Mr Haughey:	No, but you fired them at innocent itinerants.
Dr O'Brien:	I did not put these matters on record because of my specific ministerial responsibility as has been pointed out rightly.
Mr Haughey:	Judging from the state of the Department, the Minister, perhaps, had nothing better to do.
Dr O'Brien:	... Figuratively I am supposed to be all poised to set the dogs on them [journalists] as, we have been reminded by Deputy Kelly, Deputy Haughey set the dogs quite literally on Senator Noel Browne.
Mr Haughey:	That is incorrect and I shall deal with it.

Continuing the debate, with little further interruption, Dr O'Brien acknowledged that some opponents of the Bill were genuinely concerned with the civil rights issue, but he said the IRA were sheltering behind that. He noted that the practices of the IRA, arbitrary imprisonment, pistol whipping, tarring and feathering, knee-capping, random or semi-random murder by bomb and booby trap, and capital punishment without trial, were against civil liberties.

He stood by the *Washington Post* article saying that he had been quoted correctly. But he objected to the interpretations put on it. He said the Criminal Law Bill did not introduce censorship.

163

It did not give special powers to the Government in relation to the press. Rather it increased the scope of limitations on propaganda, in favour of armed conspiracies. He said these limitations, their judgement and interpretation, were entrusted to the Courts. It would be for the Director for Public Prosecutions to bring charges and not the Minister for Posts and Telegraphs.

The divisions within the Labour Party on security measures were very obvious during this debate. Mr Haughey remarked in the Dail, 'The Labour Party always wrestle with their consciences but I am afraid the Labour Party always win'. Three Labour TDs spoke against the Bill but abstained on the vote. Four Labour members who were not then in the Parliamentary Party voted against the Bill. These were David Thornley in the Dail, and Noel Browne, Michael Mullen and Mary Robinson in Seanad Eireann. But when on 14 September the Minister for Justice whose measure the Bill was, accepted a Fianna Fail amendment which would be less stringent on the newspapers, it served to further isolate O'Brien, this time within the Government, as he had been so much in favour of the measure.

A week later, speaking in the Dail, Mr Cooney, Minister for Justice, defended Dr O'Brien's contribution to the debate. Mr Cooney confirmed that the press curbs contained in the Criminal Law Bill would still stand when the Bill is enacted, despite the deletion from the Bill of the terms dealing with incitement. Mr Cooney said that the interview of the Minister for Posts and Telegraphs with the *Washington Post* which sparked off the press controversy was misrepresented. 'Dr Cruise O'Brien was not threatening censorship', he said. 'The Minister had made that clear when he stated in the Dail that this was never his intention', he added.

The President of Ireland, Erskine Childers, who had defeated the Fine Gael candidate, TF O'Higgins, by 635,867 votes to 578,771 in the Presidential election of May 1973, died suddenly on 17 November 1974. All party agreement saw the inauguration of

Cearbhall O'Dalaigh to succeed Childers on 19 December 1974. O'Dalaigh had been a distinguished jurist, appointed to the Supreme Court in 1953 and as Chief Justice in 1961. In 1973 he joined the European Court of Justice. But like most successful jurists he had a very political background also. He was a defeated Fianna Fail candidate in the 1948 and 1951 general elections. He served as Attorney-General to Fianna Fail governments in 1946 and 1951. But during his period as Chief Justice he made a major impact on the country, as he developed the law in a liberal fashion, drawing on the Constitution to place the Supreme Court as the guardian of citizens' rights. He was also a scholar and a gentleman.

When the Bill was sent to President O'Dalaigh for his signature and promulgation, he quite properly decided to consult the Council of State on the matter.

Speaking in the Dail the Minister for Justice whose Bill it was, said that, 'It had not been expected,' that President O'Dalaigh would consult the Council of State concerning the Emergency Powers legislation. If the matter were taken to the Supreme Court the Government would be represented by its own legal advisors. The Minister said he would not speculate on the President's reasons for consulting the Council of State about the legislation, but if it were brought to the Supreme Court, the Court would have first to debate its right to examine the case. His advice all along, he said, was that the Bill was within the terms of the Constitution. Article 28 envisaged a state of emergency, and provided that laws passed in pursuance of the state of emergency would be immune from Constitutional challenge. The Minister admitted that the President's action did not fit in with the Government's plans. 'We would prefer to see the Bill in operation as soon as possible. That is why the Dail was called into session during the recess,' he added[1].

But after consulting the Council of State the President did send the Bill to the Supreme Court. Though the Court acted quickly it had to fulfill its obligations in a correct way. This entailed a few weeks delay. Finally the Court found the Bill to be in accord with the Constitution. The President duly signed it on 16 October.

To put it mildly the Government was not pleased with this delay. From the beginning of his tenure, Cosgrave had not shown much respect for the new President, treating him more as a Fianna Fail politician. [2] During the delay the Government members champed at the bit, but held their peace. But two days after the Bill was signed, the undercurrent of fury came out in public. The Minister for Defence, Paddy Donegan, a publican from County Louth and a close friend of Cosgrave's, attended an army function in Columb Barracks, Mullingar. He was opening a new cook-house. There, in public, he made reference to the President as, 'a thundering disgrace'. Donegan said, 'It was amazing that when the President sent the Emergency Powers Bill to the Supreme Court he did not send the powers of the army, he did not send the seven years maximum penalty for inciting people to join the IRA to the Supreme Court. In my opinion he is a thundering disgrace. The fact is that he must stand behind the State'.

President O'Dalaigh sent a letter of protest threatening resignation to the Government the next day. The Government felt that he would not resign.

The President was, according to the Constitution, Commander-in-Chief of the army. When Donegan's remarks were reported, he offered to resign but Cosgrave refused to accept his resignation, saying that a letter of apology would suffice. Donegan had a request to see the President refused. 'In the impasse the onus was on Cosgrave to go to O'Dalaigh and apologise on his own and on the minister's behalf. If at this stage O'Dalaigh requested Donegan's resignation, it is difficult to see how Cosgrave could have refused, or if he did, how his refusal would have produced less than O'Dalaigh's resignation'[3]. The President made no statement. Cosgrave spoke twice by telephone to the President, but did not make any apology or indicate he wished to see O'Dalaigh, though the latter said he would see Cosgrave. O'Dalaigh was not agreeable to discuss such a matter on the phone. He also indicated to Cosgrave that 'he had already taken certain preliminary decisions'.

Fianna Fail naturally saw this as a great opportunity to attack the Government. It tabled a Dail motion demanding Donegan's resignation. Donegan offered an apology to the President. Some of the Government Deputies felt that Donegan should have been dismissed. But Cosgrave handled the 'controversy as a purely party political matter' and 'on the whole the Labour Party kept out of the argument'.[4] Brendan Corish said in the debate: 'I am speaking in favour of the Taoiseach's motion (That Dail Eireann affirms its confidence in the Taoiseach and his Government) and my Party are voting for it, because the overall record of the Government merits support... The issue of the Presidency is not one on which to resign. To the Labour Party, quite frankly, it is not that important'.[5]

Dr O'Brien did not speak on the matter in the Dail, though he did say that in his opinion the remarks of the Minister were not thought out but rather off the cuff in difficult circumstances. Fianna Fail made every effort in the debate to criticise Conor. David Andrews said: 'That lie was compounded by the Minister for Posts and Telegraphs on Monday, when he suggested that the Minister for Defence made his remarks in an unpremeditated fashion. Nothing could be further from the truth'. [6]

James Tully, a Labour cabinet colleague and also a member of the security committee felt called upon to defend Conor in the debate saying: 'There are some who endeavour to sneer at the Minister for Posts and Telegraphs but if there is in this House a more courageous man than he, I should like to hear who it is. Time after time the Minister has pointed to the real cause of trouble between this country and Northern Ireland, that is, the activities of the paramilitaries on both sides'.[7]

Mr Cosgrave said: 'There has been a great deal of fuss and comment here about the words of the Minister for Defence. I have said already many times and I want to reiterate it now, that what the Minister said is regrettable and regretted, but that the responsibility for accepting his resignation or, on the other hand, requesting his resignation, devolves on me'.[8]

Garret FitzGerald has written that while he was with Liam Cosgrave a message arrived that there was an important note coming from the residence of the President. FitzGerald suggested that they try to avert the expected resignation by accepting Paddy Donegan's proffered resignation. That done the Taoiseach sought to phone the President to inform him of his action. But FitzGerald reports their plan was thwarted by the unavailability of the President. The letter of resignation duly arrived.[9] The Dail motion had been passed and on 21 October O'Dalaigh sent his letter of resignation 'As the only way open to assert publicly my personal integrity and independence as President of Ireland and to protect the dignity and independence of the Presidency as an institution'[10]. Within two years he was dead. Cosgrave agreed again with Jack Lynch on an unopposed Fianna Fail person for President, Patrick Hillery. He was the natural successor to Lynch in Fianna Fail and it suited Cosgrave's political calculations to have him out of the political arena. Early on in his Presidency, Hillery decided against giving interviews. He explained: 'My main reason was because Cearbhall O'Dalaigh had resigned and I did not think we should go on as if nothing had happened. If this man resigned, it should be seen that he had to resign and that it was wrong that he had to'[11].

This episode brought little credit on anyone within the Coalition Government. Those who preached about honesty and high standards in public life looked the other way for political motives when they had an opportunity to uphold the honour of the State and its Constitution. The question was how would the people judge them? For the high honour of the Cosgrave family in

Irish constitutional history, it was a bad time.

On Dr O'Brien's behalf, it could be argued that he was completely taken up with the introduction of Section 31 of the Broadcasting Act at the time. In this he was coming under fierce opposition and journalistic attack.

Dr O'Brien's commentary on this episode makes it clear that he stood full-square behind the Government's handling of the matter, and feels Cearbhall O'Dalaigh himself made a constitutional crisis out of the situation. He writes:

> I regard the strictures in the second last paragraph as unwarranted in the circumstances, and I feel in no need of the excuse offered in the last paragraph. Paddy Donegan's 'thundering disgrace' remark was of course indefensible and if he had not publicly apologised for it immediately, I and others would have demanded his resignation. He did apologise and retract and sought an interview with the President in order to convey his apology and retraction in person. Most people would, I believe, have accepted that apology and closed the incident. I have no doubt that should a Minister use intemperate language about our present President, Mary Robinson, she would accept the minister's apology rather than allow a regrettable incident to escalate into a constitutional crisis. President Cearbhall O'Dalaigh, as we all know, chose to act otherwise. In the circumstances, I felt at no time any urge to join in the public pounding of a colleague who had erred and apologised. In fact it was I who later recommended to the Taoiseach, Liam Cosgrave, that he take Donegan back into the Cabinet as Minister for Fisheries. Cosgrave did so. Donegan was a good Minister for Fisheries and never again attracted unfavourable notice.

Chapter Seventeen

SUNNINGDALE AGREEMENT

FALL OF EXECUTIVE

The British Authorities, to the consternation of the political parties North and South, talked to the IRA again in 1972. They flew an IRA delegation of six to London. The IRA demanded that the British publicly state their support for the principle of an All-Ireland vote on the future of Northern Ireland, and an amnesty for all terrorists.[1] The British declined to meet these demands and the IRA blitzed Belfast with twenty-two bombs. The Army moved against no-go republican areas in Belfast and Derry in Operation Motorman. Political solutions were needed urgently. A referendum was to be held in Northern Ireland in March 1973 to see did the people wish to remain part of the United Kingdom. Between 29 January and 18 February, nineteen people were assassinated in sectarian murders, thirteen Catholics and six Protestants. Both the SDLP and the IRA said Catholics should boycott the referendum. Fifty-nine per cent of people voted, of whom ninety-eight per cent voted to remain in the United Kingdom. It was clear the electorate had spoken. Brian Faulkner claimed that twenty to twenty-five per cent of Catholics voted to retain the *status quo*.[2]

William Whitelaw produced Northern Ireland Constitutional proposals and an election to a new Northern Ireland Assembly followed. Brian Faulkner believed, 'Tensions were also being eased by the defeat of Lynch's government and the accession of a new Government led by Mr Cosgrave and containing such progressive thinkers as Conor Cruise O'Brien and Garret FitzGerald, who commanded some respect in Northern Ireland. A new era of neighbourly co-existence appeared possible.' [3]

The results confirmed how Unionism had fragmented under the traumatic events, with extremists well represented. Faulkner's Unionists won twenty-three seats, Paisley's and Craig's followers together won twenty-seven. The SDLP got nineteen and the non-sectarian Alliance Party got eight out of the seventy-eight seat body.

The opening of the Assembly proved farcical with the behaviour of the Loyalists dramatising the issue of wreckers versus the rest.[4] In contrast Faulkner has written that the SDLP was a responsible party with John Hume making a fine conciliatory speech.[5] Finally Faulkner's Unionists, Alliance and the SDLP had to leave the debating chamber and negotiate quietly. They agreed to form an Executive of six Official Unionists, four SDLP and one Alliance. The meetings of the Assembly which followed had to be adjourned as Loyalists had only one word to shout at the Official Unionists, 'Traitors'. Their fury knew no bounds. While Paisley harangued the Assembly, others physically assaulted the Official Unionist members.

The next part of the negotiations to set up a working Executive in Northern Ireland involved meetings between the British, Irish and the Northern Ireland parties. Paisley and his Loyalists refused to attend these meetings which were held at Sunningdale in England. Mr Heath, who chaired the four day conference, had Sir Alec Douglas-Hume, Francis Pym (the new Northern Ireland Secretary), David Howell and Sir Peter Rawlinson (Attorney General) with him. Mr Cosgrave had Brendan Corish, Garret FitzGerald and Conor Cruise O'Brien with him. All the Northern Ireland Executive were present. Everybody was aware of the historic nature of what was happening. Mr Cosgrave tried to dampen expectations before he left Dublin by saying: 'The Irish public should not pin exaggerated hopes on what these talks can produce in the immediate future. I have to tell you, and it is important that you remember, that these talks are essentially about men's lives and there is no guarantee that peace will return in the immediate wake of the talks... The danger of further serious violence is not to be excluded. We will deal firmly with such activities here'.

The Official Unionists were very happy with the outcome of the talks. They had achieved a Declaration saying: 'The Irish government fully accepted and solemnly declared that there could be no change in the status of Northern Ireland until a majority of the people of Northern Ireland desired a change in that status.' [6] The British government declared that it was and would remain, their policy to support the wishes of the majority of the people of Northern Ireland. The present status of Northern Ireland is that it is part of the United Kingdom. If in the future the majority of the people of Northern Ireland should indicate a wish to become part of a united Ireland, the British government would support that wish. Formal cooperation to defeat terrorism was agreed. The establishment of a Council of Ireland was also agreed with various structures which would not infringe on the role of the Northern Ireland Assembly. The Irish Government and the SDLP held out for this Council as something to take away from the conference, which would satisfy their constituents. Faulkner saw this as the price his group had to pay.

The Power-Sharing Executive took office on 1 January 1974. When negotiations began with the Irish Government on the structures of the Council of Ireland, the Executive took a common position and reached amicable agreement with Dublin. [7] They agreed that executive functions of the Council would be confined to non-political matters like tourism, agriculture and fisheries.

The Ulster Unionist Council came out against the Sunningdale Agreement and Faulkner resigned from the leadership of the Unionist Party. [8] Only two of the Unionist Assembly members defected from supporting the new Executive, so it still retained a majority there. But the feeling within the

Unionist community was being whipped up with the message that the Council of Ireland was the start of the road to Irish unity.

Kevin Boland, an ex-Fianna Fail minister, took a constitutional challenge against the Sunningdale Agreement. He claimed it breached the Constitution. Cosgrave defended the challenge saying the Agreement was not contrary to the territorial claim on Northern Ireland in the Constitution. The anti-Sunningdale Unionists seized on to this as proof of their view that the South did not really recognise the legal position of Northern Ireland. Cosgrave invited Faulkner to Dublin where he reassured him that despite the niceties of the legal situation, 'We accept Northern Ireland as it is, and want to cooperate with you, that's all there is to it'.[9] Cosgrave was bound by the *sub judice* situation of Boland's court case and could not go public until the final judgement was delivered on 13 March. Faulkner accepted Cosgrave's *bona fides*, but they were useless to him in his fight for political survival. In the Assembly extraordinary behaviour occurred from the Loyalist members. But the Executive went about its administrative business demonstrating that power sharing could work if allowed.

As often happens in Northern Ireland, the calling of a British general election can come at the most inopportune time. Despite protests from the Executive, a snap British Election was called for 28 February by Mr Heath.[10] The Loyalists opposed to Sunningdale united into the UUUC. They won 367,000 votes to 94,000 for Faulkner's Unionists. The Loyalists won eleven out of the twelve Parliamentary seats to Westminster. Labour won the election in Britain and Harold Wilson became Prime Minister, with Merlyn Rees as the new Secretary of State for Northern Ireland. He legalised Sinn Fein and the UVF and began to release detainees.[11] The IRA responded with violence. Wilson came to Belfast and met the Executive, reassuring them of his support. Roy Mason, Defence Minister, said the general feeling in Britain was for the withdrawal of British troops. On 14 May, after weeks of bitter debate, the Assembly voted by forty-four votes to twenty-eight for accepting the Sunningdale Agreement.

This vote provoked a Loyalist strike, which due to the inaction of Merlyn Rees as the person in charge of security, and the tacit support of most Protestants, gradually brought Northern Ireland to a standstill. This led to the resignation of the Executive. Dr O'Brien wrote that the Executive collapsed when it became plain that the Protestant participants were repudiated by the Protestant community. [12] Security considerations had let a brave experiment end. The army regarded the strike as political and not terrorist and therefore not its primary concern to stop.[13] Cosgrave had urged Rees to act.[14] Wilson insulted all Unionists by referring to them as spongers. [15]

The Assembly duly collapsed and Merlyn Rees took control of running Northern Ireland. A new convention was called in 1975 and elections were held. Faulkner's supporters won five seats to forty-six for the UUUC. The Convention discussed power sharing, but rivalries within the UUUC did not make that possible again. The convention collapsed in November 1975, Paisley running the Democratic Unionist Party and James Molyneux in charge of the official Unionist Party. Each party always had to watch how the other reacted to any new situation. Each seemed to vie with the other in negative and sterile politics. More than two hundred people died in violence in each of the years from 1973 to 1976. Roy Mason succeeded Merlyn Rees in September 1976. Constitutional reform had proved impossible. Both the British and Irish governments realised that security measures had to be uppermost in containing the IRA and the by then vibrant Protestant para military terrorist groups.

In 1977, Brian Faulkner was of the same opinion as was Conor Cruise O'Brien in 1972. Faulkner wrote: 'The only real alternative to working together is to live separately. That means repartition and a form of sectarian apartheid which will bring shame on the name of Ireland'. [16]

Despite being a critic and writer, Conor Cruise O'Brien did not make any notes or keep diaries about his time in Government. He always deplored the *Crossman Diaries* way of going on: taking detailed notes of statements made in confidence by colleagues, and then publishing same. Dr O'Brien had not written in any detail about this period until shortly before Garret FitzGerald, who was Minister for Foreign Affairs in that Coalition Government, published his autobiography. Then he decided to do a little reminiscing too.

He said that he and Garret FitzGerald got on well and still do, except on the subject of Northern Ireland. In practice, he wrote:

> During the lifetime of the 1973-77 Coalition, Garret did and said whatever John Hume advised him to do and say. The divergence between myself and Garret became most marked on the run-up to Sunningdale in 1974. Garret argued in favour of a high-profile Council of Ireland; a thing with two tiers and executive powers. Hume wanted this so that the agreement would have an all-Ireland dimension and be capable of leading to 'an agreed Ireland'. I argued that the important thing about Sunningdale was the power-sharing Executive. The more the Council was emphasised, the more the Executive would be in danger. The idea of a Council of Ireland was alarming to the Unionist grass-roots. The more we raised our sights on that matter, the greater the risk of discrediting our interlocuters, with their own constituency and wrecking the whole deal.

Garret replied kindly but with a touch of condescension, as one might use towards a person who was venturing into a field with which he was imperfectly acquainted. 'There were no grounds for fear that events would take the turn that I was suggesting. Northern Ireland had changed. Specifically the Unionist community had changed. The proposed arrangements complete with Council of Ireland, executive powers and two tiers, would be quite acceptable to them.'

That was it pretty well, as far as the Cabinet were concerned. Liam Cosgrave was prepared to leave it to Garret, and hope it kept fine for him, without much confidence that it would. The rest of the Cabinet showed little sign of interest in the whole arrangement.

After the Executive fell, Liam Cosgrave turned to Conor and said: 'The Protestants have won. Isn't that it?'[17]

Dr O'Brien went on to say that Garret FitzGerald subsequently acknowledged that he had been wrong. But O'Brien adds that Garret believed that this experience was bad for O'Brien, in that he appeared to Garret (and many others) to believe he was infallible. Dr O'Brien continued, 'In fact, I don't believe in anyone's infallibility, not in me, not Garret's, not John Hume's and not even the Pope's. '[18]

Dr O'Brien clearly believed then that the sovereign Irish Government, of which he was a Minister, was being unduly influenced in its Northern Irish policy by John Hume. He continued to hold this view and believed the same held for successive Irish governments. In April 1993, writing of the recent meeting between John Hume and Gerry Adams, of which Garret FitzGerald gave mild approval, Dr O'Brien wrote:

> John Hume is not indeed a member of any government. But he is something much more important than a member of a government. He is, and has long been the *de facto* leader of nationalist Ireland. Successive Governments in Dublin have deferred to him for more than twenty years now. No politician in our Republic – with the minor, and temporary exception of myself – has ever maintained a public difference of opinion with Mr Hume. The only leading politician who ever even risked Mr Hume's displeasure was C J Haughey. In opposition in 1985, Mr Haughey publicly opposed the Anglo-Irish

Agreement, Mr Hume's brainchild. But when he became Taoiseach again, Mr Haughey hastened to make peace with Mr Hume by embracing the Agreement which he had once denounced.

Garret FitzGerald himself, both as Taoiseach and as Foreign Minister, was John Hume's undeviating disciple. Our Department of Foreign Affairs, under every minister since 1970, has never known any other language than Hume-speak in relation to Northern Ireland. Anything else is politically incorrect and would be a bar to promotion.[19]

Noting that the Hume-Adams meeting of 1993 took place in the presence of a number of Catholic priests and was therefore in the tradition of the Confederation of Kilkenny, apart from the presence of the Nuncio, O'Brien added, 'People sometimes refer to Mr Hume in jest as Pope John, yet the parallel is, in fact unnervingly apt'.[20] There is a double irony in this jibe. The last Pope John was of course a most successful Vatican diplomat over a thirty year period, in such sensitive places as Bulgaria, Turkey and post-war France. As the Pope who called the Second Vatican Council he established a good relationship with Mr Khrushchev. In 1962, when the latter almost went to a nuclear war with President Kennedy during the Cuban Missiles Crisis, Pope John was able to facilitate the Russian leader in devising an acceptable formula for ending of the Cold War.[21]

Dr O'Brien continued his criticism of the Hume-Adams meetings the following month when he spoke to the Northern Ireland Labour Party organisation. This time he widened his comments to include Hume's Social and Democratic Labour Party, which, he said, had used unfounded protestations that it was non-sectarian to persuade the British Labour Party that it was unnecessary to organise in Northern Ireland. He then went on to make a most devastating critique of John Hume and his Party, saying, 'The Adams/Hume pact shows the SDLP up for what it has become under John Hume's leadership; a coldly sectarian party which is not above doing a deal with the accomplices of terrorists in order to gain a collective communal and sectarian advantage'. [22]

Though, no doubt, like others in different circumstances, John Hume might have preferred to avoid rising to O'Brien's bait, he could not possibly risk refusing to answer publicly such grave charges. This he did some days later in an article in the paper in which O'Brien writes his weekly column, the *Irish Independent*. His tone was one of anger and even exasperation, accumulated over many years, as he wrote, 'The most recent statement by Conor Cruise O'Brien is a powerful example of both irresponsibility and deep prejudice. If I were seeking advice on how to be sectarian, then one of the first people I would consult would be Conor Cruise O'Brien'. [23] Hume then went on to give several examples to rebut the charges of sectarianism. He also noted that Northern Loyalists sometimes quoted Dr O'Brien's writings to bolster their own actions.

In his autobiography, Garret FitzGerald wrote of O'Brien in the context of his role of advising the Coalition Government on Northern Ireland policy. He said:

> He was more nearly right than I and the rest of us were in the run-up to Sunningdale and in his judgement of the Conference itself... his presence in that Government helped to promote a balance in our assessment of the complex Northern Ireland issue that previous governments lacked... At Sunningdale both Faulkner and the Alliance leader, Oliver Napier, urged deleting Articles 2 and 3 of the Irish Constitution... Conor responded that a simple proposal to delete them would certainly be rejected by the people in the referendum... the Irish Government should not be pushed on the issue, he said. [24]

John Boland, a Fine Gael Senator of that Parliament, and future government Minister, has written of the relationship between Conor Cruise O'Brien and Liam Cosgrave in that Coalition Government. He has shown how the Taoiseach, even at meetings of the Fine Gael Parliamentary Party, supported his Minister. Boland writes: 'No two men could, in the context of that time, have come from positions further apart. One, a liberal literary agnostic, the other a conservative Catholic pragmatic'.

The Cruiser, as he was dubbed by political colleagues not particularly enamoured of his outlook, was given to occasional sallies in the public domain where he aired his views on the need for change in Ireland's social, moral, and other attitudes. More often than not these remarks, from a Labour Party Minister, led to a bumpy ride for his Fine Gael colleagues and, especially for those backbenchers representing essentially rural and conservative constituencies. Not surprisingly this, in turn, provoked occasional grumblings at meetings of the Fine Gael Parliamentary Party. One recalls suggestions to the effect that he should open more telephone boxes and shut his own. To all of these complaints the then Taoiseach was impassively unmoved. His answer, on the several occasions they were raised, was always the same. He himself was not always in total agreement with all of Conor's statements, yet he respected his right to have such views. Cosgrave said that if any member of the Parliamentary Party could stand up and say that Minister O'Brien's comments were contrary to, or damaging of, Government policy then the Taoiseach would take action. Even more tellingly, he would ask his colleagues whether anything the Minister had said was untrue. Nobody, during those four years of that Government, was ever able to answer these challenges for the very simple reason that both Conor Cruise O'Brien and Liam Cosgrave knew what their roles were, as Minister and Taoiseach respectively, in a Coalition Government. And because they did, they very quickly came to have a mutual respect and understanding. Within a short time, the conservative and the liberal defended each other in public and formed a friendship in private, because they trusted each other. [25]

179

Chapter Eighteen

---◆---

---◆---

The 1976 Labour Party annual conference gave the go ahead for a manifesto between it and Fine Gael on which to fight the forthcoming general election. In June 1976 Labour had won its first by-election since 1965. The portents looked well for the Coalition to remain in office.[1] The main problem to be resolved, as always, was when precisely to hold the election. The drawing up of the second manifesto put pressure on the Government to go earlier than necessary to the country. Fianna Fail said the Government was afraid to let the people have their say. Some members of the Government, including Dr O'Brien, preferred a date later rather than earlier.[2] They believed the economy was gradually improving. The prerogative to name the date rested with the Taoiseach. As was his form, Cosgrave did not show his hand until quite late in the day. But Fianna Fail had guessed correctly and the Dail was dissolved on 25 May. They were ready with a detailed manifesto which appealed to a wide cross section of people. The media in general expected the Coalition to have a resounding victory. Jim Tully had recently completed a constituency revision which was expected to favour the government parties.[3]

The early Fianna Fail campaign and the disunited Labour Party (Noel Browne, selected as a Labour candidate though an ardent anti-Coalitionist, was refused official backing and stood as an Independent Labour) soon made the election an open one.

Fianna Fail proposed the ending of motor tax and rates. These were radical and almost unreal fiscal proposals. Their cost was shrouded in political verbiage. By contrast the Coalition manifesto appeared to offer nothing new. The Government had come through difficult economic and security problems during its period of office. They had remained united. They expected the people would see and be grateful for their hard work. But as often happens when people leave the factory floor for administrative positions they can easily lose touch with the reality on the ground. The stolid Cosgrave government, full of earnest sober men, were taken aback by the positive public reaction to the unrealistic Fianna Fail manifesto. A commentator wrote of its presentation, 'as if victory was certain and the issues did not matter. They offered an economic programme which had not been costed. And they did it with a suave smiling confidence which was staggering'.[4] The Coalition then, feeling under pressure, offered to phase out rates, making a twenty-five per cent reduction in 1977. The person of Jack Lynch was also much more appealing than 'the constipated image of Cosgrave'[5] and the electorate seemed content to deal in images.

Some Government ministers had not given as much time to their constituencies as they might. Among these was Dr O'Brien, who now began to see the danger of a Government defeat. He found it difficult to accept that a man who had been dismissed from government in 1970, was still very much to the fore in public life and possibly biding his time for a return to high office. Conor no longer had to expect the indignity of trailing in behind Mr Haughey, as Jim Tully had arranged the constituency revision, so that the latter was then fighting the Dublin North constituency. Conor's Dublin Clontarf constituency appeared to be ready made for a resounding victory for himself. It was solidly middle income with two minority groupings, working class and well off. The only question to be determined was how would Conor, with ministerial charisma, fare against George Colley. It was expected that there was one seat each for Fianna Fail, Fine Gael and Labour, from the

181

forty thousand voters. Election commentators were agreed that the election result in Clontarf was only of academic interest as both O'Brien and Colley were virtually certain of being elected, though one newspaper ran a story on the Clontarf constituency, asking the question, 'Is Dr O'Brien really such an unpopular politician?'

Conor was surprised to find that the North and security issues in general were not perceived as important election matters. He decided to raise that topic and point out Fianna Fail's record. In a BBC interview he spoke of Mr Haughey's involvement in the Arms Crisis of 1970. He accused Haughey of being sympathetic to the objectives of the Provisional IRA. He said it must be assumed that a government of which he was a member, would be less inclined to clamp down on the Provisionals, than would the Coalition or a Fianna Fail government without Haughey. The latter said that Dr O'Brien's unfounded allegations were simply a repetition of those which the Minister had based his campaign in the 1973 general election on. He added, 'By giving me the second highest vote in the country in that election my constituents showed what they thought of the allegation. I believe they will treat them in the same way on this occasion'. Dr O'Brien also gave an interview to the London *Times*, again attacking Mr Haughey. O'Brien had said that if Mr Haughey were to become a Minister again, 'There would be a feeling that certainly existed in 1969-70, among members of the Garda that if you saw "the boys" preparing for some exercise in Northern Ireland, you really did not see them'. Mr Haughey responded with a nice historical allusion saying 'that Dr O'Brien should go to the London *Times* to launch a piece of character assassination against a fellow Irishman, is not surprising in view of that newspaper's role in Irish history.' This strategy of Conor's did not work as the electorate were not interested in the North. Security questions were sufficiently peripheral, that the only current affairs television programme allocated for a discussion on them, was dropped in favour of a debate on the coalition package, designed to appeal to voters in Dublin.[6] A National Opinion Poll found that both Dr O'Brien and Mr Haughey were least favoured for government leadership, whoever won the general election. Conor, naturally, after the ordeal he and his colleagues had been through on the security front, found it difficult to accept that the people could so blithely go on, as if the whole Northern issue did not really impinge on the South. For Mr Haughey to be able to walk away so effortlessly from his past, was also hard, but Dr O'Brien never forgot that democracy was no simple methodology for governing a country.

Towards the end of the campaign an *Irish Times* poll said fifty-four per cent to twenty-nine per cent of voters preferred Lynch to Cosgrave as Taoiseach. But forty-two per cent to thirty-four per cent felt the Coalition had better ministers than Fianna Fail would have. This gave the Coalition the impetus to again attack Fianna Fail on the personality of Haughey and the fact that some Fianna Failers still seemed to be sympathetic to the IRA. On 14 June the question of Mr Lynch's control of the Fianna Fail party was mentioned by the Minister for Posts and Telegraphs, Dr O'Brien, who described Mr Haughey's presence on the front bench 'as the tip of the iceberg' and without naming him suggested that he had led a faction within the opposition party which sympathised with the IRA. [7]

Polling day was on 16 June 1977. Very early that morning a new set of election posters appeared in Dublin, allegedly on behalf of Conor. These were a scandalous final attempt by his political enemies to smear him personally. It was one of the most outrageous attacks on any Dail candidate on the day of an election. The posters read: Election Special from the Cruiser. Abortion on Demand; Private Facilities for Alcoholic TDs; Suppression of the Irish Language; Easy Divorce; Legislation of Drugs; Congolese Call Girls; – Issued by a Friend of Conor Cruise O'Brien'. Dr O'Brien immediately issued a statement seeking to minimise the effect of this attack. He said, 'This is clearly a black propaganda campaign aimed at damaging the Labour Party. The fact that the printed posters have been widely and quickly distributed, shows that there is an organisation behind this scurrilous and despicable campaign. We call on the Fianna Fail party on the eve of this election to repudiate and condemn this vile propaganda'.

The day after the election, *The Irish Times* headlined:

75% POLL TO BRING NARROW ELECTION WIN FOR COALITION'. [8]

The following day the same paper headlined:

'FIANNA FAIL SWEEPS TO BIGGEST VICTORY'. [9]

The results of the election were sensational. Three ministers lost their seats: Conor Cruise O'Brien in Dublin Clontarf, Justin Keating another Labour Party minister in Dublin West County and the Minister for Justice, Mr Patrick Cooney in Longford-Westmeath. In the previous fifty-five years only three ministers in toto had lost their Dail seats thus. Fianna Fail got 50.6% of the vote and 84 out of the 148 seats, the biggest majority ever recorded in the State. Fine Gael went from 53 to 43 seats, while Labour went from 20 to 17. [10]

The result of the first count in the Dublin Clontarf constituency, which had three seats, 75% turn out and a quota of 7,741 was:

Colley George, FF	– 8,768
Cosgrave Michael, FG	– 3,991
Cruise O'Brien Conor, Lab.	– 3,588
Woods Michael, FF	– 3,093
Loftus Sean, Community	– 3,003
Nealon Ted, FG	– 2,821
Manning Vincent, Community	– 2,076
Fitzsimons, FF	– 1,590
Duffy, Lab.	– 917
Melia, FG	– 549
Bell, Independent	– 527
Malone, Independent	– 40

On the tenth count a distribution of Loftus' vote went thus:

Cosgrave	+	1,114	7,662
Woods	+	1,323	7,352
Cruise O'Brien	+	1,263	6,629

Cosgrave and Woods were then deemed elected without reaching the quota.

O'Brien had been defeated by 723 votes. [11]

People who have experienced it, recount that there is no experience quite like losing one's Dail seat. At the time even death might seem kinder. But for a Minister to lose a Dail seat is the final political ignominy. To be running the country one day, and to be unemployed the next, is a shattering experience which takes time to recover from. The sense of a recurring personal rejection, for Dr O'Brien, was immense and his initial reaction was to counter it by rejecting politics itself. That Mr Haughey's personal prediction of his own success proved so accurate was another cross to bear. When he had time to recover sufficiently, Dr O'Brien felt that the North was probably a factor in his own defeat. While people did not basically disagree with much of what he had been saying about it, he believed that they found the North an 'uncongenial topic', and didn't want to hear him going on about it. His reading of the Fianna Fail victory, was that the mood of the public was, 'to trust Mr Lynch, and that if they had any unease about Mr Haughey, they thought Mr Lynch could control him'. [12] He declared himself very proud to have served in a Government over which Liam Cosgrave had presided. David Thornley commented that he imagined himself and Dr O'Brien to be in a race for the publication of their memoirs.

Reaction to Dr O'Brien's defeat in Britain was rather severe. The *Sunday Telegraph* commenting on the election result said, 'Nothing can compensate for the disappearance of Conor Cruise O'Brien from the scene'. [13] The *Observer* wrote quite reasonably, 'According to public opinion polls, the North was not an issue of any importance. Nevertheless individual Ministers, most notably, Conor Cruise O'Brien, have lost their seats because they were outspoken and honest in facing the Irish people with ambiguities in Irish attitudes. Hypocrisy, it seems, is the best policy. Ireland has wounded herself by losing Dr O'Brien from the Dail'. [14]

There were probably many reasons why O'Brien lost his seat, but luckily for him, there were plenty of options available to him. He thanked the electorate for affording him the opportunity to continue his career as a writer [12]. Of party policies he later said: 'It's a terminal sickener. A politician is constrained to lie. Politics went sour for me after I was on the Northern Ireland Committee. Then the electorate put me out of my misery. I had the pain of losing the seat, and I wondered why I'd wanted to be in politics at all. Now wild horses couldn't drag me back. [15] I did speak my mind more than most politicians do, and my colleagues were generally, though not invariably, patient with me. But by the end of eight years in politics... the constraints were telling'. [16]

That Dr O'Brien was a public representative of rarity there can be no doubt. His intellectual, moral and physical courage stood out on almost every occasion. No one had such style and wit whether speaking or writing. He was a performer *par excellence* and whether one agreed with him or not, his rapier-like thrusts at opponents was high entertainment. But therein lay part of a weakness that grew with time. The media is a voracious consumer of personalities who will entertain. O'Brien's style always made for that. Whatever platform he was on, whatever the subject, sparks would fly. There would be confrontation. But gradually over the years with O'Brien, because he was so good, people got used to him, as they get used to other personalities who are continually pleading the same cause. The public feel they know where he stands, so there is no need to listen, to be persuaded, only to be entertained, whether outrageously or subtly.

The image becomes the message. Everyone knew where Conor stood on Northern Ireland and the IRA so they stopped listening to him and watched his performance. Whether he persuaded one person to change his inherited views on these topics is debatable. But he certainly influenced public opinion by raising the issues in a stark way. As a Minister he played an enormously important role in containing violence with a Government under siege. He castigated Fianna Fail for its ambivalence on violence and Northern Ireland. He castigated all of nationalist Ireland for the same thing. But he became a zealot on the subject. As Senator John A Murphy wrote: 'He concentrates his attack on the excesses of nationalism and the ambivalences indubitably inherent in Irish nationalists attitudes but in doing so he indicts the whole nationalist population and especially anyone who articulates a unity aspiration. His attack on nationalism is a stalking-horse for an assault on nationality itself'.[17]

The whole basis for his attacks on nationalists was flawed. He continued to believe that the 1916 Rising need not have taken place and that Home Rule would have delivered as much to the country. This mistaken view meant he had less respect for the 1916 mythology than his fellow citizens, who regard the 1916 leaders as the Founding Fathers of the modern state. This was the perceived wisdom which a people had of itself. To attack this so vehemently was a futile and foolish exercise. As Terence Brown wrote: 'What Cruise O'Brien believed was a false view of history, dangerous in as much as it stimulated a current campaign of violence the only outcome of which would be civil war. He challenged by speculation of a curiously unhistorical kind.' [18] But O'Brien believed he had the truth and he proved incapable of treading carefully with it. This was due to the importance he attached to the truth as he perceived it, due also to his inflated ego and to the dire consequences he saw for the people of Ireland, his own people, unless major changes occurred. The fact that there was so much merit in what he said, combined with the audacious and pugnacious way he said it, had the paradoxical effect of making him an almost Cassandra type figure in Irish life. Again as Terence Brown has argued: 'It may well be that O'Brien, instead of hastening a demythologising of Irish history, contributed to a continuation of it.' [19] People must defend their sacred cows, they cannot see them slaughtered by the person who is just too intelligent by half. Liam de Paor has argued that the economic boom of the 1960s had broken the chain of historical myths and the Irish were ready to regard economic growth as paramount[20]. But, though ready to loosen its connection with the past, it had to hold on firmly for another while under the onslaught of Conor Cruise O'Brien.

In two articles published in *The Irish Times* in August 1975, Dr O'Brien saw and wrote of an unhealthy 'intersection between literature and politics which he believed to be a facet of the Irish dilemma. The connection between the Irish republican movement and a version of literature goes back to the foundation of that movement. The Phoenix Literary Society of Skibbereen, County Cork, was a vigorous group which prepared the way for the Fenians, from which the present IRA originate. A permanent feature of such a movement is the conception of history as a series of blood sacrifices enacted in every generation and therefore capable of being entered by people in the current generation who will repeat the blood sacrifice. Now this', Dr O'Brien wrote, 'is most essentially a literary invention. Yeats was the great propagandist of this notion. To minds that are possessed by that idea of sacrifice it is irrelevant to prove that a campaign like the current IRA campaign, for example, cannot possibly accomplish any desirable political objective.' He went on to say that, 'Ours is a small country much afflicted by ballads and by persons shooting and bombing their way to a place in the ballads to be. I have heard Yeats' line 'A Terrible Beauty is Born' used to glorify or better to bedizen the sordid horrors which the Provisional IRA and their competitors have brought to the streets of Belfast.

'In these conditions', he continued, 'one develops – or at any rate I have developed – a resistance to romanticism, an aversion to the ballad form, a horror of the manic passages in the poetry of

Yeats, and a tendency to see the influence of literature over politics, in the tragic mode as a contagion to be eradicated where possible. No doubt these propensities may carry me too far and perhaps that has been the case with this essay'. [21]

Another weakness in O'Brien's contribution to the debate on nationalism was his apparent willingness to be more harsh on the Republican State than on the Unionist one. He appeared to make more demands of nationalists, especially those in Northern Ireland, than on Unionists. [22] Though this was a tactical and possibly a realistic position, it further removed him from being a figure nationalists could empathise with or even listen to. He was regarded as being almost anti-national and pro-unionist. His easy access to and brilliant use of British media tended to bolster up this feeling. An old attitude that if you had dirty linen, (and who did not?) the place to wash it was not in a public place and definitely not abroad.

Dr O'Brien's commentary defends himself on two of these criticisms. He writes:

I was addressing the community I belonged to, with a message about the danger of collusion with the men of violence in that community. The principle involved is one which I expressed at the conclusion of one of my speeches to the Annual Conference of the Labour Party: 'We do right to condemn all violence but we have a special duty to condemn the violence which is being committed in our name'. I may add that that Conference, by its applause, expressed its warm approval of that sentiment.

Dr O'Brien comments on the phrase that he was a figure that nationalists can't 'even listen to'. He writes:

This is certainly true of particularly fervent nationalists and especially fellow travellers of the IRA. But it demonstrably is not true of ordinary Irish people with the normal quota of nationalist feeling. For a number of years now I have been writing a regular weekly column in Ireland's largest circulating daily newspaper, the *Irish Independent*. In that column I have repeatedly taken the line which you say has made nationalists unable even to listen to me. The *Irish Independent* is run on strictly commercial lines and if my column displeased or bored their readers it would have been discontinued long ago.

Desmond Fennell, a nationalist commentator, speaking at the 14th Lipman Seminar on Ireland held in April 1992 at Ruskin College, Oxford, spoke of the life of the Coalition Government. He said that Dublin liberalism's finest hour against republicanism had been under Liam Cosgrave's 1973-77 Coalition, which pursued republican organisations and their supporters, real or imaginary, with obsessive zeal. 'The republic came so close to being a police state that, on election night in 1977, when Conor Cruise O'Brien and Patrick Cooney fell and Jack Lynch won an overall majority for Fianna Fail, citizens of all parties everywhere danced and sang'. [23]

J Bowyer Bell, who has made a life's study of the Irish conflict wrote of Dr O'Brien: 'For all varieties of Republicans he has become a figure combining the vices of Attila the Hun, Judas and Brutus. And well he might, for he has little time for Republican pretensions or their more simple-minded scenarios for a united Ireland. These he sees as bad history, bad politics, dangerous and even, if possible, a dreadful prospect given his own vision of the black and bleak soul of the Northern Protestant. And he has as little time for sentimental Southern Nationalists, for a good many recognisable political figures, spokesmen and pundits, and for the innocent and ignorant in general'. [24]

Chapter Nineteen

◆

EDITOR OF THE OBSERVER

EWART-BIGGS LECTURES

◆

Before the month of June 1977 was out the resilient Dr O'Brien issued a statement saying that he ·was anxious to stay in Ireland and to have a voice in public life. 'A number of people with whom I have been in touch in Trinity College, have told me that there is support among Dublin University graduates for public positions which I have taken'. He therefore announced his candidacy for election to the Senate on the T C D panel [1]. He was duly elected along with Mary Therese Winifred Robinson and Trevor West. In October he resigned the whip of the Parliamentary Labour Party, so that he could be free to say exactly what he wished on Northern Ireland. He remained a member of the party, continuing to attend and speak at party conference. He spoke in the Senate on a Telephone Capital Bill twice on the same day in November. [2]

In the middle of December the *Sunday Times* of London announced that 'Dr Conor Cruise O'Brien, aged sixty, is joining the *Observer* in the newly-created post of Editor-in-chief. The former Irish diplomat and minister will join its board and will have responsibility for overall policy – effective early next week'. [3] The next day the London *Times* sneered at the Irish. It was headed:

INTELLECTUAL OF MANY PARTS TO START NEW CAREER.

It read:

Orator, academic, literary critic, former diplomat and one of

191

the most influential members of the last Dublin government, Dr Conor Cruise O'Brien, is a perfect example of the type of Irishman whose talents and intellectual ability completely belie the traditional saloon-car caricature of a race of dim wits... (He had resigned from the UN) to be free to criticise publicly the Congo policy of the British government, an acerbic attack that was given considerable coverage in the *Observer*, and thus began his association with that paper.

In the London *Times* in 1978, he said, 'I shall be responsible for major issues of policy. This will be mainly in the political sphere, with particular emphasis on international politics'.[4]

In the ordinary way this appointment would have been a source of great pride to most Irish people. But, in the circumstances, many took a begrudging attitude, if not declaring that at least now he was taking the Queen's shilling out in the open. This was totally unjustified but was an indication of the depth of feeling he had engendered on the national question.

Conor explained the rationale and mechanism of his association with the *Observer*. He said that in 1978 the ownership of the paper changed to the family Astor Trust. It was losing money and the Trust proposed selling it. An American company, Atlantic Richfield bought it. David Astor was very anxious that the policy of the paper would not change under the new ownership. He proposed that Donal Telford remain on as Editor, but he recommended that Conor be brought in as Editor-in-Chief. This was accepted by the new owners.

One of the main changes O'Brien made at the *Observer* concerned its coverage of Irish affairs. The paper had from the outset of the Northern Ireland Troubles been very supportive of the Irish nationalist cause. Its correspondents had been at the forefront of writing about the situation in the North, which up to then had been neglected by the British media. Mary Holland was the foremost of these writers. But Dr O'Brien naturally wished his own view of the Irish problem to be reflected in the *Observer*. Part of this involved seeing matters from a unionist perspective with the question of a united Ireland being left on one side and with it the position of the Catholics of the province. This was to cause much dissension within the paper as the violence in Ireland showed no sign of abating and various efforts were made to solve the problem constitutionally. Lord Longford, the British Peer who took such a keen interest in Irish affairs, was very unhappy with Dr O'Brien's policy. He wrote: 'The *Observer* pleasantly surprised me this morning by turning forcibly to the idea of power-sharing. I look up to Conor Cruise O'Brien, but I have deplored his influence over the *Observer* while he was Editor-in-Chief. Has he departed now?' [5]

During these *Observer* years, Dr O'Brien gave a major series of addresses putting the Irish situation in an international context. He spoke from the standpoint of an historian, academic and retired politician. They have stood the test of time, and twenty years on remain a realistic exposition. These were given in memory of the assassinated British ambassador Christopher Ewart-Biggs, whose widow, Jane, devoted much of her life to an understanding of the Irish problem. They were titled:

1. Outlook from West to East
2. The Northern Connection
3. Ireland, Britain and America
4. Britain, Northern Ireland and the Republic: Attitudes, Options and a Positive Programme

The first lecture was delivered in Trinity College, Dublin in January 1978, the second at Queens University Belfast in June the same year, the third at New York University in November 1978 and the fourth at University College Oxford in October 1979.

In these lectures he told how he had talked – earnestly, but as it proved, inaudibly, – to Sir Harold Wilson on the day he saw the Provisionals in Dublin and to Mr Whitelaw in London the day

193

before he saw them. He declared he was against British withdrawal from Northern Ireland because what might replace it might be a lot worse. He saw Britain's committment to Northern Ireland as reluctant and unwanted on the part of the British public. He had no doubt that there was not a simple solution to the Northern Ireland impasse. But the worst of that was that it was men of goodwill who had the greatest tendency to flinch from this self evidence, thereby producing a kind of intellectual paralysis at that very point, where intellectual vigour was most needed. He chided Sir John Peck, British Ambassador to Ireland prior to Ewart-Biggs, for seeing an Anglo-Irish Council as an initiative likely to end the IRA violence. How could it, he asked.

He said that Mr Lynch, the Taoiseach, and Mr Currie (SDLP) suggested a power-sharing executive and some recognition of the Irish dimension like at Sunningdale. O'Brien said he was proud to have taken part in the Sunningdale Conference, but it failed. It did not bring peace. IRA violence increased. The Protestants believed it was a step towards Irish unity. Brian Faulkner knew it was not but 'important Catholic and Nationalist participants in Sunningdale and the Dublin media said otherwise'. According to O'Brien the Catholics of Northern Ireland had been the principle victims of the Home Rule and anti-Home Rule struggles and of the consequent political division of the British Isles and of Ireland. Catholics in Northern Ireland were discriminated against in housing and jobs and in the local franchise. They were also humiliated by certain ritual commemorative ceremonies and in other ways. From the 1970s the Provisional IRA moved in to exploit the situation, to eliminate the British, coerce the Protestants and to unify Ireland. But the Catholics have suffered most from this campaign. If the British withdrew, an independent Protestant dominated Northern Ireland would result.

He said devolved government was gone, as were all forms of State discrimination against Catholics. He claimed that Direct

194

Rule was becoming more acceptable in both communities. He argued that continuing pressure from the Republic on the British to introduce fresh initiatives, which would only end in violence, should cease. Otherwise the British would eventually withdraw and an all Ireland civil war would ensue.

He suggested that the way forward should be initiatives in the economic and social spheres to tackle unemployment and diminish sectarian resentments. A Consultative Assembly to assist Direct Rule would also help the situation.

On 13 June 1979 the Cathaoirleach of the Senate announced to the members that he had received a letter from Dr O'Brien, announcing his resignation from the House. This was not unexpected as the gentleman was not in a position to attend the sittings of the Senate, and felt that another person should fill his Trinity College seat, though of course Dr O'Brien continued to have some participation in public life in Ireland. At a Centenary Debate on Patrick Pearse in November 1979 he did not hold back on his views of 1916, describing Pearse as 'a manic, mystic nationalist with a cult of the blood sacrifice and a strong personal motivation towards death. A nation which takes a personality of that type as its mentor, is headed towards disaster'.

The end of that year brought about a change in the Irish political scene, which might well have been dubbed as a nightmare scenario by O'Brien. His long time political enemy, over whom he had the gravest doubts, Charles J Haughey, took over as Taoiseach from the retiring Jack Lynch. Mr Haughey's nomination was confirmed in the Dail on 11 December, though not before he endured a bitter attack on his 'flawed pedigree' both from the Fine Gael and Labour benches. It is doubtful even if O'Brien himself had been present could he have been so opposed to Haughey as those who remained TDs. Among the ministers dropped by Haughey was Jim Gibbons.

A rather unfortunate libel action occurred during O'Brien's tenure at the *Observer*, when he and the paper were sued for libel by the well-known Irish actress Siobhan McKenna. The case arose over an article, entitled, *On Being A Jewish Wild Goose*, written by Dr O'Brien and published on 3 June 1979. Miss McKenna felt that the article repeated a suggestion made by some television viewers after an American interview in 1956, that she had some prejudice against Jewish people. When the case came before the London High Court in January 1981, the *Observer* accepted that Miss McKenna's original remarks were not intended to be offensive to the Jewish people and that she was not anti-Semetic. It expressed regret for any unintended impression given by the article and agreed to pay Miss McKenna's costs. Miss McKenna, who had brought the action to clear her good name, was content to let the matter rest. Mr Justice Jupp agreed that the record of the action should be withdrawn.[6]

Conor had devoted almost four years to the *Observer*. At first he stayed in London, being a sometime resident on a houseboat in Chelsea. Then he began to commute between Dublin and London, flying out on Tuesday and home on Saturday. As we have seen both Conor and Maire placed a high premium on their family life and particularly the welfare of their children. Commuting was difficult for them all. After three years, he decided that was enough. His children were still quite young and needed a father figure on a more permanent basis. Besides, he felt that he had completed a certain job at the *Observer*. He proposed to the Board that he resign his position, but continue to contribute a regular column. This was accepted and he resigned in January 1981. The Chairman of the Board said: 'Conor Cruise O'Brien has provided effective leadership in a period when the sales of the newspaper have risen substantially. I am delighted that he will continue to make a distinctive contribution by writing regularly for the *Observer* '.[7] Conor reiterated that his resignation was due entirely to family considerations. He preferred to live in Ireland. Dr O'Brien's resignation provoked speculation about whether he had future political intentions. It was noted that he remained a member of the Kilbarrack Branch of the Labour Party and represented the branch at annual Conference. A Labour Party spokesperson indicated that the party did not expect Dr O'Brien to stand for public office again.

Two months later the British newspaper world was amazed to find that Atlantic Richfield had decided to sell the *Observer* to Tiny Rowland of Lonhro conglomeration. Conor was shocked by the announcement saying that he had serious misgivings about the deal. He said that he would, however, continue to write his weekly column for the paper, as long as Lonhro's guarantee of editorial independence to *Observer* journalists held. He feared a clash between Lonhro's interests in the City of London, in South Africa and the Middle East, and the paper's editorial freedom to write about those areas. He said that nobody on the Board or in the staff had any advance warning, but learned about it from the press. He added that Atlantic Richfield had been good proprietors. David Astor also objected to the proposed sale and the deal was referred to the Monopolies Commission. Both O'Brien and Astor argued that Tiny Rowland was not a suitable owner for the paper, but the sale went ahead, and Dr O'Brien said to me, 'Tiny Rowland then naturally felt that we were not suitable people to be associated with his paper'.[8]

Dr O'Brien continued to warn the country against Charles Haughey. In early 1981 he warned that if Fianna Fail were reelected under Mr Haughey, after a few years the country would begin to resemble Mayor Daley's Chicago. 'There would be bossism, not just rule by party, but of one man of very authoritarian temperament, with a party around him. Every vacancy would be filled by his men', he said. [9]

To the great surprise of many, Dr O'Brien then favoured an electoral alliance between the Labour Party and Sinn Fein the Workers Party, if the latter had really broken their paramilitary links. He believed his influence was perhaps greatest among supporters of Sinn Fein the Workers Party, than in the Labour Party. The former had moved to the position where they accepted much of his analysis of the Northern Ireland situation. He declared himself to be proud of the influence he had in their circles. If he could be convinced the tie between Sinn Fein the Workers Party and the secret armies of the North, were broken, he would be drawn towards them, he said. [10]

The next few years saw several changes of government leading to a very unstable political situation. Events in the North with the Hunger Strikes and the ten dead men caused almost anarchy across the country. Mr Haughey had a famous meeting with Mrs Thatcher, the British Prime Minister, which for a time seemed to open up a possibility of a unique relationship between the two countries. [11] Mr Haughey continued to be a hostage to misfortune and from the sidelines of journalism. Conor continued to flagellate him, warning of dire consequences for the country unless he was watched endlessly. The most famous occasion the two became juxtaposed in the public eye occurred in 1982, when a man wanted for questioning on murder, was discovered staying in the apartment of Haughey's Attorney General, Patrick Connolly. Though Haughey and Connolly spoke together after the man's arrest, Connolly departed the country for London and New York. Haughey described the resulting crisis as, 'grotesque, unprecedented, bizarre, unbelievable'. O'Brien made a mnemonic of the words and GUBU entered the language, a word that would continue to haunt Mr Haughey. [12]

Chapter Twenty

---◆---

INTELLECTUAL TERRORISM

IRISH TIMES COLUMNIST

---◆---

In January 1982 *The Irish Times* carried a picture of Dr O'Brien on its front page, announcing that he had joined the paper as a regular contributor. 'In his first column', the notice said, 'he writes about the crisis caused by the bad weather, and points out that in winter, it snows.' This first column was a good example of the format of his contributions, in that it was funny, aggressive, and introduced much information about the writer's personal situation. He attacked the *Irish Press* saying, 'You probably don't read the *Irish Press,* and I don't blame you, but it is still around and has been for just over fifty years'. He then gave a detailed account of what it was like living on Howth summit, with the water and electricity supplies cut off, by a heavy snow fall. He and his family only survived, thanks to a friend arriving from low lying Balscadden, with a portable loo and eight gallons of water. Dr O'Brien was grateful for good neighbours. He presumed, in charity, that the Government was doing its best, but he could not see his way to extend any such hypothesis to Dublin Corporation, which he threatened to 'deal with, unless our water is back'. This was a strange contribution for a prestigious writer to make to a high brow newspaper like *The Irish Times*, but it remained indicative of his style and content. Of course Dr O'Brien's main topics continued to be the ongoing political situation in the North and the need for the Republic to be more generous minded to the Unionists. On the Falklands War, he saw the Taoiseach, C J Haughey, take an anti-British stand and apparently sacrifice local

199

Irish interests. Conor criticised the Government's stance as no more than traditional 'Brit-bashing', and was duly chided by Senator John A Murphy, who wrote: 'It is sad to see that Conor Cruise O'Brien, who contributed substantially to the evolution of our independent foreign policy twenty years ago, should see the government's present stance, as Brit-bashing'[1].

Conor's contributions to *The Irish Times* soon aroused serious criticism, particularly when they were set against his renewed contributions to the *Observer*. No less a person than Denis Donoghue, former Professor of English and American Literature at University College Dublin, and current Henry James Professor at New York University, took him to task in the *London Review of Books*. Donoghue asked in caustic terms:

> Why does Dr O'Brien exercise his intelligence when he writes for the *Observer*, and turn out such vulgar rubbish for *The Irish Times*? Is it merely that he despises the Irish readers who were sufficiently stupid and unworthy to turn him out of office? Or that he assumes that what Irish readers want is the repetition of personality, in any familiar form, week by week?

Conor was naturally stung by such fundamental criticism. He often adopted the tactic of diverting personal criticism to include as wide an audience as possible, with a view to minimising its effect on himself. Donoghue's criticism, he therefore said, insulted his Irish readers and the Editor of *The Irish Times*, as well as himself. He argued that Donoghue did not take into account the art of writing for two different audiences, on a regular basis. He argued that for Donoghue to suggest that he turned out vulgar rubbish, likened his column to what appeared in the *Sun* newspaper, which again was a terrible insult to his readers and *The Irish Times*. 'Clumsy fellow, this Professor', Conor wrote. He then emphasised that he was writing for two entirely different audiences:

> To write for two publics is to be conscious of connections and disconnections. It is like standing on a heaving deck,

with sudden changes in perspective, and perceived proportions. At one moment it is an anti-abortion referendum that is important, next it is an independent nuclear deterrent, at one moment most of your audience are religious believers, the next you are amongst a crowd of agnostics. That last is the most important of all. It would be restful, I suppose, if I could switch off my mind, when writing for an Irish public, as my academic critic assures his English readers I do. But this doesn't happen. I like writing for *The Irish Times*, because I have many more things I want to say about Ireland, than most *Observer* readers want to hear, and because I want to say those things to an Irish audience. My critic suggests that I despise you, who read this. You are the ones who know best that I don't. How could a writer despise his audience, unless he also despised himself? and I am not in the least inclined to do that.

Thus he concluded in high jest[2]. As usual Dr O'Brien admonished, with style and wit, a would-be critic, though there is little doubt that his *Irish Times* contributions often appeared to be overly self-indulgent and repetitive, as he approached his audience with an almost proprietorial air. As if to show his contempt for the clumsy Professor's criticism, the next month of June he wrote a long piece on the situation of his own Howth home and the vagaries of the Irish summer, which undoubtedly his readers would thoroughly enjoy.

Another example of his interest in affairs other than politics occurred in relation to the workings of the Dublin to Sligo train. In 1994 there remains much disquiet about the level of service given to passengers on this route. This came to Dr O'Brien's attention ten years ago when he had the bad luck, he might say, to travel the route. He and his family were travelling to Donegal and decided to go by train as far as Sligo. He tells us that Maire, who he says is of an optimistic disposition, unlike himself, checked about the availability of a buffet on the train. The positive reply she got was technically correct. However, in the overcrowded conditions on the trip which lasted for four and a half hours, with most of the lights not working, neither Cruise O'Brien parent had the temerity to voyage forth in search of the buffet carriage. But their son Patrick, whom Dr O'Brien describes as being slim, fit and fearless got through to the buffet car and returned with sandwiches and beer to his parents. Patrick was hungry enough to make a second safari to fend for himself. Dr O'Brien in the light of this experience, did admit that the entry on himself in *Who's Who*, listed his recreation as travelling. He announced that this entry would have to be amended forthwith.[3]

Of course Conor wrote about the big stories too. He wrote regularly about the 'Let's Pretend Forum' and other political matters. He disapproved strongly of the New Irish Forum, launched in the aftermath of the Hunger Strikes of 1981. The forum sought to bolster Irish nationalism and strengthen the position of the SDLP within the North where Sinn Fein was taking more and more of the nationalist vote. Conor objected so much to the process in Dublin Castle that he resigned his membership of the Labour Party who was then in government with Fine Gael. He felt that Labour had adopted a different, and distinctly greener line, than the one he had defended over eight years, with the approval of successive party conferences. Conor delayed the announcement of his resignation, at Dick Spring's request, until after the upcoming European elections. Even then he did not seek any publicity about the matter. He declared that he would not support Labour in the forthcoming general election because it had no objection to supporting C J Haughey as Taoiseach, according to Dick Spring speaking about the prospect of a hung Dail[4].

The most memorable piece Dr O'Brien wrote for *The Irish Times* during his four years as a weekly contributor, for me, was penned early in 1984 and was in the best crusading fervour of his late cousin Owen Sheehy-Skeffington. It was entitled 'Victims of

Silent Panic' and concerned the harrowing story of Ann Lovett. Conor took his text from an article in the *Longford Leader*, which in desperate circumstances sought to dress the tragic incident in excessive religiosity, writing foolishly:

> Could it be that an intelligent teenager, who presumably was fully aware of all the facilities available to unmarried mothers, deliberately decided that was not for her? Could it be that she decided that the Virgin Mary meant more to her than all these things? Who is to say Ann Lovett did not die happy? Who is to say that she and her son are not in heaven? Who is to say that she has not fulfilled her role in life as her God had decreed? As Our Lord said: "Suffer Little Children to come Unto Me'.

Conor wrote passionately:

> What the writer of the above prose is talking about, of course, is a young girl who died of exposure, as a result of giving birth in the rain, at the foot of a statue, in a Christian community. 'Everybody knew', said one of her contemporaries... The Bishops last week were talking to the Forum about 'the moral quality of life' in these parts... Religion and human sexuality have – traditionally, and in all parts of the world, and in all faiths – had an uneasy and sometimes hysterical relationship – but the relationship has to be particularly fraught where the education of the young, including such sexual education as children get – and they even got some in Granard we are told – is under the control of celibate religious of both sexes. In these conditions, sex becomes a more explosive subject than it need be. Sex education becomes a matter of pregnant silences: sometimes leading as in this case, to silent pregnancies.
>
> Many generations of this kind of thing have caused the whole subject of sex, in some regions, to be covered with layers of shame and guilt. When the wind of secular society all around us beats against these layers, strange flappings occur. What seemed to have happened in Granard was a bad

case of culturally induced silent panic. Those who have done most to shape the culture in question must take the main responsibility for the silent panic.

The culture set an excessively high value on the closing of eyes and ears. If you refuse to see something, it may go away. Afterwards, you can hope to hush up the manner in which it went away. What you don't know, won't hurt you. It might hurt someone else. The publicity is rather widely held to be rough on the survivors. This view of the matter is characteristic of the hush-up culture. What's done can't be undone: least said soonest mended.

In this case, the more said, the sooner mended. The publicity which has surrounded the deaths of Ann Lovett and her son carries a message into every community in Ireland where such things have happened and been hushed up. The message is that the good old hush-up system may be beginning to break down. If you turn a blind eye these days, you may find yourself in the full spotlight of publicity. That realisation may help to save other Ann Lovetts in other towns of Ireland. It would be better, of course, if they were saved by watchful compassion – as some are ...'.

The entry in *Who's Who* listing Conor's hobby as 'travelling' was a genuine one. He travelled to many parts of the world on a regular basis in connection with books or articles he was writing. But the most time he spent out of Ireland was spent in the USA, which, in its vastness, lent itself to plenty of internal travel. Having been divested of his political commitments and his full time journalism, he became free to take up several academic positions in American Universities. These sometimes lasted for just a semester, but on occasion for a full academic year. One such institution was Dartmouth College in Hanover New Hampshire, where he taught during 1984-85. Because his wife was also an academic, she was sometimes able to get a suitable posting also. During these periods he continued to contribute his weekly newspaper columns as well as travelling around the USA lecturing. He also made several trips to Jerusalem, being engaged on a monumental history of the Jewish people. South Africa was another country he visited on a regular basis. In fact it has been widely noted that he has had a longtime fascination for three white beleaguered peoples, the Jews, the Afrikaners and the Ulster Unionists.

His weekly columns usually reflected wherever he was, which at times gave them a welcome cosmopolitan aura. He passed on a message to his readers from his wife, somewhat with tongue in cheek, on the status of Catholicism in the USA: 'Catholics are *in* this Fall... My wife who listens to more sermons that I do, asks me to point out that the intellectual character of Catholicism here is "old-fashioned" as compared with the Catholicism we have at home, God help us all... I am writing this on the morning of Sunday October 7th. You must forgive me if I break off now. I have to go to Mass'.[5] Still on a religious theme, he once attacked the inheritance of 1916 Rising, saying, 'The majority vote for Barabbas against Jesus had no validity for Christians. The majority vote in the Dail for the Anglo-Irish Treaty had no validity for the tradition of 1916'.[6] Though to his credit, he also identified one of his heroes, Parnell, as bringing discredit on the democratic process, when he refused to accept the will of the Irish Parliamentary Party after his divorce case. For this reason Conor distrusted all forms of retrospective Parnellism as it chose to glorify the romantic and destructive phase of his career.[7]

As has been mentioned previously, Conor always strove to be guided by reason. On occasion he was criticised for this laudable aim, being reproached as if there was a better way, a better Irish way. 'I find it strange, you have never appreciated the importance of thinking with your guts... the gut reaction of any Irish person, save the Unionists, is to desire separation from Great Britain on one island', he was admonished by a correspondent. Conor likened this notion as akin to the Nazi approved analogue of 'thinking with your blood', which blurred the consideration of the relation between gut/blood reaction and the surrounding reality. He pointed out that we all use our heads and not just our guts in relation to the choices of our daily life: infants think with their guts and roar accordingly but the infants must be protected by the adults, who must use their heads, or the infants will not live. Dr O'Brien admits that Emmet, Pearse and even Yeats on occasion, had told us to think with our guts, and we have been damaged in a number of ways. Some have seen it as a valid licence to slaughter, taking Pearse literally. But, Dr O'Brien concluded, there were others who pretend to think with their guts/blood and really think with their brain, for their own substntial advantage and in power and material rewards. These latter, he suggested, dedicate their lives supposedly to the ideals of Pearse and Connolly. [8]

In pursuit of his intellectual integrity, Dr O'Brien was very upset to be publicly accused of 'intellectual dishonesty' by political journalist Bruce Arnold. Arnold had been commenting on a lecture Conor had delivered at Oxford. Conor was angry... 'and I wanted to sue the guy'. He consulted his friend and legal advisor, the late Alexis Fitzgerald. Fitzgerald told Conor that if the charge was one of straightforward stealing, an Irish jury would sympathise with him, but he explained that an Irish jury would not understand such a charge as intellectual dishonesty.[9]

The continuing problem of Northern Ireland continued to be Dr O'Brien's main concern in later years. When in 1985 the British and Irish governments embarked on the Anglo-Irish Agreement as a way forward, he opposed it because the Unionists were not involved. He held that the main trouble with the Agreement was that it weakened the perception of the United Kingdom and proportionately weakened Protestant inhibition against eventual recourse to Holy War. Protestant opposition to the Agreement, he wrote, was unconditional.

In Northern Ireland there is probably not a single

person who feels happy with the province's relation to the rest of the UK. The Agreement tends to end alienation only in the sense that it tends towards the political conclusion that can alone end the alienation of nationalists: the dissolution of the United Kingdom of Great Britain and Northern Ireland... Northern Ireland is in a state of latent civil war: independent Northern Ireland would be in a state of real civil war'. He also remained one of those who continued to argue for reintroduction of internment. He wrote, 'If the Agreement was used for the Joint Implementation of internment, then the Agreement could become acceptable to Protestants. Nothing less will do it[10].

Dr O'Brien continually remained on guard for anything he regarded as slipsliding towards a softening of people's attitudes to violence and the IRA. In November 1985 he entered a confrontation on the matter with his criticism of a book edited by a Professor of Philosophy at University College, Dublin, Dr Richard Kearney, called *The Irish Mind : Exploring Intellectual Traditions.* Conor wrote:

> The version of Cultural Nationalism that is represented by *The Irish Mind* has no room for Ulster Protestants... It is fundamentally hostile to them... but also to those Catholics who were insufficiently British. Kearney is far too sophisticated to call O'Faolain (Sean) a shoneen... I prefer old DP Moran: a bigot, but a plainspoken one.

Conor goes on to call the book's title and its celebration in the Editor's introduction a graven image. He says the idea of *The Irish Mind* is a manifestation of cultural nationalism which in the Irish context would be 'the Gaelic mind'. But the efforts to restore the Gaelic language foundered and *The Irish Mind* then had to display its essence in the English language, which is pure heresy in terms of continental cultural nationalism. Dr O'Brien continued:

The Irish Mind sets out to show, not only that Irishmen can think, but also that they think in some special way. Having read *The Irish Mind*, I still haven't the faintest idea of what that special way is supposed to be... These cultural nationalists are the latest generation of what used to be called 'the Literary side of the movement' – a term employed – with genial derision, by the military leaders of the movement in question: the IRA.

Some of those concerned have talents which should not be wasted on this sort of guff, or tied into these sort of knots... they could speak and write Irish and become serious cultural nationalists. Or they could follow the logic of their political rhetoric and join the liberation of Northern Ireland[11].

Subsequently at a round table debate in Monaco, Richard Kearney answered O'Brien when he said:

But at the same time there is a tremendous danger in trying to debunk myths in the rational way of somebody like Conor Cruise O'Brien, without wishing to personalise the matter. There is a sort of intellectual terrorism in the attitude of certain people who will denounce any attempt to reinterpret our heritage, our traditions, our myths, as conservatism, reactionary nationalism and even gun-running republicanism. In my view, this kind of intellectual terrorism foments violence instead of protecting people from it.

Senator John A Murphy, another participant added:

Yes, there are two extremes here to be guarded against. One is the insistence of the intellectual wing of the IRA, that the past is a corpus of sacred truths, which must not be tampered with... But the other extreme, as Richard Kearney has rightly pointed out, is the line taken up by people like Conor Cruise O'Brien (one has to personalise it, because he is the revisionist *par excellence*). Though he exposed our ambiguities brilliantly, he went further and demolished people's self-confidence in their own nation, in their own nationality. So beyond a certain stage, you can't debunk myths without damaging the very fabric of people's national pride.

Richard Kearney, in the same book comments that, 'Conor Cruise O'Brien was wonderful in opposition. Given power, he became a disaster[12].'

Chapter Twenty-One

❖

BREAKS ACADEMIC BOYCOTT OF SOUTH AFRICA

RIOTS

❖

In March 1986 Dr O'Brien moved to the *Irish Independent* newspaper, where he contributed a lengthy weekly column to the editorial page each Saturday. The *Irish Independent* proudly informed its readers, 'Dr Conor Cruise O'Brien, the distinguished international political commentator, writes his first column in the *Irish Independent* today. He analyses the effect that the Anglo-Irish Agreement is having on American politics, where support for the Provos is waning. He also looks at the way in which Irish-Americans are increasingly just Americans. They are so well integrated now, he says, that their need to stick together to survive isn't what it was'[1]. The twin topics of the continuing civil war in Northern Ireland and its political repercussions in the south, together with O'Brien's reporting on American politics, were to form the bulk of his writing for that paper up to the present. But his interests were worldwide, as were his travels. Over the following months his columns carried datelines from New York, Mexico City, El Salvador, Managua, Costa Rica. This exotic flavour fitted in well with the glamour which the *Irish Independent* sought to convey in the paper. The *Irish Independent*, which Conor had such harsh things to say about in his famous 1966 article in *The Irish Times*, was then owned by that well-known Irish capitalist, A J O'Reilly, and was hell bent on achieving maximum commercial success. Conor was just one of the major personalities brought in to write for the paper. Of course he was well versed in the freedom of the press from many viewpoints and speaking of his tenure with the *Irish*

210

Independent, he said: 'I do see a certain responsiveness within the culture. Just the fact that the largest selling daily newspaper in the country is prepared to give me a column, and allow me the freedom, almost without restraint, to express my view without interference I see that as hopeful.'[2] Though at the same time he knew how the owners of newspapers could influence matters when he said: 'Few, if any, editors of newspapers in western society could afford to ignore altogether the views of their proprietors, on political and other matters. And these views are likely to be prevalent in the social class to which the proprietors belong. The press as a whole reflects those views to a greater extent, and with greater stability, than they are generally reflected in the electoral choices of the public which reads it'[3].

From the very beginning Conor introduced himself, his life and his family into the column in a far greater way than he had done at *The Irish Times*. Writing from Managua he told his readers that he and his wife had been in the congregation at the Cardinal's Mass, when the murdered Archbishop Romero had been commemorated. When the divorce referendum was held that same year of 1986, he penned two open letters to the Catholic Hierarchy in which he said, '...Like you, I have feelings, and not just abstract thoughts about this matter. I was divorced and remarried – outside this country – and my second marriage – entered into twenty-four years ago – is a happy one'[4].

Dr O'Brien, of course, did not confine himself to matters Irish. He was a regular traveller to various points of conflict around the world, writing and lecturing widely about them. Among these was South Africa. He had long been interested in apartheid and in 1970 was one of the leaders of a six thousand march of anti-apartheid protesters to Dublin's Lansdowne Road rugby ground where the Springboks were playing Ireland. *Circa* 1984 he received an invitation to lecture at the University of Cape Town. He accepted on condition that his son, Patrick, who was black, could also go. He satisfied himself that they were going to a completely integrated campus. But the Irish anti-apartheid movement regarded this visit as a betrayal of the anti-apartheid boycott of South Africa then in being worldwide. Their leader, Kadar Asmal, said: 'The authentic movement that speaks for the people of South Africa have asked people like him to stay away'. This upset Conor as a long-standing member of the movement. He reacted in his usual confrontational manner by vigorously attacking the Irish anti-apartheid movement as run by Kadar Asmal saying that it had a representative of Provisional Sinn Fein on its executive. He therefore saw the movement as partly under the control of people who were publicly committed to giving 'unequivocal support to the armed struggle' meaning the murders and other criminal actions perpetrated by the Provisional IRA. He wrote: 'I am as firmly opposed to apartheid and all forms of racial discrimination as I ever was. My family is a standing demonstration against the whole value system upon which apartheid is based. My resentment of Mr Asmal's vicious insult is proportionate to that existing commitment'.

The *Irish Independent* had little option but to give Kadar Asmal the freedom of reply. The controversy would do the paper no harm. Asmal noted that Dr O'Brien had resigned as a sponsor of the Irish anti-apartheid movement in 1984. Before that time, he said, Dr O'Brien had not raised a single query about any campaign or statement issued by the movement. He noted that it was the movement that had initiated the international campaign for the academic boycott, as far back as 1967, the same year Dr O'Brien became the movement's Chairman. More than one hundred and fifty Irish academics made a public declaration that they would not work in South Africa, as long as apartheid existed. Asmal said that the response to O'Brien's breaking the boycott was not a sudden inspiration to hound O'Brien, nor was it the result of a transformation by which radical revolutionaries push through their restrictive resolution. He noted that the movement had some ninety affiliations, none of which has a right to be represented on the executive. He said that Trinity College supported the boycott in 1982 and University College Dublin did so in 1986. Asmal ended his convincing response by noting that in the face of this collective international process, individuals must make their own choices and decisions, and Dr O'Brien must not ascribe ulterior and conspiratorial motives to those who disagreed with him[5].

This visit was Dr O'Brien's fourth visit to South Africa. Patrick discovered that when it was clear that he was a foreigner, public attitudes to him were not hostile, since he was not seen as a threat to whites. The only visible on-campus protest at his own presence, Conor detected initially in the University of Cape Town, was one graffito in a lift. But that was to prove illusory as he moved out of that campus. At another university he accepted an invitation from the Social Science Students Committee on the subject of 'The Academic Boycott'. About two hundred and fifty mainly white students crammed the hall. Conor soon realised that he had been set-up as he was grilled by a group of about fifteen students working in relays. These were supported by a larger group who hissed, yelled, and laughed nastily at Conor's replies. The interrogation was led by an Irishman named Patrick Bulger[6]. Conor found it a gruelling but instructive experience and was reminded retrospectively of what those Chinese professors had to endure during their Cultural Revolution. Soon the issue of Conor's presence at the campus of the University of Cape Town became a matter for protest, with leaflets branding him as 'a stinking scoundrel and rogue'. A 'Day of Action' was organised. Efforts were made to stop his lectures with campus policemen protecting his classes. This went on for a week with O'Brien and his undergraduates besieged by howling mobs, many of whom were from outside the campus. Eventually the Vice-Chancellor of the University asked Conor for authorisation to say that he had cancelled his remaining classes on campus. Conor felt that he had little option but to accede to this request. He and Patrick returned home shortly afterwards. Dr O'Brien wrote his *Independent* column from South Africa and included a dialogue between himself and Patrick on their experiences there. He also included these articles in his book, *Passion and Cunning*, published in 1988.

Subsequently a three-man Commission, appointed by the University of Cape Town, investigated the protests which surrounded Dr O'Brien's visit. They put much of the blame on Dr O'Brien himself, citing his 'mercurial and volatile temperament' which provoked the student reaction. This finding was later formally repudiated by the senate of the University of Cape Town[7].

The week after his last South African piece appeared, Dr O'Brien had moved on and filed his contribution from Santa Barbara California. He commented that Americans were less prone to resentful envy than Europeans and were more inclined to better themselves. Two months later, also from Santa Barbara, he recalled that he had spent a year, not long ago, living in New England and the favourable aspects of American life left more impressions on him than the unfavourable. But, writing about California he said he had got more conscious of the unfavourable, the corruption, the frivolity; frivolous corruption and corrupt frivolity. He realised that such things exist everywhere, even in Ireland, but in California, he found, there seemed to be more of them, no doubt because there was more of everything there. That month of November he spent on a lecture tour visiting California, Texas, Arizona, Ohio, Florida, Connecticut and New York. Early in 1987 Conor and Maire were based at Williams College, Massachusetts, where he was a Bernard Fellow. While there he also gave a series of lectures at Harvard and the University of Pennsylvania. On one occasion he travelled into New York State where he ran into trouble, which reminded him of his South African experience. His two public lectures were picketed by people, all from off the campus, who handed out leaflets, asking, 'Why Is This Man On Campus?'. Part of the leaflet read, 'It is the height of irony that respected institutions of learning should court The Cruiser. Academia is nourished by the exchange of ideas. Conor Cruise O'Brien believes in smothering ideas contrary to his own and strangling debates... The University represents the spirit of freedom, Conor Cruise O'Brien is the supporter of slavery in Ireland and South Africa... Conor Cruise O'Brien is a liar, a political bigot, an opportunist and a moral coward. Conor Cruise O'Brien should be ignored'. The leaflet carried a footnote inviting, 'For more information, write, 'The Cruiser' in care of: Ancient Order of Hibernians, 1021 Ninth Avenue, Watervfliet, New York, 12189, or Irish Northern Aid, P.O. Box 12243 Albany, New York, 12212.[8]

During the summer of 1987 Conor and Maire went on a cruise in the eastern Mediterranean. They were accompanied by their sixteen year old daughter Margaret and Conor's granddaughter, Sarah, who celebrated her eighteenth birthday on the last day of the cruise. Ever one to include the family in his newspaper column, Conor commissioned/dragooned the three of them to put pen to paper, on the cruise. Margaret certainly gave the authentic view of a sixteen year old, writing, 'I enjoyed the cruise as a short well-organised holiday. Although at first I wasn't too keen on the lectures and tours of ancient sites, the way in which they were presented made the cruise far better than it sounded..'. Sarah wrote, '... although I have studied ancient Greece from a political standpoint, I found the social side of life now loomed much more sharply in my life...' Maire wrote, '...Our first stop is Olympia... I think of Gougane Barra and Clonmacnoise... You cannot help feeling that here is a most privileged part of the globe, where the material and the spiritual have been in harmony since the beginning of time'.[9]

Chapter Twenty-Two

CONOR AT SEVENTY

AGNOSTICISM

During the secessionist war in Nigeria in the late sixties, when the Ibo people sought to establish an independent Biafra, their cause received much sympathy in Ireland. Supplies were often flown into the beleaguered province at great danger. Journalists sometimes used this route. Dr O'Brien travelled on one such journey, flying over Nigerian lines, in a plane full of salt. During this potentially fatal flight, he experienced, not for the only time, a mystical phenomenon, which was to afford him a lifelong feeling of safety. He described it thus: 'I remember not being afraid at all and having an inward conviction that my life was protected for some purpose. I could give no cerebral account whatever; it didn't make any sense to my conscious mind. Somewhere, down there, it was there, and I felt it more than once, but never more acutely than in that plane full of salt'[1].

Some years later, Dr O'Brien had a direct contact with religion which left him rather uneasy. His second wife was involved in a serious car accident, which left her life in danger for some time. She was being cared for by nuns who always ended their bulletin on his wife's condition with the phrase 'Please God'. Conor recalls that, 'For a while I sullenly resisted saying that phrase "Please God" too. Then when the news was better, the nuns used the phrase, "Thank God", and I used it, feeling something equivalent to that, whatever there is for an agnostic to feel about: it was there. I had the experience of finding myself praying. I haven't

216

had it since and I don't want to have it either. As a result of that experience, I no longer feel the deep cold resentment that I once had towards the Catholic Church: only a much milder form of exasperation at the way the hierarchy carry on'[2]. When questioned about the reason for his agnosticism, O'Brien replied that he felt there was no data on the existence of God. He admitted to being humbled by the work of religious believers among the poor, saying, 'My agnosticism may be very grand. It does not impel me to do work of that order. On the contrary I have led most of my life most comfortably. I am no kind of agnostic saint'.[3]

One regular line of attack on Dr O'Brien, from his adversaries at home, was that in some obtuse way he was not truly Irish. This was a ridiculous suggestion, but it rankled, particularly as he got older and became more prone to recall his roots. He once made the declaration: 'I am proud of being an O'Brien. I am proud also of my mother's family, the Sheehy family and the part they played in Irish history... I am proud – quite irrationally proud – of being Irish, even to an extravagant degree'[4]. He noticed one day that his grandfather's old house at 2 Belvedere Place was up for sale – with tax concessions – and he would have liked to buy it.[5]

To attain the age of seventy years is indeed an occasion to be commemorated with thanksgiving. As Conor's seventieth birthday approached in November 1987, Maire was busy with the preparations. She assembled all his children at their home in Howth and had a wonderful party. Conor deemed it a great success, the best party he ever had. Champagne was served. His mind turned to the bible as he took stock, feeling that a certain amount of adjustment was needed. The words of the psalmist about the allotted span being three score and ten, came to his mind. He said, 'One is conscious of having crossed a limit'.[6]

But Dr O'Brien introduced some humour into the occasion. He indicated that he did not believe in any religion and made it clear he did not want people of religious persuasion using the occasion to send him greetings of a devotional nature. He assured

217

them that such efforts, however well intentioned, had in fact the opposite effect. He made it clear that he was not saying he disbelieved in God, but that the idea of God had always been opaque. Strangely he used the occasion to confess that he was a great liar when he was young. He recalled that when at school he used to lie with great fluency and aplomb, to get himself out of difficulty. At university, he still retained this facility, though he used it more sparingly.

He declared that unless he had taken two specific measures earlier in his life, he would never have lived to be seventy. He named them as, telling the truth about his time with the UN in Katanga, and leaving politics.

He spoke of the people and things that were important to him at his time of life, saying, 'I am happily married. My wife is interested in my work, and I in hers. We also find the same things funny, which is important. I have the joy of witnessing the ties of affection which join my three married children and their spouses to my two younger children, and those in turn to the four grandchildren. My home is in one of the most beautiful places in Ireland, overlooking moorland, cliffs and the sea, yet within half an hour's drive of some of the great libraries of the English-speaking world. I am allowed to park my car in the grounds of Trinity College, and when I go for a walk on the Hill of Howth, with my springer dog, Greta, – acquired on Greta Garbo's eightieth birthday – I often meet and talk with Gay Byrne, a nice neighbour, who tells me he is in the broadcasting business. So all in all, quite a lot to be thankful for. I can't help feeling that somewhere along the line, I must have done something right'.[7]

His son Patrick was then an undergraduate at Trinity College, where in the tradition of Owen Sheehy-Skeffington, he rowed for College. Maire and Conor were proud parents as they and Margaret went down to the Liffey, at Islandbridge, to see him row. Quite soon afterwards Conor, as a Pro-Chancellor of Trinity College, would have the pleasure and privilege of conferring Patrick with his degree.

Chapter Twenty-Three

───◆───

WORKING FOR TONY O'REILLY

───◆───

Far from withdrawing from the public arena in his later years, or even slowing down his output, Dr O'Brien has continued to be very active, sometimes directly, though most often as a writer and commentator. The following academic year, 1988-89, saw him teaching at the University of Pennsylvania, where Maire also got an academic post for the year. Celtic studies were spreading southwards from Canada and westwards from Europe. At Pennsylvania they both found strong interest in Ireland. Maire found several students who knew Irish well. Many of them, though not all, were of Irish descent. They both attended meetings of the American Council for Irish Studies in Philadelphia and Syracuse New York. From Philadelphia Conor issued a New Year's greeting for 1989, with a New Year's wish for Ireland, on a familiar theme:

> My wish for 1989 is that in that year the representatives of the two communities in the island of Ireland will at long last begin to talk to one another. To one another and not at one another, as has been the practice in the past, with disastrous consequences. I don't mean that they should talk to one another about a United Ireland. In this context, a United Ireland is not a subject for conversation. It is a comprehensive conversation stopper. What they should be talking about is how to share an island in peace and with mutual respect. It may be said that the eventual disappearance of the Anglo-Irish Agreement will open the way for such a dialogue. If so, the death of the Agreement will have done more for the

reconciliation of the two traditions, than the Agreement ever did during its lifetime[1].

Conor never fitted into an accepted persona with which traditional Irish-Americans could be entirely comfortable. He certainly would never doff the cap to them, and his uncompromising line on republicanism would be most difficult for them to swallow. Though he might have been read or even consulted by some of their political leaders on rare occasions, there was little meeting of minds in these encounters. Tip O'Neill, one of the foremost of these, published his memoirs early in 1989. Conor said of it: 'Tip O'Neill's personality comes through whether you like it or not. Some of the interesting bits concern not Ireland, indeed, but the Irish. The real Irish – the ones who live in America'[2]. It was little surprise that Mr O'Neill referred to Conor as 'a silly senile son-of-a-bitch' in a conversation with the *Observer*[3]. Conor was later to say of Senator Edward Kennedy: 'Ted Kennedy neither knows or cares anything about Northern Ireland. I once spent a half an hour with him to discuss that subject and it was long enough to satisfy me on both those points'[4].

Dr O'Brien derived great pleasure in the late 1980s as his youngest daughter from his first marriage, Kate, became a successful novelist and a fellow contributor to *Independent Newspapers*. One of her earliest memories of her father was when the Howth train to Dublin would sometimes be held up, waiting for 'the doctor', who was still coming down the hill[5]. She was subsequently to be appointed Literary Editor of the Poolbeg Publishing Press in Dublin. During those years too, George Hetherington, his first wife's second husband, published a book of poetry entitled *Delphi and other Poems*. This slim volume, dedicated to Christine Foster, contained poems for Fedelma Cruise O'Brien and her husband Nicholas Simms, Donal Cruise O'Brien and his wife Rita, their daughter Sarah and Alex Foster. Another poem was an *In Memoriam* for Alex Foster.

Conor remained one of the star contributors to the Saturday

edition of the *Independent* and often contributed to the *Sunday Independent*. The front page of the Saturday *Independent* normally carried his photograph with a summary of what his article covered that day. Only rarely did his views appear to conflict with the editorial stance of the paper. The following notice appeared under an article he wrote on 'Facing up to Terrorists': 'The views expressed here are the personal opinions of Conor Cruise O'Brien and do not represent the editorial stance of the *Irish Independent*'[6]. Some of his comments on individuals in his contributions reflect the wide scope of his interest, the acidity of his pen and sometimes his low-key wit.

> Gary Hart is a Yuppie lightweight with a couple of good speech-writers and an astonishing incapacity to understand that the fooling has to stop when you are running for President[7].

> Herbert Hoover knew where all the bodies were buried, and let it be known that he would dig them up whenever he felt like it... Hoover was unsinkable[8].

> Mr Carson (Johnny) is the principle purveyor of what is probably the most mindless form of spoken entertainment that ever existed[9].

> If Nancy and Raisa were in charge, instead of Ronald and Mikhail, there would be a Cold War of Arctic intensity. Let no reader take offence at this observation. It is not a question of gender but of personality[10].

> Strategically, Hitler was a revolutionary, but tactically he was a pragmatist. In the long term he was radically hostile to all the churches; he told intimates that he would 'annihilate Christianity' once he had won the war[11].

> So when Dr Waldheim, long afterwards said that he didn't know the Germans were committing any atrocities in Bosnia, at the time when he was there, I knew that the

old pro wasn't telling the truth[12].

Shortly after Tom King took over the Northern Ireland post he has just vacated, I put the question: 'Does intelligent life exist in Tom King?'[13].

Cyril Ramaphosa, Secretary-General of the ANC led that demonstration in person, so that courage is one quality he cannot be accused of lacking. Common sense is another matter[14].

To the general public Noel Browne appears as the epitome of compassion, and I am sure that is exactly what he is, in his personal life... But in a Committee of his political peers, Dr Noel Browne, when moved by fury, can be like something out of a German horror movie[15].

Don't blame Ray Burke. Instead we should be sorry for him. He has been quite a good Minister up to this week when he seemed to make an exhibition of himself[16].

Jim Mitchell, in his conduct of this campaign, is in the running for the mantle of the late Joe McCarthy, but adapted to local conditions[17].

Gerry Collins is a grandmaster in this genre. He must have done more with the Blarney stone than kiss it. But let me follow that metaphor no further in this family newspaper[18].

The election of Sean Doherty as Cathaoirleach of Seanad Eireann is a public scandal[19].

There is nothing petty or vindictive about Nelson Mandela, as you can tell from his utterances[20].

Ban-Gharda Ann Reddy, to her eternal honour, broke the long sinister spell, and got the young victim to talk[21].

In the nineties Dr O'Brien has continued to speak his mind on major events at home and abroad. He pointed out that when Saddam Hussein invaded Kuwait, Arab nationalists everywhere did

not see him as having attacked an Arab nation or State. Dr
O'Brien said that Kuwait was originally a British client state and
creation and, after the elimination of British power from the
region, it became the client of the Western alliance, headed by the
USA.

Dr O'Brien encouraged Jack Lynch to run for the Presidency
in 1990 saying that, 'Jack Lynch is not a vindictive man. But he is
human enough, and politician enough to enjoy paying off an old
political score with an unbeatable political stroke. And President
Lynch would be a credit to us all'[22]. Of course as long as Mr
Haughey continued to hold political office, Conor kept up the
attacks in a variety of forms. He accused Mr Haughey of inheriting
a flourishing party, and doing nothing to enhance its appeal,
concluding that the centenary of Haughey's downfall was unlikely
to be noticed[23]. Using a literary flourish he wrote of his hounding
of Haughey: 'I do not have a vengeful disposition (laughter) and if
I had... I know that I have not been pursuing a personal vendetta
but I also know – and am deeply concerned at the knowledge –
that many people do think I am so motivated. My position
essentially is that of Brutus in Shakespeare's *Julius Caesar (Act Two
Scene One)*, "I know no personal cause to spurn him, but for the
general"...'[24]. When Mr Haughey's political career was over, Conor
sent him birthday greetings[25].

Vinnie Doyle, who became Editor of the *Independent* in 1981,
had a tremendous regard for Charlie Haughey , describing him as
his favourite politician. Doyle, though, was often depressed at the
level of criticism which the paper, through its columnists, carried
of Haughey . He explained his predicament in August 1993 saying:

> But if you hire somebody like Conor Cruise O'Brien or
> Bruce Arnold, who were ultra-critical of Haughey , you
> have to give them their say – you hire them for their
> views and their writing. If you are going to muzzle them,
> you might as well not hire them. Coming up to a recent
> election, the Cruiser had two scathing attacks on
> Haughey , bordering on the personal and definitely on

the vindictive. In the middle of the last week I rang him and said, 'Conor, I think enough is enough. If you cannot do a positive piece on Charlie Haughey , which I am sure you can't, can you pick another subject?' Conor said that he would let me know, of course, he never did. He just sent in his column, which was a scathing attack, mark three. I spiked it. We put in something else and the following day Conor rang me at home and said, 'Vinny, I'm deeply disappointed you spiked my column'. I said, 'Conor, I told you enough was enough – you were not being fair to Haughey , particularly in the last week before the election'. Conor said, 'I'm sending the column you spiked to *The Sunday Tribune*. Is that all right with you?'. I told him no way was that all right with me, he would be breaking his contract and we would probably sue him. In the end, he sent the column to *The Sunday Tribune* who, with great delight, used it[26].

Chapter Twenty-Four

---◆---

NO COMPROMISE

---◆---

As he approached his seventy-fifth birthday, Dr O'Brien remained as active as ever, believing that the Northern Ireland situation proved a great danger still. In 1991 he travelled to Belfast to speak at a meeting of the Young Alliance Party. He said that the Republic's territorial claim to the North was poisoning the atmosphere of the current talks aimed at securing a new British-Irish Agreement. He said:

> I would like to see the Brooke talks culminate in constitutional amendments by the Republic on Articles 2 and 3, followed by Unionist acceptance of cross community devolved government in Northern Ireland, with the Anglo-Irish Agreement still in place, since the most serious ground to Unionist objections to that Agreement, has been its association with the Republic's territorial claim[1].

In June of 1991 the Secretary of State in Northern Ireland, Mr Peter Brooke, was engaged in finding an acceptable Chairman for talks between Britain, Ireland and the various Northern Ireland parties. Many names were being mentioned. On a programme on RTE called *Questions and Answers*, the moderator, John Bowman, asked Dr O'Brien, who was a participant, about the rumour that his name had been mooted as possibly chairing the talks. Dr O'Brien replied that he would not be acceptable to the parties. He elaborated by saying that neither the Irish government nor the SDLP, nor possibly the Democratic Unionist Party, would be happy to accept him.[2]

On 28 August 1991 a protest was held outside the Sinn Fein office in Dublin against IRA intimidation in Northern Ireland. Among those on the picket was Conor Cruise O'Brien.[3]

In the early months of 1992 a Constitutional battle developed over a woman's right of freedom to travel outside the jurisdiction of the State, especially as she was leaving to seek a possible termination of pregnancy. The issue arose when the Attorney-General sought a High Court injunction restraining a young girl, allegedly a rape victim, from travelling abroad to procure an abortion. The High Court granted the injunction, but the Supreme Court overturned that judgement and allowed freedom to travel. The Constitutional case rested on the interpretation of the anti-abortion clause inserted in the Constitution after the bitterly fought referendum of 1983. Dr O'Brien had strong views on the matter and saw once again an alliance at work between two old enemies of his, the Catholic Bishops and Fianna Fail. He wrote:

> The tragic story here is the state of our laws and traditions, concerning human reproduction, as a result of a tacit alliance between those two forces which together have dominated our national life over the last sixty years. That alliance was sealed more than fifty years ago by the prohibition of the sale and distribution of contraceptives under a Fianna Fail Government Act of 1935.

He believed that the change in the Constitution in 1983 was brought about by the tacit but effective alliance of the Bishops and Fianna Fail. The latter did it 'for cynical reasons for party advantage. The Bishops may have acted out of conviction. But it is not a kind of conviction that can inspire much respect in those of us who don't share it'. He continued that the fact that 'the Bishops, by letting it be known that they did not support the

226

injunction and thus (in practice) favoured the right of the rape victim to leave the jurisdiction, even though they knew that the purpose of the journey was to obtain an abortion...' showed that the bishops 'are accomplices-before-the-fact in the mass-murder of the unborn conceived in this country... not in fact... but in terms of the rhetoric of the anti-abortion lobby'[4].

Once more it might be difficult to argue against Dr O'Brien's logic, but his reasoning was leading him into positions which would be offensive to many people. It was almost a position of over-kill, which unfortunately had become more and more his hallmark. He was putting an almost insurmountable barrier between the people he wished to influence and himself. Once again he was being seen as a performer and an all too predictable one. But he still retained his father's tradition of being able to say wounding things in a memorable manner. Those attacked rarely saw the need to reply as time went on, believing that silence was the best defence. But occasionally a riposte was delivered his way. Another newspaper columnist, Rev Colm Kilcoyne wrote: 'Conor Cruise O'Brien is so outrageously consistent in his comments on Catholic values that he should be filed under comedy. His piece lately on the Catholic bishops crossed some line between fair comment and downright nastiness. You can't do that and still ask to be read seriously'[5].

Conor had earlier expressed genuine sorrow for having hurt the feelings of Fr Kilcoyne, 'and no doubt of many other readers as well. Yet I cannot honestly promise not to repeat the offence. You see it's not a question of examining scars. It's more probing a sensitive area of our culture... where religion and nationalism meet'[6].

During the British General Election of April 1992 Dr O'Brien actively supported Laurence Kennedy and Leonard Fee, who were standing in Northern Ireland as candidates of the British Conservative Party. He said, in the North, 'I am a citizen of the Republic of Ireland who rejects the efforts of the Republic's political parties to disrupt the union between Great Britain and Northern Ireland, contrary to the known wishes of a large majority of the people of Northern Ireland'[7]. He believed that the primary emphasis in the North should be on security and not on a quest for a political solution which was likely to remain elusive while the violence continued. He supported selective and even-handed internment. He argued that a conservative victory in north Down could spell the end of the presence of the Official Unionist Party at Westminster. The election of Conservative and later Labour candidates from Northern Ireland would lessen the likelihood of British disengagement from Northern Ireland. Without some development that would lessen that likelihood, British disengagement seemed probable in the first decades of the new century. In the event of British disengagement there would be full scale civil war, beginning in Northern Ireland and then drawing in the Republic. The stabilisation of the United Kingdom, of Great Britain and Northern Ireland is in our vital interests, he said. [8]

This dramatic intervention, when he declared, 'I believe the Union would be strengthened by the return of Conservative MPs from Northern Ireland to Westminster'[9], appeared to *The Irish Times*, to bring Dr O'Brien the full political circle. For others it was a grotesque, unbelievable, bizarre, unprecedented political act, which nevertheless was in line with the man's cold logic, so alien to so many of his country people.

Dr O'Brien predicted correctly in June of 1992 that the new Taoiseach, Albert Reynolds, successor to Mr Haughey, wearing the fresh laurels of the Maastricht Treaty, would go for an early election, hoping to ditch his recent allies and coalition partner, the Progressive Democrats[10]. Conor was appalled at the subsequent Fianna Fail-Labour Coalition Government. When it subsequently became clear that peace moves had been occurring involving the republican movement and the Irish Government, Conor was highly suspicious. When it became known that John Hume was involved in negotiations with Gerry Adams of Sinn

Fein, with the tacit support of the Irish Government, Conor smelt the whiff of treachery. His longtime attitude to John Hume made him almost incapable of believing anything good could come out of his negotiations. He was also on record as believing that successive Irish Governments gave too much status and deference to John Hume. O'Brien and other commentators, mainly from *Independent* Newspapers, wrote vociferously against what was termed the Hume-Adams Agreement of 1993. This led to the Chairman of the Oireachtas Foreign Affairs Committee, Brian Lenihan, attacking the role Dr O'Brien was playing. Lenihan argued that the public debate about the North, in the Republic, had become blinkered from reality. He said that that was highlighted by the unreasoned attacks launched by a coterie of commentators and politicians in the Southern media against the Hume-Adams talks. Lenihan went on:

> The columnist and former Minister Conor Cruise O'Brien has led these attack which have intensified in recent weeks to a degree that hatred and personal viciousness have replaced reasoned argument. In effect he has become a terrorist intellectual, who increasingly employs rhetorical devices, labels and slogans that are as undemocratic and 'hate filled' as the very men of violence he so often condemns. His attempted intellectual cleansing of John Hume's courage and integrity is both misguided, and against the interests of peace on this island. He has acted as an intellectual 'Godfather' to other columnists pursuing a quasi-political agenda of their own making. Yet the net effect of this very public campaign, if it is succcessful, against the Hume-Adams peace initiative will be the further prolongation of violence and misunderstanding well into the future. I appeal to the ordinary members of political parties, voluntary organisations, and the public at large to make their presence felt. Write to your politicians, but particularly the media, and tell them you support the

peace process currently underway. The voice of ordinary members of the public needs to be heard in this very public debate, about the relevance of the current Hume-Adams peace initiative[11].

As was so often the case in recent years, Dr O'Brien was on a year's fellowship in the USA, this time at The National Humanities Centre, Durham College, North Carolina. This distance would not have assisted him in assessing the real import of Lenihan's statement and he would naturally be fearful lest his family be put in any danger. Reacting publicly and vociferously, Dr O'Brien said:

> I do not accept that the law, civil or criminal, permits Mr Lenihan to incite others, with emotionally charged language to 'make their presence felt' whether in relation to me or to other commentators or politicians. I think it is plain to any reasonable person that Mr Lenihan's words were calculated to influence an emotional response, the eventual consequences of which are unpredictable.

> Mr Lenihan's calumnious and emotionally charged statements have caused serious apprehension to members of my family, and I clearly cannot leave the matter there. I am, in consequence, taking legal advice to see what redress may be open to me. I am making it known here and now that I am taking this step, lest others feel that they can with impunity follow Mr Lenihan's inflammatory lead, with regard to me and to others[12].

That statement certainly seemed to have had its desired effect and public criticism of Dr O'Brien's attitude to the peace initiative appeared to come to an immediate halt. The incident did not make Conor, himself, draw back one whit from his continuing attacks on the peace process. He continued to insist that the Irish Government should finally take his advice and put a great distance between itself and John Hume. He doubted that Hume would disengage himself from the political embrace of Gerry Adams. He saw the Hume-Adams initiative as representing an agreement between two wings of the same community, a non-violent wing and a violent wing. He then saw the leaders of the other community being invited to accept a platform jointly adopted by their non-violent and violent enemies, as a basis for discussion between the two communities[13]. A month later he railed at the Irish Government claiming that it was in regular touch with the IRA Army Council and even taking its orders from that illegal institution, to a degree unprecedented in the history of our State... The line of communication, he said, was at third hand, through Mr Hume and Mr Adams[14].

Then when, in the aftermath of the Downing Street Declaration, Gerry Adams was allowed to visit New York, Dr O'Brien, still in Durham, North Carolina, watched his triumphant performances on the American media. With a certain amount of bitterness, he saw the spectacle taking place as a result of the collusion of a democratically elected Irish government. Dr O'Brien felt sick at heart, and thought 'of others who would feel likewise, if they had lived to see the same: Frank Aiken, Sean MacEntee, Brendan Corish. And their revulsion would be deepened by the knowledge that their own parties had sunk so low as to engage in collusion with the IRA[15].'

When on 31 August 1994, the IRA declared a complete ceasefire, Dr O'Brien was isolated in his almost total scepticism of the intentions behind this move. The subsequent proposal that John Hume be nominated for the Nobel Peace Prize for his efforts in bringing about the ceasefire, may be a cause for additional scepticism by Dr O'Brien.

Dr O'Brien celebrated his seventy-fifth birthday in November 1992. Though his physical prowess has slowed down considerably, his mental alertness remains as sharp as ever. In a birthday tribute, he was asked about his attitude to death and an afterlife. As usual he was forthright in his reply saying:

I'm not altogether convinced that there is not an afterlife in some kind of way; I can't convince myself that my consciousness will just disappear like that. It seems quite a reasonable proposition that it should, but I don't feel that it's going to: I feel that it's going to go on in some kind of way. I also feel that there is some kind of purpose in the universe, though I cannot fathom it and I don't believe the people who claim to have information about it. At the same time, I don't believe myself to have had an unhappy life. In many ways I am singularly blessed, not least in where I live, here, a happy place to live and my present marriage and the children. I would like to put death off as long as I am *compus mentis,* as long as I'm writing well. I want to live. But if anything were to happen to upset my mind, I would want to be seen off as speedily as possible[16].

One of Dr O'Brien's latest literary performances, from which he derived great pleasure, and may have been his greatest work, was a monumental thematic study on the life of fellow Irishman, Edmund Burke. This large book is a work of historical revisionism, in that it liberates the subject from being seen as 'a snob and toady despised by his associates, and a person of exceptional ability but of commonplace type'[17]. By delving into Burke's youthful Catholic Irish ethos, where religious and civil persecution were commonplace, O'Brien has shown Burke 'to have been a truly independent spirit, willing to sacrifice his own and his party's interest in the pursuit of principle, a towering genius'[18].

As has happened in the past with the historical work of Dr O'Brien, there are parallels between himself and his subject, which transport him into an ecstatic state as he writes. The 'betrayal' of Parnell by O'Brien's maternal grandfather, can be contrasted with the apostasy of Burke's maternal grandfather leading to an underlying sense of guilt in both. O'Brien says:

If you are very much into a book, and believe in what you

are doing, you get a sort of exalted feeling which is not too far away from being a bit crazy, and in that mood from time to time I have felt that everything I have been doing throughout my life has been a preparation for this book, a preparation for the better understanding of Burke, in bringing out that my work as a historian, as a diplomatist, as a parliamentarian, you name it, the whole thing, they all sit in to some bit of Burke[19].

Unlike Edmund Burke and many other gifted Irish people, before and since, O'Brien was given the facility to achieve his potential while remaining domiciled in his native country. Some Irish people believed he should have been grateful for this, even humble for it. But this was not the case, nor should it be so. O'Brien was so confident of himself and his abilities, that this kind of Irish doublespeak would be totally alien to him. In this way, though essentially Irish, he was very different from his contemporaries. He was more mature and more civilised than they. But this is no great credit to himself. Though never very wealthy, he came from a very privileged cultural background and was able to use the educational and career opportunities of the new Irish state to the maximum. This is what a mature and civilised society should be able to offer its citizens. O'Brien was lucky enough to be able to almost take this for granted.

Far from expecting his thanks for this, Irish society should be grateful that he chose to remain in Ireland. It has been the richer by far for his presence and the truth of this will become more apparent as time marches on. Unlike Edmund Burke in England, O'Brien had no need to cover his tracks. Rather he continues to emblazon them on several continents. But, as ever, he remains naturally controversial and provocative.

Let's put it this way, [he says], 'I've never spent an entire year outside Ireland. In every year of my life I have been able to come back here for some part of the summer. What the lawyers call *animus revertendi*. It's quite strong.

But if a law was passed, as under our legal system it well might, you won't be able to get out of Ireland at all. I'd get out of Ireland before that law came into force. I can't be happy unless I can spend a lot of time here, and a lot of time outside it. Which has mostly meant Britain and America and more often America than Britain. [20]

References to the Text

I have used abbreviations for the following frequently cited books and newspapers.

SI :   *States of Ireland,* Conor Cruise O'Brien, Hutchinson 1972 hardback edition

TK :   *To Katanga and Back,* Conor Cruise O'Brien, Hutchinson 1962

WP :   *Writers and Politics,* Conor Cruise O'Brien, 1965

PC :   *Passion and Cunning,* Conor Cruise O'Brien, Weidenfeld 1988

Skef: *Skef,* Andre Sheehy-Skeffington, Lilliput 1991

Irl :   *Ireland 1913-1985,* JJ Lee, Cambridge University Press 1989

Memoirs: *Memoirs of a Statesman,* Brian Faulkner, Weidenfeld and Nicholson 1978

ILP :   *The Irish Labour Party in Transition,* Michael Gallagher, Manchester University Press 1982

II :   *Irish Independent Newspaper*

IT :   *Irish Times Newspaper*

DD :   *Dail Debates*

Introduction

1. The student, Patrick E O'Keeffe, reproduced the album on the occasion of the Silver Jubilee of the class of 1967, at Maynooth in June 1992.
2. *TK,* p. 158
3. Lecture by Dr O'Brien, Waterstones, Dublin, October 1992
4. Lecture by Dr O'Brien, Peacock Theatre, October 1992
5. *Questions & Answers,* RTE, 5 April 1993

Chapter 1

1. *SI* p. 82
2. *James Joyce*, Stan Gebler Davies, Granada 1982 p.51
3. *Ulysses*, James Joyce,
4. *Enigma of Tom Kettle*, J.B. Lyons, Glendale 1988 p. 203
5. *S.I.* p. 82
6. *Letters of James Joyce*, Volume 2,
7. *Lady Gregory's Journals 1916-1930*, Ed. Lennox Robinson London 1946
8. *PC* p. 33
9. RTE, *Questions and Answers*, 5 April 1993
10. ibid
11. ibid
12. ibid
13. ibid
14. *Sunday Independent*, 28 July 1991
15. *SI*, p. 109
16. RTE op. cit.
17. *States of Ireland*, Conor Cruise O'Brien, Panther 1974 p. 114, paperback edition
18. ibid p. 114
19. *Weekly Independent*, 9 April 1938
20. *Skef*, p. 90
21. *States of Ireland* op. cit. p. 137
22. Interview with Christine Foster, 16 December 1993
23. *SI*, p. 21
24. *WP* p. 117
25. Letter to *Irish Times* 24 July 1971

Chapter 2

1. Irl. p. 176
2. *Formulation of Irish Foreign Policy*, Patrick Keatinge, IPA Dublin p. 24
3. *DD*, 18 June 1936
4. *IT*, 9 February 1982

5. Interview with Christine Foster
6. *Sean MacBride*, Anthony Jordan, Blackwater 1993 p. 122
7. *West Briton*, Brian Inglis, Faber 1962 p. 141
8. ibid p. 143
9. *Ireland since the Famine*, FSL Lyons, Fontana p. 591
10. *SI*, p. 145
11. *A Concise History of Ireland*, Conor Cruise O'Brien & Maire MacEntee, Thames & Hudson 1972 p. 160
12. *IT*, 9 October 1982
13. *Maria Cross*, Donat O'Donnell, Chatto & Windus 1952 p. 259
14. Interview with Christine Foster

Chapter 3
1. *DD*, 24 July 1946
2. *Ireland since the Famine*, FSL Lyons, Fontana p. 593
3. *WP*, pp 195-212
4. *TK*, p. 15
5. *Irl*, pp. 369-370
6. *Ireland 1945-70*, JJ Lee, Ed. Gill & MacMillan 1979 p. 139
7. *Ireland at the United Nations, Speeches* by Frank Aiken, Dublin 1959 p. 29
8. *TK*, p. 19
9. ibid p. 23
10. *Ireland 1945-70*, JJ Lee, Gill & MacMillan 1979 p. 144
11. Aiken Speeches op. cit. p. 29
12. *Irish Times* Interview 6 August 1991
13. *Irish Press*, September 1960.

Chapter 4
1. *The Rise and Fall of Moise Tshombe*, Ian Colvin, Leslie Frewin 1968 p. 23
1. *II*, 9 January 1961
3. Ian Colvin, op . cit. pp. 42-47

4. *TK* p. 65 and The *Observer,* 10 December 1961
5. *TK,* p. 65
6. Ian Colvin, op. cit. p. 55
7. *TK,* p. 14

Chapter 5

1. *TK,* p. 134
2. ibid p. 214
3. ibid p. 221
4. Ian Colvin op. cit. p. 73
5. *TK,* p. 236 and Ian Colvin op, cit. p. 74
6. *TK,* p. 256
7. Ian Colvin, op. cit. p. 77
8. ibid p. 84
9. *TK,* pp 262-263
10. Ian Colvin, op. cit. p. 85
11. ibid p. 85
12. *TK,* pp 260-261
13. Ian Colvin, op. cit. p. 86
14. *TK,* p. 284
15. *The Mysterious Death of Dag Hammarskjold,* Arthur Gavshon, Walker New York 1962 p. 130
16. *TK,* p. 270
17. Ian Colvin op. cit. p. 86
18. ibid p. 91
19. *TK,* p. 299
20. *IT,* 5 October 1961
21. *TK,* p. 304
22. Interview with Christine Foster
23. *Peacemakers of Niemba,* Tom McCaughren, Browne & Nolan 1966 p.11
24. Colvin op. cit. p. 97
25. *Katanga Report,* Smith Hempstone, Faber 1962. pp 143-5
26. Titus Oates – invented the conspiracy of the Papist plot which led to the execution of many Catholics in England and their exclusion from Charles II's Parliament.

27. *Katanga Report*, Smith Hempstone, Faber 1962. p.152
28. Ian Colvin, op. cit. p. 98
29. *IT*, December 1961
30. *TK*, p. 328
31. ibid pp. 347-349
32. *IT*, 4 December 1961
33. National Archives Dublin
34. Patrick Keatinge, op. cit.
35. Patrick Keatinge, op. cit. p.226
36. National Archives Dublin
37. *Skef*, p.209
38. *IT*, 11 December 1961
39. The *Observer*, 10 December 1961
40. Information from Dr O'Brien

Chapter 6
1. *Challenge of the Congo*, Kwame Nkrumah, Nelson 1967
2. *TK*, p.297
3. *Reap the Whirlwind*, Geoffrey Bing, McGibbon & Kee 1968 p.459
4. ibid p. 358
5. ibid p. 359
6. *WP*, p.234
7. *To Be a Pilgrim*, Robert Collis, Secker & Warburg 1975 p.159
8. Geoffrey Bing op. cit. p.364
9. *WP*, p.250
10. ibid pp. 256-257
11. Geoffrey Bing op. cit. p. 364-365
12. ibid p.365
13. P.C. p.273

Chapter 7
1. *WP*, p.234
2. *Lyndon Johnston & the American Dream*, Doris Kearns, Andre Deutch 1976 p.275

3. ibid .281
4. *IT*, p.310
5. *IT*, 5 December 1967
6. *IT*, 6 December 1967
7. *IT*, 7 December 1967
8. *Sunday Independent,* 28 July 1991
9. *IT*, 14 February 1967
10. *A Historical Review of the Men and the Women and the Politics of the Easter Rising – Irish Times Supplement,* Easter 1966

Chapter 8
1. National Archives Dublin
2. *II,* 2 January 1990
3. *Neighbours, Ewart-Biggs Memorial Lectures,* Conor Cruise O'Brien, Faber 1980 p. 72
4. *SI,* p. 148
5. *Memoirs* p. 27
6. ibid p. 28
7. ibid p.39
8. *Political Murder in Northern Ireland,* Martin Dillon & Denis Lehane, Penguin 1973 pp. 28-35
9. *SI,* pp. 252-253
10. *The Peoples Democracy,* Paul Arthur, Blackstaff 1974 p.107
11. *SI,* p.162
12. *Memoirs,* p.51
13. ibid p. 54

Chapter 9
1. *IT,* Easter 1966 supplement
2. *IT,* 20 December 1968
3. *Ireland,* Basil Chubb, Longman 1982 p.23
4. *IT,* 27 January 1969
5. *II,* 7 November 1987
6. *ILP,* p. 90
7. ibid. p. 137

8. *DD*, 2 July 1969
9. *IT*, 5 August 1991
10. *SI*, p. 199
11. *Memoirs* p. 61
12. *SI*, p.183
13. *The Price of my Soul*, Bernadette Devlin, Pan 1969
14. *DD*, 23 October 1969
15. *SI*, p.209
16. ibid p. 226
17. *States of Ireland*, Panther 1974 pp. 223-227

Chapter 10
1. *Irl*, p. 459
2. *SI*, p.211
3. RTE, *This Week*, May 1990
4. *SI*, p.247
5. ibid p.257
6. *DD*, 4 November 1970
7. ibid 4 November 1970
8. *ILP*, pp. 113-114

Chapter 11
1. *Memoirs*, p.87
2. *SI*, p.260
3. ibid p.264
4. *Memoirs*, p.109
5. ibid p.119
6. *The Uncivil Wars*, P.O'Malley, Blackstaff 1983 p.208
7. *SI*, p.276
8. *Irish Press*, 21 September 1971
9. *DD*, 21 October 1971
10. *ILP*, p.147

Chapter 12
1. *SI*, pp. 283-284

2. *DD*, 4 February 1972
3. *IT*, 26 February 1972
4. *IT*, 28 February 1972
5. *ILP*, p.147
6. *Memoirs*, p.163
7. *Sunday Press*, 4 June 1972
8. *SI*, pp. 298-316, passim
9. *IT*, 3 October & 16 october 1972
10. *IT*, 12 October 1972
11. *ILP*, p.150
12. *II*, 14 September 1991

Chapter 13
1. *IT*, 20 January 1969
2. *DD*, 2 July 1969
3. *IT*, 11 & 13 May 1969 & DD. 4 November 1970
4. *ILP*, p.195
5. *Irl*, p.472
6. *What Kind of Country*, Bruce Arnold Jonathan Cape 1984 p.94
7. *II*, 14 September 1991
8. *All In A Life*, Garret FitzGerald, Gill & MacMillan 1992 p.197
9. *IT*, 3 December 1977
10. G. FitzGerald op. cit. p.308
11. *IT*, 31 March 1976
12. *DD*, 12 October 1966
13. *IT*, 29 March 1979
14. *Ireland at the Polls: Dail Elections of 1977*, H. Penniman (ed). American Institute of Public Policy Research 1978 p.109
15. *IT*, 19 October 1976
16. *II*, August 1992
17. *IT*, 5 August 1992
18. *IT*, 7 August 1992
19. *IT*, 7 August 1992
20. *Labour the Price of Power*, John Horgan, Gill & MacMillan 1986 pp. 56-57

21. *IT*, 27 January 1981
22. *ILP*, p.221
23. *II*, 28 October 1975

Chapter 14
1. *IT*, 9 October 1982
2. ibid 8 September 1970
3. ibid 21 September 1970
4. ibid 21 September 1970
5. Interview with Michael O Dubhslainte, April 1994
6. *IT*, 8 June 1982
7. *Siolta Filiocht & Pros*, Brid Nic An Fhailigh & Rosemary Day, Comhalcht Oideachais 1991 p.22

Chapter 15
1. *IT*, 1 July 1974
2. *IT*, 25 September 1974
3. *ILP*, p.211
4. *The Crane Bag 2 1978 Further Reflections on Irish Nationalism*, John A Murphy p.159
5. *The Visual Arts in Ireland*, James White p.101
6. *The Crane Bag*, op. cit. p.157
7. *I.T.* 21 August ;1975
8. *Ireland A Social and Cultural History 1922-1985*, Terence Brown, Fontana 1987 pp. 289-291
9. *SI*, p.121
10. *IT*, 28 January 1977
11. *IT*, 14 January 1974
12. G. FitzGerald op. cit. p.197

Chapter 16
1. *II*, 20 September 1976
2. *Them and Us; Britain, Ireland and the Northern Ireland Question 1969-1982*, James Downey, Ward River Press pp. 157-158
3. Bruce Arnold op. cit. p.124

4. *Irl*, p.482
5. *DD*, 28 October 1976
6. ibid
7. ibid
8. ibid
9. G. FitzGerald op. cit. p.316
10. *IT*, 22 October 1976
11. *IT*, 5 August 1991

Chapter 17
1. *Memoirs*, p.171
2. ibid p.185
3. *Irl*, p.442
4. *Memoirs*, p.187
5. ibid p.201
6. ibid p.125
7. ibid p.243
8. *Irl*, p.444
9. *Memoirs*, p.247
10. ibid p.249
11. ibid p.255
12. *PC*, p.209
13. *Northern Ireland, A Personal Perspective*, Merlyn Rees, London 1985 p.80
14. ibid p.73
15. *Memoirs*, p.275
16. ibid p.278
17. *II*, 14 September 1991
18. ibid
19. ibid 24 April 1993
20. ibid
21. Pope John XXIII, Peter Hebblethwaite, Chapman 1984 pp. 445-448

22. *II*, 15 May 1993
23. *II*, June 1993
24. G. FitzGerald op. cit. p.213
25. *Sunday Press* December 1992

Chapter 18
1. *Irl*, p.481
2. *ILP*, p.216
3. *Irl*, p. 481-482
4. *II*, 28 May 1977
5. *Irl*, p.483
6. H. Penniman op. cit. p.145
7. *IT*, 14 june 1977
8. ibid 17 June 1977
9. ibid 18 June 1977
10. *Irl*, p.p. 484
11. *IT*, 20 June 1077
12. RTE *This Week* 26 June 1977
13. *Sunday Telegraph* 19 June 1977
14. The *Observer* 19 June 1977
15. *Sunday Independent* 28 July 1991
16. ibid 7 October 1990
17. *The Crane Bag 2 1978 Further Reflections on Irish Nationalism*, John A Murphy p.159
18. Terence Brown op. cit. p. 290
19. ibid p.291
20. *Atlantic No. 3* November 1971 *The Ambiguity of the Republic*, Liam de Paor.
21. *IT*, 21 & 28 August 1975, Politics and the Poet, by Conor Cruise O'Brien
22. *Irl*, p.477
23. *Sunday Press* 5 April 1992
24. *The Gun in Politics*, J Bowyer Bell, Transaction publishers 1991 p.288

Chapter 19.
1. *IT,* 29 June 1977
2. *DD,* November 1977
3. *Sunday Times,* 18 December 1977
4. London *Times,* 19 December 1977
5. *Diary of a Year,* Lord Longford, Weidenfeld 1982
6. *IT,* 26 January 1981
7. ibid
8. Interview with Dr. O'Brien.
9. *IT,* March 1981
10. ibid.
11. *Irl,* p.504
12. *Irl,* p.509

Chapter 20
1. *Sunday Independent,* 8 June 1982
2. *IT,* 24 May 1983
3. *IT,* 31 January 1984
4. *IT,* 5 February 1981
5. *IT,* 9 October 1984
6. *IT,* 8 February 1983
7. *II,* 7 January 1989
8. *IT,* 9 August 1983
9. *IT,* 21 January 1986
10. *IT,* 28 July 1986
11. *Times Literary Supplement,* 1 November 1985
12. *Irishness in a Changing Society,* Princess Grace Library, Colin Smythe 1988 p.215

Chapter 21
1. *II,* 22 March 1986
2. RTE *Questions & Answers* June 1991
3. *IT,* 23 August 1991
4. *II,* 4 May 1986
5. *II,* 20 September 1986

6. *PC,* p.242
7. ibid p.15
8. *II,* 17 April 1987
9. *II,* 5 September 1987

Chapter 22
1. RTE *Would You Believe* 29 October 1992
2. ibid
3. ibid
4. *IT,* 31 August 1982
5. *II,* 1/2 January 1988
6. *II,* 7 November 1987
7. ibid.

Chapter 23
1. *II,* 24 December 1988
2. ibid 11 February 1989
3. ibid 11 February 1989
4. ibid 2 October 1993
5. *Sunday Independent* 28 July 1991
6. *II,* 24 May 1989
7. *II,* 12 September 1987
8. *II,* 15 August 1987
9. *II,* 16 July 1987
10. *II,* 4 June 1988
11. *II,* 4 February 1989
12. 13 February 1988
13. *II,* 29 July 1989
14. *II,* 12 September 1992
15. *II,* 23 January 1988
16. *II,* 2 June 1990
17. *II,* 20 October 1990
18. *II,* 15 December 1990
19. *II,* 4 November 1989
20. *II,* 3 February 1990

21. *II*, 6 March 1993
22. *II*, 26 May 1990
23. *II*, 8 December 1990
24. *II*, 24 June 1989
25. *Sunday Independent*, 19 September 1993
26. *Talking to Ourselves*, Ivor Kenny, Kenny's Bookshop and Art Gallery 1994, p.23

Chapter 24

1. *IT*, May 1991
2. RTE, *Questions & Answers*, June 1991
3. *II*, 23 August 1991
4. *Sunday Independent* 19 April 1992
5. *Sunday Press* 5 April 1992
6. *II*, 23 January 1988
7. *IT*, 3 April 1992
8. *II*, 4 April 1992
9. *IT*, 3 April 1992
10. *II*, 20 June 1992
11. *II*, 10 October 1993
12. *IT*, 16 June 1993
13. *II*, 13 November 1993
14. *II*, 11 December 1993
15. *Sunday Independent*, 6 February 1993
16. RTE, *Would you Believe*, 29 October 1992
17. *IT*, 12 September 1992
18. ibid
19. ibid
20. ibid

Index

Ibo 216
Ileo, Joseph 41
Inglis, Brian 20

John XXIII, Pope 177
Johnston Lyndon 80
Joyce, James 1-3
Joyce, Stanislaus 1-3

Kasavubu, Joseph 33-8
Keane, Ronan 82
Kearney, Richard 207-8
Keating, Justin 133
Kelly, Captain James 110
Kelly, John 110, 163
Kennedy, Eamonn 26, 37
Kennedy, Edward 220
Kennedy, John F 177
Kennedy, Laurence 226
Kennedy, Ludovic 145
Kennedy, Paddy 122
Kenny, Colum 142
Kettle, Tom 1-5, 14, 84
Khiary, Mahmoud 42-5, 50-5
Khrushchev, Nikita 34, 177
Kibwe, Jean-Baptiste 45
Kilcoyne, Fr. Colm 226
King, Martin Luther 80
King, Tom 222
Kirwan, James 69
Kissane, Fr 147

Lee, Joseph 25, 135
Lemass, Sean 31, 62-3, 85-8, 97, 100,
            123, 140
Lenehan, Joe 113
Lenihan, Brian 114, 229-30
Lennon, JG 21
Lester, Sean 17
Lindsay, Mayor 81
Linner, Sture 50, 53
Loftus, Sean 184
Longford, Lord 19

Lonhro 197
Lovett, Ann 203-4
Loughnane, Bill 127
Lumumba, Patrice 33-8, 63, 97
Lynch, Jack 98-115, 120-4, 131, 140,
            168, 170, 181, 223
Lynd, Robert 13, 84

MacAteer, Eddie 21
MacBride, Sean 19-25, 87, 95
MacEntee, Maire 28, 53-8, 63-4, 69, 81,
            127, 146-150, 196,
            201, 205, 211, 216
MacEntee, Seamus 105-6
MacEntee, Sean 21, 54, 63, 99, 230
McGee Case 137
McGelliot, JJ 17
McGowan, GL 10-11
McHugh, Roger 86
McKenna, Siobhan 196
MacKeown, Sean 31, 35, 50, 58, 63
MacMillan, Harold 51, 64
MacNeill, Eoin
MacQuillan, Jack 63
Major, John 143
Mandela, Nelson 222
Manning, Vincent 184
Manseragh, Nicholas 84
Mason, Roy 173-4
Maudling, Reginald 120, 127
Mitchell, Jim 222
Mitchell, Tom 105
Mobutu, Colonel 35-6, 41
Molyneux, James 174
Moran, DP 207
Mullen, Michael 164
Munongo, Godefroid 34, 42-8
Murderous Angels 97
Murnaghan, Mr Justice 83
Murphy, John A 156, 187, 200-209

251

OTHER

▦ POLITICAL BIOGRAPHIES ▦

FROM

BLACKWATER PRESS

▦ **SEAN MACBRIDE**
Anthony J. Jordan · £9.99 (Hbk)

▦ **MARY ROBINSON: THE LIFE AND TIMES OF
AN IRISH LIBERAL**
Michael O'Sullivan · £9.99 (Hbk) £6.99(Pbk)

▦ **SEAN LEMASS: MAKER OF MODERN IRELAND**
Michael O'Sullivan · £12.99 (Hbk)

▦ **ALBERT REYNOLDS: THE UNAUTHORISED BIOGRAPHY**
Tim Ryan · £7.99 (Pbk)

▦ **DICK SPRING: A SAFE PAIR OF HANDS**
Tim Ryan · £9.99 (Hbk)

▦ **MARA: PJ**
Tim Ryan · £7.99 (Pbk)

▦ **NEIL BLANEY: A SOLDIER OF DESTINY**
Tim Ryan · £8.99 (Pbk)

▦ **JACK LYNCH**
T.P. O'Mahony · £8.99 (Pbk)

All of the above titles can be ordered from:
Blackwater Press, C/O Folens Publishers, Unit 8,
Broomhill Business Pk, Broomhill Road Tallaght, Dublin 24.
Tel: (01) 4515311. Fax: (01) 4515308.

Cheques payable to Blackwater Press